HANDBOOK
for the
SOUL

HANDBOOK
for the
HEART

Edited by
RICHARD CARLSON
and
BENJAMIN SHIELD

ONE SPIRIT
NEW YORK

HANDBOOK
for the
SOUL

HANDBOOK
for the
HEART

*EDITED BY RICHARD CARLSON
AND BENJAMIN SHIELD*

Healers on Healing
For the Love of God
Handbook for the Soul
Handbook for the Heart

BY RICHARD CARLSON

You Can Be Happy No Matter What
You Can Feel Good Again
Shortcut Through Therapy
Don't Sweat the Small Stuff

HANDBOOK
for the
SOUL

Foreword by
MARIANNE WILLIAMSON

To Pamela DuMond Shield, Richard Carlson,
and to those souls who have encountered mine along our paths:
know that your gifts remain treasured
—BENJAMIN SHIELD

To Sathya Sai Baba and Jesus Christ, constant reminders to me
of that which is soulful in the world. And to
my wife, Kristine Carlson, and my dear friend
Benjamin Shield, the two people who so often lovingly
put up with me when I am less than soulful!
—RICHARD CARLSON

Contents

Contents

Contents

Contents

Foreword

by Marianne Williamson

I can think of no other time when it has been more important to consider the needs of the human soul. The twentieth century has been dominated by a worldview that glorifies a mechanistic, rationalistic focus at the expense of the inner life. The ravages that have been wreaked on the planet as a result of this dissociation from the essential self have reached crisis proportions. Yet, just as the individual unconscious knows when a person's survival is threatened, I believe the collective unconscious knows when group survival is in danger. Beyond the level of the rational mind is an awareness that without our souls, we are without our power, and without our power, we will die.

Carl Jung said that the psyche is inexorably driven to seek balance. I believe that modern consciousness is now seeking its soul — not because it's a new trend, but because it's literally our only survivable alternative. This book speaks to a yearning for balance, a mass willingness to rekindle our souls. This may represent a more important historical unfoldment than we as a culture have known for centuries.

All the great religious and philosophical systems are paths to this understanding — different, yet equally valid, paths. And spiritual ideas, like any ideas, are strengthened as they're shared. For those to whom many of these ideas are new, our hope is that they will fill you with wonder and delight, as they surely inspired those who wrote these pages. And people who are already quite familiar, at least intellectually, with this ageless wisdom can join other pilgrims in sharing it, embracing the ideas even more deeply, making them part of our daily spiritual practice, and trying to apply them to all we say and do.

Our soul is our life. Everything else is a fiction — a mind game, inauthenticity. Without nourishing our own souls, we can't nourish the world; we can't give what we don't have. As we attend to our souls, we emanate invisibly and involuntarily the light we have received. The book is dedicated, then, to increasing the spiritual potency in each of our lives, so that what begins as individual nourishment might become nourishment for our communities and for our countries and for our world. As the ancient mystical doctrine, the Cabala, says, we receive the light and then we impart it . . . and thus we repair the world.

Acknowledgments

If the impossible became possible and we could use a single word to summarize our feelings about the creation of this book, it would be *gratitude*. Gratitude for the loving support, intelligence, and talent of the following individuals:

Jennifer Josephy, our editor, whose vision of the highest possible quality for this book reflected our own devotion. And to her assistant, Abigail Wilentz, for her skill and kindness.

Mark Lipsman, our copyeditor, whose vision far exceeded the words on the page.

Barry Fox, Janet Bailey, Gay Edelman, Judy Carroll, Dr. Pamela DuMond Shield, Penny Popkin, Steve Hasenberg, and Bernie Asbell, who put words to that which defies definition and helped us share our vision.

Sheree Bykofsky, our literary agent, who showed us

through her friendship and professionalism that one never has to veer from the path of soul.

Linda Michaels, our foreign rights agent, who enabled people around the world to share this book.

Janet Rosen, for her assistance and skill in the initial presentation of this book.

We especially wish to offer our appreciation and respect to all the participants who shared their souls and so freely gave of their time. They reminded us that the best way to teach is by example. Our heartfelt thanks to all who were involved with this project.

Introduction

"When you are old and gray and full of sleep,
And nodding by the fire, take down this book,
And slowly read, and dream of the soft look
Your eyes had once, and of their shadows deep . . ."
— WILLIAM BUTLER YEATS

This book is the collective effort of some of the most accomplished minds of our age. It was born of their quest to explore and understand the world of Soul and how each of us connects with it. Together, their contributions weave a tapestry of warmth, wisdom, and insight about the most important relationship in our lives.

Since the publication of our first two anthologies, *Healers on Healing* and *For the Love of God*, we have received countless letters from readers all over the world. These letters have convinced us that a desire to pursue and understand Soul in the life of individuals is woven into the fabric of our world. The primary purpose of this anthology is to create an environment of understanding and possibility as we explore together this mysterious and powerful universe.

"Soul" has different meanings to different people. Many would accept that Soul suggests an invisible dimension of experience. It has a lot to do with love, depth, and reflection. To feel nurtured on a deep and sustained basis, we must attend, beyond our physical needs and worldly aspirations, the life-enhancing nature of the Soul. In doing so, we bring a sacredness to every moment of our day.

We all seek Soul. While Soul is always present, it doesn't appear in our lives automatically. Soul requires our attention and reflection. Offering our respectful regard to the Soul is a way of loving it, caring for it, nurturing it.

With this in mind, each contributor to this collection has created a personal vision of nourishment for and from the Soul. The various visions and the tones they adopt cover a great range. That is because, in a real sense, each had to invent the subject.

Perhaps the most definitive framework for writing about the soul was expressed by Phil Cousineau in his book *Soul: An Archaeology*, when he paraphrased British author W. Somerset Maugham: "There are three rules for writing about the soul. Unfortunately, nobody knows what they are."

Yet this is a book that we could not *not* do. In traveling our own journeys, we have found others, like us, like you, searching their own depths for understanding not only of who they are but for the fulfillment of all they can be. We hope this book helps them in tending this need.

Our gratitude goes to the contributors of this work. As we contacted them, we were greeted, almost universally, with great enthusiasm for the invitation to address this subject. Repeatedly, they told us that this book was addressing one of the most important issues of the day. In all cases, they demonstrated humility and love. Now and then one of the authors would call us, sometimes from the other side of the globe, to share an expanded insight. We hope that these considered reflections of people who have dedicated their lives to the study of the Soul may change the way you think about your life.

We approach this subject as students, not experts. We come with "our cup empty." We created this book not in an effort to put forth any particular point of view but to cultivate a greater understanding of, and appreciation for, the possibilities open to all of us, and to offer a gift to humanity.

This project unfolded as a gift. The cultivation of this project provided us with the opportunity to share, reflect, and grow on a daily basis. We wish it to be a gift to others as well. Profits from this book will be donated to an international humanitarian organization. We hope it will affect many lives in a meaningful way.

Treasure yourself.

BENJAMIN SHIELD, PH.D.

RICHARD CARLSON, PH.D.

1.

Soul in Everyday Life

———— ••• ————

*"For a long time it had seemed to me that life
was about to begin — real life. But there was
always some obstacle in the way, something to
be got through first, some unfinished business,
time still to be served, a debt to be paid. Then
life would begin. At last it dawned on me that
these obstacles were my life."*

— FR. ALFRED D'SOUZA

WINDOWS
of the SOUL

by Jean Shinoda Bolen, M.D.

*"While everyone has a different experience of what
is soulful, these experiences do share similar beginnings.
We start by giving ourselves permission to be soulful,
to take seriously this aspect of ourselves, our soul
and our soul needs."*

WHENEVER I EXPERIENCE something beautiful,
I am with Soul. That moment of inward breath,
that pause and awareness of "how beautiful this
is" is a prayer of appreciation, a moment of gratitude in which
I behold beauty and am one with it. I have come to appreciate
that having an aesthetic eye takes me effortlessly into soul.

The beauty of where I live is the emotional equivalent of
being in a cathedral with light streaming in through stained-
glass windows. My first impression on awakening is usually
"How beautiful it is." Living as I do on the side of a mountain,
I have a panoramic view over the San Francisco Bay and often
see the sun rising over the East Bay hills. Sometimes the fog

obscures the view and lends a mysterious, private quality to where I am. It's always different, always special, and always beautiful.

To look out my windows and feel as I do in response to what I see is an effortless spiritual practice. There is a timelessness and serenity to my unhurried mornings. Just about every morning, I sit with a cup of coffee, gaze outward, and am in a receptive space in myself. Ideas, thoughts, and feelings come to mind. They rise to the surface, where I can think about them or make further intuitive connections. The experience is like being a still pool in the forest and simultaneously being at the edge of the pool, observing what arises from its depths. It is the same when I am doing my best writing (which I also do in the mornings), or, more accurately, when writing has to do with being totally absorbed in the shaping of what comes effortlessly to mind from my depths. In the timelessness of these moments of creativity, there is always a fullness of soul as well.

Another place where I find soul, one of the strongest places, is in the presence of other people whom I meet at soul level. It happens whenever a dialogue takes place in which both people are truly present, tuning in to really hearing each other and reflecting back. A sense of discovery occurs, as when musicians get together and improvise a musical dialogue, a dialogue that depends on letting go of ego and defenses. To voice something you're feeling and put observations into words with another person who is totally present is a creative act embodying soul and love.

When people come for therapy, soul is present. When they speak to me of the experiences that have affected them deeply, trusting me with their vulnerability, or tell me dreams rich with symbolic meaning, or reveal what they have never shown another person, I know that we are meeting at soul level, that we are not just in an office but in sanctuary, and that an invisible, transpersonal healing energy enters our space. They speak with a natural eloquence and, emotionally, an expressiveness and trust that touch my heart. If I'm also listening with an ear for prose poetry, very often a beauty of form comes through in their phrases.

I think that whenever soul is present, it's because what you're doing, whom you're with, where you are, evokes love without your thinking about it. You are totally absorbed in the place or person or event, without ego and without judgment. You are in what the Greeks call *kairos*. When you are in kairos time, you are totally absorbed in what you are doing; you lose track of time. Whether you are in love with a person or in love with a project, it's the same quality. Time may expand — you feel that the experience has been happening for hours and it's really been forty-five minutes. Or maybe you've spent hours, and it seems that only forty-five minutes have gone by. Time is not measured. You are participating in time as you make a connection through the deeper, creative parts of yourself. And that connection nourishes the soul, always.

What particular experiences will nourish your soul? No one can prescribe that for you; it is something only you can know and experience. What is satisfying for one person may be just the opposite for someone else. Being out in nature, by the seashore, or on a mountaintop works for me. Communing with nature brings me into soul time. But for others, being out in nature is something to be tolerated, or even an ordeal, or just what you do if you're a member of a family that goes camping. For some people, listening to or playing music is a soulful experience, while for others, music is a way to mark time until they can get on to something productive.

While everyone has a different experience of what is soulful, these experiences do share similar beginnings. We start by giving ourselves permission to be soulful, to take seriously this aspect of ourselves, our soul and our soul needs. You have the need and the right to spend part of your life caring for your soul. It is not easy. There are many obstacles. You have to resist the demands of the work-oriented, often defensive, element in your psyche that measures your life only in terms of output — how much you produce — not in terms of the quality of your life experiences. We live in a materialistic culture that emphasizes being productive. We get messages that something is wrong with spending time attending to the soul. To be a soulful person means to go against all the pervasive, prove-yourself values of our culture and instead treasure what is unique and internal and valuable in yourself and your own personal evolution.

Sadly, some people wait until they have a heart attack or ulcers, or have a teenage child who gets into trouble, or until their spouse leaves them, or the like, to attend to their soul needs. The disastrous experience pushes them to it. But you don't have to wait for disaster. You can open yourself to the possibility of nourishing your soul, and you can make it a priority. Take careful stock of the ways you spend your life energies doing things that are not so nourishing. Often, in the middle adult years especially, people find that they have been busy being productive in some task-oriented way, some way in which their souls were excluded. The responsibilities of everyday life — taking the kids to school, paying the bills, doing the grocery shopping, all the stuff that life requires of mature adults — expand to fill the entire life. When you're so consumed, you don't have very many moments in which to experience the soul.

There is a little myth about how if you were on the road to Athens, you had to pass Procrustes and his bed. He would place you on his bed, and if you were too tall, he cut off your feet. If you were too short for the bed, he stretched you as if you were on a medieval rack until you filled it. The myth is a metaphor for how we are shaped to fit expectations of our cultures and families. The qualities that lead to success are stretched — we concentrate on developing them. To fit in, we cut ourselves off from what is unvalued by others and lose part of our souls in the process. What we reject of ourselves, we bury alive in the unconscious.

Loss of soul creates a void, an emptiness, that people fill with addictive activities — because it is the path of least resistance to sit in front of the television, or work a couple of hours more, or complete something from the "to do" list. Yet it is very possible to make changes that will lead back to the lost parts of yourself, back to those lost parts of your soul. The decision to reconnect with your soul is similar to any choice to change things for the better, whether it's to stop smoking or to lose 20 pounds.

Become aware of how deprived your life is of sources of joy, sources of beauty, and sources of creativity, which are all soul sources. Find the silent parts of yourself, the parts of you that have atrophied from disuse: ask yourself, What gave me pleasure as a child? Maybe it was fishing or gardening or working with your hands or sculpting things or whittling or painting. Go down into your unconscious and reconnect with dismembered parts of yourself that were important. Remember and reconnect with what really gave you pleasure when you were younger and had more time, for going back to it may lead you to soul. When you recover or discover something that nourishes your soul and brings joy, care enough about yourself to make room for it in your life. A woman I know loved dancing but hadn't danced for decades because she lacked a partner. She recently began ballroom dancing. All it took was the realization that she could take a class to bring dancing back into her life. The decision to do so followed, which reanimated a wonderfully soul-filled source of pleasure for her.

When you attend to the needs of the soul, you experience a sense of freedom. In the midst of absorption in a soul-nourishing activity, we are liberated, creative, unaware of time, and in harmony with ourselves. When we attend only to work and neglect the soul, we may dream of being imprisoned and we are often tense, because we carry the weight of our joyless world on our shoulders. Soul-satisfying experiences open us to respond to the beauty around us, in others and in the world. As I experience it, appreciation of beauty is access to the soul. With beauty in our lives, we walk and carry ourselves more lightly and with a different look in our eyes. To look into the eyes of someone beholding beauty is to look through the windows of the soul. Anytime we catch a glimpse of soul, beauty is there; anytime we catch our breath and feel "How beautiful!," the soul is present.

PAY ATTENTION

by Robert Fulghum

"For all my good intentions, there are days when things go wrong or I fall into old habits. When things are not going well, when I'm grumpy or mad, I'll realize that I've not been paying attention to my soul and I've not been following my best routine."

LTHOUGH THE PURPOSE of this anthology is to explore the notion of nourishing the soul, I must begin by confessing that "soul" is a word I rarely use. I understand that within the context of Christian theology, the soul is the immaterial essence of a person that precedes one's earthly existence and continues after that existence has concluded. But this is not the meaning of "soul" as I would use it. I don't want to lead anyone to think that I believe in a separate entity, called the "soul," that needs care and feeding, as does the family dog. Although I would never quarrel with anyone who uses the word "soul" in the classic manner, I'd like to find a different way in which to talk about what the word "soul" means to me.

If someone were to ask me whether I believed in God, or saw God, or had a particular relationship with God, I would reply that I don't separate God from my world in my thinking. I feel that God is everywhere. That's why I never feel separated from God or feel I must seek God, any more than a fish in the ocean feels it must seek water. In a sense, God is the "ocean" in which we live.

The same attitude applies when it comes to discussing matters like the soul, spirit, heart, and mind. I don't divide myself from these things; they are not separate from me. But in the same sense that we use the word "mind" to talk about a particular function of the brain, I can use the words "soul" or "spirit" or "heart" to talk about a particular function of my life. I use these words to describe a particular set of activities in my life.

"Soul" is found in the quality of what I am doing. If my activities have a sense of truth and integrity, if they are deep in meaning, then they are rich in soul, and so am I. Thus, for me, "nourishing the soul" means making sure I attend to those things that give my life richness and depth of meaning.

Rather than launch into an abstract discussion of the philosophy and theology of enriching one's existence, I'll tell you about a day in my life. Certain activities, structures, and ritual patterns have become woven into the fabric of my daily life because they have been so consistently useful to me — because they nourish my soul.

I arise about six o'clock every morning. Instead of turning on the light or the radio, my wife and I light candles or oil lamps. We like to begin our day with this softer, gentler light. We listen to music as we build a fire in the fireplace, especially in winter. After the fire has been built, the next hour of the new day is spent in talking to each other. These morning rituals bring us into the day in a gentle, nourishing manner, so unlike the hurried and panic-stricken way we began our days when we were much younger. Now we open our day with a consciousness of attitude. We're together, and we pay a lot of attention to each other.

After breakfast I go to my office, where I have what an anthropologist might describe as an altar. I don't call it that, but it's a place on top of a cabinet where I put things of importance. Right now, there's a brick on my "altar." As I look at it, I remember walking along the seashore in Seattle. Right along the edge, where the water and shore meet, I found this brick. And this brick had a history. It was once earth. At some point, fire and water were added to the earth, and it became a brick that was used in a building — perhaps someone's home. Eventually, the building was torn down and the brick was cast aside, becoming a bit of rubble on the beach. As I was walking along the water's edge that day, I saw in this ordinary object the eternal pattern of our lives, the coming and going of use, the coming and going of energy.

A Buddhist would say that I saw the Buddha nature in the little brick. I don't think of it that way, but I understand what it means — that this brick is a physical metaphor for the processes of life. And so, as people often do, I picked up an interesting object and brought it home, putting it in this place where I look at things that have meaning to me. It's been there a while now. In time, I suppose, it will be pushed aside by something else. I think that we have all, consciously or unconsciously, placed items like this in our houses – something we have picked up while walking along the beach, or a leaf we have found during the change of seasons, or a flower, or a fruit.

I enjoy lighting incense every day, as much as for the sensory smells as for the gesture of fire. Rather than using Oriental incense, I've found wonderful incense smells from my own culture — mesquite, cedar, and piñon pine. The smells remind me of quiet evenings by the campfire, sitting outdoors in nature in a thoughtful state of mind. The incense I light is not a symbol of prayer to the gods, as in Eastern religions. Instead, it is a way for me to recollect fine times in my life through the smells that bring to mind pleasant memories.

Sometimes during the day, I consciously focus on some ordinary object and allow myself a momentary "paying-attention." This paying-attention gives meaning to my life. I don't know who it was, but someone said that careful attention paid to anything is a window into the universe. Pausing to think this way, even for a brief moment, is very important. It gives quality to my day.

Through many years of trial and error, I have learned that my conscious brain is efficient for only about an hour. No matter what intellectual task I'm performing, my performance begins to deteriorate after about sixty minutes. Forcing myself to continue does not improve my performance or add to the pleasure of the task. So, every hour or so, I get up and do something else, especially something physical. I'll go out and pick up firewood, or carry out the trash, or go for a walk. I'll do almost anything that gives my brain a break and employs my physical sensations, my eyes and ears and nose. By the time I come back to work, I'm cooking again.

I have also learned that my intellectual activity is strong in the morning, so that's when I turn my attention to the day's thinking tasks. I never force my brain to do what I know it does not do well in the afternoon. Instead, I focus on physical activity, task activity, and mindless things. And then I do something that you would not be surprised to hear I learned in kindergarten — I take a nap. I lie down in the afternoon and quiet myself for half an hour. Napping improves all the other aspects of my life (and my wife says the world is better for it, as well). I don't always sleep, but I have learned that if I'll just be still for half an hour, I may enjoy the feeling of meditation, or prayer, or simply restfulness. Perhaps sleeping isn't as important a goal as stopping — stopping the thoughts and the pressures.

After my nap, I usually walk for an hour. The walk is exercise for my body, but also a time to consciously forgo trying to do anything with my brain. I leave my thinking mechanisms alone; I let my mind wander. I talk to myself as I walk, and sometimes I talk out loud. I'm always surprised at the thoughts that pop into my head at inopportune times. I've learned to carry a very small tape recorder and a pencil and paper with me as I walk. I pay attention to ideas that appear in my mind during these walks. I'll sit down and take notes, or I'll talk into the recorder, or talk out loud to myself.

Sometimes I have an unexpected feeling of connection with the universe, with the seasons of the year, with what's going on in the world, and with what's right in front of me. All of a sudden I'll have a deep emotional experience, because I gave myself an opportunity to have feelings, to let things happen in my mind as they will. Letting go of life's deliberate activities allows me to see what my subconscious wants to do. And so I nourish my soul by paying it careful attention.

Later in the day, as we sit down to dinner, my wife and I hold hands before we eat. As we look in each other's eyes, we tell each other without words that we love each other very much. That moment of stopping and holding hands is a powerful statement of affection and well-being. If we have company, we tell them that the finest blessing of any meal is to share it with friends, and invite them to join us in our ritual.

After dinner, my wife and I do the dishes together, often singing as we do. We'll begin singing as we wash the dishes, and then we sit down (not for too long) to play my guitar and her autoharp as we continue harmonizing (but not too well, unfortunately). This is one of the loveliest times of the day. Singers are those who love to sing.

Before I go to bed, I always go through the house, closing the doors and turning out the lights. Then I sit down in the rocking chair in the living room for a few moments. I sit there, in the dark, collecting my thoughts and trying to focus. I have no purpose in this. I couldn't describe to you, or even to myself, exactly what I'm doing, other than to say it is a deliberate effort to allow the pace of my life to slow down and to let things happen in my mind.

To end the day, I do a funny thing before I go to sleep. I read something humorous in bed. Joke books, cartoon books — I'll read anything to help me go to bed with a laugh in my mind. This annoys my wife, because I get to laughing and shaking the bed, and then I have to read her the story or the joke.

So there's what I do every day that I can. I must confess, however, that I don't always manage to do all of these things, or even any of these things. For all my good intentions, there are days when things go wrong or I fall into old habits. When things are not going well, when I'm grumpy or mad, I'll realize that I've not been paying attention to my soul and I've not been following my best routine. But if I stick to my routine regularly, even four days out of seven, my life goes well.

I have a weekly ritual to complement my daily rituals of paying attention to my soul. For fifty years, first as a child and later as a minister, I went to church almost every Sunday. For about the last ten years, I have not been active as a minister. Still, I try to observe the Sabbath in two ways. First, I visit churches. Some Sunday mornings you'll find me at the Greek Orthodox church, even though I am neither Greek nor Orthodox, because I love the chants, the aesthetics, the whole rich-ness. Or I might go to the very last compline service at the Episcopal cathedral, which is a thirty-minute sung liturgy, with no sermon. In going to these churches, I am consciously put-ting myself into a place where richness comes to me in a way that's beyond words.

My wife and I also try to live Sundays as if they were a different kind of day. I take this concept more from the Jewish tradition than from the Christian. We don't go anywhere; we don't have any obligations; we don't do any work. Instead, we listen to music, we read, we go for walks. We try to set our-selves aside from our busy lives on this day, allowing ourselves to simply enjoy being alive. We've noticed that having one sane day a week really makes a difference. We don't always manage to observe the Sabbath in this way, but when we do, it is indeed a special day.

And so, every day, I make a conscious effort to wake gently, relive pleasant episodes in my life, participate in physical ac-tivity, do meaningful work, let my unconscious mind speak to me, and focus. One day a week I set aside as a Sabbath. All of these simple-yet-rich rituals nourish my soul. If I fail to do these things, I don't sleep well, and my days do not go well.

The older I get, the more I realize the importance of exer-cising the various dimensions of my body, soul, mind, and heart. Taken together, these aspects give me a sense of whole-ness. I want to be a whole human being rather than one who limps on one leg because I don't know how to use all of my parts. Intellectual, emotional, and physical activity are not sepa-rate entities. Rather, they are dimensions of the same human being.

All this takes some conscious effort. At the same time, I am fully aware of the extraordinary power of the unconscious. As I write these words, for example, some part of my brain is controlling my liver. If I were to take over conscious control of my liver, I'd be dead before this page was completed, because I don't understand how my liver works — yet somehow I cause it to function. This same split with unity is true for the activity of my whole being. If I were to attempt to rationally run every aspect of myself, I couldn't. The conscious part of my mind simply cannot control all the mysterious activities of my humanity.

I don't have all the answers, and I certainly do not live a superior life. But there are some things that one begins to figure out after almost sixty years of life. Life often goes well at this point because we have made our mistakes and survived our failures, and because we know what it's like when life goes wrong.

One final thought on nourishing the soul. I try to make sure that I see the real news of the real world that's right in front of me, not just the recitation of disasters that passes for news on television. The real news, the knowledge of what's going on in my immediate world and immediate life, sustains life. I ate today, and I was not eaten. All the people in my world treated me with great civility and respect today. This news is nourishing to the soul; it should be sought out and welcomed. Now, I'm not a Pollyanna, I know that bad things do happen. As I look across the room, I see a very large poster hanging on my wall that shows a chicken being held upside down, about to have its throat cut. Underneath the picture it says, "Don't forget, sometimes things are just as bad as they seem." But right alongside that is a rubber chicken, and looking at it makes me laugh.

I guess the key questions to ask are, "What do you expect out of life?" and "What will you settle for?" I don't expect that anyone's life will be lived exactly according to plan. But I do expect that life will go well if I simply pay attention to the positives, as well as to the negatives, of the mixture that is in me and is in the rest of the world. And if I focus on my soul, if I allow it to speak to me and if I listen to it carefully, then it is I who am nourished at the center of my being.

GOD'S FINGERPRINTS
on the SOUL

by Rabbi Harold Kushner

"When your life is filled with the desire to see the holiness in everyday life, something magical happens: ordinary life becomes extraordinary, and the very process of life begins to nourish your soul!"

EVERYTHING THAT GOD created is potentially holy, and our task as humans is to find that holiness in seemingly unholy situations. When we can do this, we will have learned to nurture our souls.

Think about it: it's easy to see God's beauty in a glorious sunset or in ocean waves crashing on a beach. But can you find the holiness in a struggle for life?

I recently had a conversation with a woman whose daughter is suffering from kidney failure. The girl has had three transplants — all were rejected. She is on regular dialysis. Yet is this a tear-jerking story of despair? On the contrary. What the woman tells me is how brave and strong her daughter has been throughout her ordeal and how "in awe" she is of her own child's ability to cope and still remain cheerful and full of life. My friend has found the "holiness" in her daughter's situation.

We must remember that everything in this world has God's fingerprints on it — and that alone makes it special. Our inability to see beauty doesn't suggest in the slightest that beauty is not there. Rather, it suggests that we are not looking carefully enough or with broad enough perspective to see the beauty.

Can you see the holiness in those things you take for granted — a paved road or a washing machine? If you concentrate on finding what is good in every situation, you will discover that your life will suddenly be filled with gratitude, a feeling that nurtures the soul.

With practice, you will be able to see holiness in areas not usually associated with holiness. You will be able to see the beauty in the "circle of life" — even when someone you love is sick or dying. You will begin to sense the holiness in the everyday problems that force you to grow and develop. When your life is filled with the desire to see the holiness in everyday life, something magical happens: ordinary life becomes extraordinary, and the very process of life begins to nourish your soul! With each new circumstance that comes your way, another opportunity presents itself to nourish your soul. As long as you can find even a kernel of holiness in a situation, your soul will grow and feel cared for.

In my book *To Life!*, I define the Jewish religion as the science of taking the ordinary and making it holy. The idea is to try to find some bit of holiness in everything — food, sex, earning and spending money, having children, conversations with friends. If we are rooted in the belief that everything God created is potentially holy, we have the capacity to notice that which is beautiful and holy in everyday life. Everything can be seen as a miracle, part of God's plan. And when we can truly see this, we nourish our souls.

Nourishing your soul can be compared to eating, or nourishing your body. Sometimes you pause during a meal and truly savor the food. You realize how really wonderful the food is; you appreciate it and count your blessings. Other times, you simply shovel the food into your mouth while you're watching the news or reading the paper, unaware of the fact that you're nourishing your body.

The same is true of spiritual nourishment. Sometimes we are simply "blown away" and in awe by finding ourselves in the presence of God. Other times, however, even when we are participating in acts of kindness — complimenting others, writing a check to charity, donating time to a good cause — we are oblivious to the miracle of what is happening at that moment. But this is OK too. In fact, there is something innately wonderful about doing nice, warmhearted things for others even when we are not "spiritually awake," when the momentum of what we have done in more awake moments carries us through.

You will notice that when you carry out acts of kindness, when you pray, study, give to charity, or forgive someone who may have hurt you, you get a wonderful feeling inside. It is as though something inside your body responds and says, "Yes, this is how I ought to feel!" I've often said that the feeling you get from a simple act of goodwill can be compared to the rush of endorphins you get from an hour-long workout at the gym.

Why do we get this wonderful feeling? What is its purpose?

I believe that each of us was put on this earth to fulfill his or her potential for humanity, and the soul is that part of us that makes us truly human. The soul is what makes a human being a human being and not simply another living creature on God's earth. The soul is not a physical entity, but instead refers to everything about us that is not physical — our values, memories, identity, sense of humor. Since the soul represents the parts of the human being that are not physical, it cannot get sick, it cannot die, it cannot disappear. In short, the soul is immortal.

You nourish your soul by fulfilling your destiny, by developing the potential that the soul represents. When you fulfill your soul's destiny, you will feel "right."

Conversely, when you ignore your soul's destiny, when you get caught up in your own self-interests and forget to care for others, you will not feel "right." Instead, you will feel empty and unfulfilled. During these times, you are neglecting your soul — you are depriving it of nourishment.

When I talk to people who feel this emptiness and lack of fulfillment, I recommend that they find a source of balance in their lives. I suggest that they find some way to "give back" to the world in order to feel a sense of completeness.

If, for example, you are very busy with your career, try not only to find the holiness within your work, but also seek something outside your nine-to-five job as an additional source of fulfillment and as a way to feel the joy of helping others. You can do any number of things to fulfill this goal — volunteer at a community hotline, coach a Little League team, donate your time to a public school, visit the sick. Whatever you choose, you will gain a sense that you are giving of yourself, that you are sharing yourself with the world, that you are fulfilling the destiny of your soul.

Let's look at the case of a typical middle-aged man who is in the midst of a midlife crisis. He feels that he is "going nowhere" with his career, and he is filled with despair. Buying a faster car or dating a younger woman won't erase this despair. Instead, he needs to reach beyond the competitiveness of the business world, to spend time connecting with people rather than seeing them as rivals. This added dimension in his life is often the single change that is needed for him to feel that sense of soul nourishment.

Too often, people make the mistake of believing that if they only had more money or more sex or a different partner or a better-looking body, they would feel the sense of "wholeness" they have always craved. Virtually without exception, this is not the case. What is actually lacking is the dimension of giving and kindness as a means of nourishing the soul. To add this dimension to your life is to nourish your soul.

The soul craves two distinct types of nourishment — public and private. Each person requires a different balance between these two types of nourishment.

I tend to be a very public person. I feel that I nourish my soul and grow as a human being through my contacts with others. I have found that, for me, congregational prayer is usually a much richer spiritual experience than private prayer. I like to feel I'm part of a team. I need contact with, and feedback from, other people.

On the other hand, I know very spiritual people who nourish their souls in a much more private manner. They tend to their souls through meditation, contemplation, study, and self-improvement. I believe that everyone needs a little bit of both types of nourishment, but the balance will vary from person to person.

Virtually all individuals have the potential to grow spiritually and nourish their souls on a day-to-day basis. There is hope and great possibility even for those who are severely disadvantaged.

When a retarded child is born, the religious question we often ask is, "Why does God let this happen?" The better question to pose is to ask, "What kind of a community should we be so that mental retardation isn't a barrier to the enjoyment of one's full humanity?"

One of the messages I share time and time again is a verse in chapter 40 of Isaiah: "Those that return to the Lord will have their strength renewed."

When you are despairing, when you are confronted with a situation you fear will overwhelm you, don't ask God to take away the problem, but instead, pray that He gives you the strength to deal with it.

For me, the proof of the existence of God is that I am constantly witnessing ordinary people doing extraordinary things and coming up with strength they never knew they had. A perfect example is the sick daughter I mentioned earlier, who is still full of life and courage despite her ordeals. My own son was able to do the same thing at the end of his life. These are examples of God's intervention: He doesn't take away the problem, but rather gives us resources to cope with it.

In one of my books, I said, "Religion can't change the facts, but it can change the way you relate to facts."

One distinction I like to make, originally made by Martin Buber, is on the difference between theology and religion. Buber defines theology as "talking about God" and religion as "experiencing God."

I believe that what we need in American spiritual life today is less "theology" and more "religion" — less concern about belief in God, the nature of God, and the existence of God, and more opportunities to find moments in our lives when we feel that we just met God.

We "meet" God when we pray, when we are helpful and kind, when we overcome nasty habits, addictions, and pettiness in our lives.

God's Fingerprints on the Soul

Ultimately, I see spiritual growth as climbing a ladder. You climb slowly, step by step. With each step you take, you solidify your footing, then move on to the next step. Each step you take up the ladder nourishes your soul. In time, you will feel completely nourished and connected to God. You will have truly met God.

EMBRACING the EVERYDAY

by Thomas Moore, Ph.D.

*"I think we would be able to live in this world more peace-
ably if our spirituality were to come from looking not just
into infinity but very closely at the world around us — and
appreciating its depth and divinity."*

I'VE COME TO BELIEVE, through many years of reading and
thinking about this issue, that the soul is really very broad,
much broader than we tend to think. It encompasses not just
the higher or transcendent level of consciousness, the realm
that we traditionally call spirit, but also what we might refer to
as the lower level of consciousness — the soul in ordinary experience, the soul in everyday life.

The higher level has to do with developing an overview
or philosophy of life, a sense of moral conviction, an idea of
what the world is all about and our place in it. These concerns
have long been highly valued and addressed through worship,
prayer, and other traditional forms of spirituality.

I have devoted most of my writing and teaching to emphasizing the lower part of the soul, not because I believe the higher part is unimportant — it is indeed important — but because the lower aspect has been so neglected. What I mean by this lower level is the value of living one's day-to-day life with attention to essential everyday qualities such as beauty, intimacy, community, imagination.

I sometimes refer to a famous dream of Carl Jung's in which he was going downstairs, descending from one level to the next. This dream was associated with a period of profound discovery. In our culture, however, we are so focused on success and progress that everyone talks about going *up* the ladder — no one talks about going *down* the ladder. We have lost the sense of how we might find religion and piety in the most ordinary experiences.

Many theologies, including Christian, Jewish, Buddhist, and the ancient Greek religion, suggest that divinity exists deep within everyday experience. For example, Christian theologians have talked about the "immanence" of God — immanence meaning God residing within us. Part of the ancient Greek religion was a sense that gods and goddesses inhabited not just heaven or the deep underworld but nature itself — they were to be found right within ordinary life.

We need to rediscover this awareness. To me, for example, a dwelling is truly a sacred space. I don't mean this romantically or fantastically, but I think there is a kind of spirit, an inherent sacredness, within a home . . . within a region . . . within trees, bodies of water, any particular place or terrain. We don't have to look up to the sky, to some infinite emptiness, in order to find the sacred. That search has its place, but a sense of the infinite is only part of a much fuller spirituality that can encompass ordinary experience as well.

I think many of the troubles we run into are due to our

treating the sacred as something abstract. This attitude is part of what allows us to do great harm to nature and ourselves. If our religion is completely ethereal, we may become numb to the consequences of, for example, building a chemical plant that could be toxic to children in the community. Not only that, but restricting religion to a high-in-the-sky place tends to make people polemical about their own moral positions — to the degree that they can justify harming others who disagree with them. We've seen this phenomenon take place in country after country. I think we would be able to live in this world more peaceably if our spirituality were to come from looking not just into infinity but very closely at the world around us — and appreciating its depth and divinity.

When we are so estranged from the everyday presence of the sacred, how can we rekindle a relationship with the soul? There are many ways, though they're not necessarily easy. A good beginning is to stop what we're doing every so often — take time out from the crazy pace we're caught up in — and use that time to contemplate, whether through formal meditation, or by talking to each other more deeply, or simply by enjoying nature. Even a vacation can be a form of contemplation if you do it in a way that's not hyperactive — though a lot of people find this difficult!

A related idea is not to be too active or forceful about planning our lives. I don't mean we shouldn't think about the future at all, but it's so easy for our ambitions to get in the way of caring for the soul. What I have tried to do, rather than let my ambitions drive me, is to listen to what's going on around and within me as an indication of which direction I should go. What I find is that this process of listening and responding often leads me back in the direction of my family. People I deal with in the media are often surprised that I'll put family needs before some potentially grand media success. I could be away

Embracing the Everyday

from home every day of the year if that kind of success and excitement were my first priority, but it's terribly important to me to protect those things that are most intimate. Ultimately, my family gives me more pleasure than whatever outside opportunity looks alluring at the moment.

Our close relationships with others — family and friends — are possibly the most soulful aspects of our lives. These relationships do not always bring immediate gratification — in fact, they can be quite difficult — but they help ground us.

We need people in our lives with whom we can be as open as possible. To have real conversations with people may seem like such a simple, obvious suggestion, but it involves courage and risk. I think it's a big mistake to think of the soul as strictly an internal experience. To be able to express our most intimate feelings and thoughts without fear of betrayal is one of the great quests of the life of the soul. And an important step in soul care is to give time and attention to those relationships that allow us to do this.

When we express ourselves, I think it's valuable to use a language that is our own. These days, a lot of people talk to each other in the language they hear on television or in magazines and books, and we end up sounding like an armchair psychologist or an anthropologist or some other kind of "expert." We need to work at speaking from the heart rather than from this mind that is so influenced by the culture at large. The discovery of our own language, our own way of thinking about and describing things, can help us be truly present — more fully open to others and receptive to experience.

Another way to encourage the opening of the soul is to notice where we feel we are going wrong, where the symptoms are. We can look around and see where our relationships are failing, where our depressions or other emotional troubles seem to be focused, where our addictions lie. By looking carefully at what's wrong, we discover the exact areas that need attention.

Take loneliness, for example. Loneliness is rarely a matter of not having enough people around. In fact, many folks say they're lonely even though their lives are filled with people.

Our inclination is usually to treat loneliness in a narcissistic way, as a personal problem — "Okay, come into therapy with me and we'll explore the roots of your loneliness and try to understand it so you won't have it anymore." But if we look carefully at what loneliness is telling us, we can see it as an invitation to respond to the world, to become more fully engaged with it and put ourselves out for it. There are so many ways in which we're needed, so many ways to become engaged — whether it's volunteering at a soup kitchen, or offering a foster home to children who need one, or visiting someone in the hospital. I think we need to look for community not just in the superficial sense of gathering in the same place to have fun, but also by feeling compassionately what others are going through and responding with our time and hearts.

Another aspect of loneliness has to do with an understanding of solitude. Loneliness is sometimes a sign that we need to learn what it takes for us to be constructively alone, grounded in our own natures, willing to take responsibility for making our own decisions and shaping our own lives. Dealing thoughtfully with both these aspects of loneliness — connection and solitude — can be so much more nurturing than the search for a quick fix that is so common in our society.

Another way to become more attuned to the divinity around us is by turning to the arts and the great religions for education and inspiration. For example, I spend a great deal of time reading ancient Greek tragedy and poetry, because I think these expressions of belief and emotion have so much to say about the life of the soul. Or I'll read books and look at paintings from the Italian Renaissance, because I think that's a particularly soulful period in European history. I'll look at African art very closely, or listen to the music of India. Each person has his or her own way of knowing which forms of art offer greatest nourishment for that person's soul.

There are so many rich sources of art and reflection all around us — you could spend several lifetimes feeding your soul just within the walls of a public library or museum. Unfortunately, our society has reduced the life of art to entertainment. We don't need to be entertained nearly as much as we need to give the soul the images it craves. Yet we allow Hollywood and the entertainment industry to distract us, to sell us superficial stories with exploitative characters and formulaic plots. I don't mean this in a snobbish way at all — truly excellent popular songs can be nourishing, as can a film that stimulates reflection or stirs your heart. Even the occasional television sitcom penetrates below the surface and touches something deeper. But I do think we should demand only the best and be willing to shut the television off; to go to movies we believe will be worthwhile and walk out if they aren't; to read books that offer depth.

In making these various suggestions, I don't want to imply that I view caring for the soul as making a project out of your life. There is already much judgment against oneself, either implied or explicit, in magazines, newspapers, and television these days. Popular psychology has put a terrible weight on people with this kind of moralism that says we should continually be improving ourselves, becoming something other than we are.

If people are having trouble finding ways to care for the soul, it may be that they imagine this task is too big a project. It really isn't. All you need to do is look right at this moment and ask yourself, what around you is requesting your attention? Is it that you would like to take a bath? Is it that your neighbor across the street is having some trouble and needs your time for a while? Is it that your house needs a little bit of paint on the side wall? Is it that your city council needs someone to speak up about what's going on in your community? The key is to give up the project of making yourself something shiny and big and to recognize that we are very ordinary people. By learning to discover and value our ordinariness, we nurture a friendliness toward ourselves and the world that is the essence of a healthy soul.

SOUL MOMENTS

by Marion Woodman, Ph.D.

*"We all experience 'soul moments' in life — when we see a
magnificent sunrise, hear the call of a loon, see the wrinkles
in our mother's hands, or smell the sweetness
of a baby. During these moments, our body, as well as
our brain, resonates as we experience the glory of being
a human being."*

WHEN I TAKE a walk on a crisp autumn day and
see scarlet leaves against a brilliant azure sky,
my soul is nurtured as I see God incarnate in
the vivid colors of nature.

Every time I arrange fresh flowers, I choose the blossoms
from my garden and the vase from my shelf so that color and
form complement each other. Four days later, I see the vermil-
ion rose is developing a silver sheen that would be enhanced in
pewter. I choose a new vase; I honor the aging; I create a new

form. Just as order and beauty are crucial to a floral arrangement, so order and beauty are necessary for the well-being of my soul. They mirror each other.

When I create a room in my home, I express that beauty in the colors I choose and how I use them. And when I walk through that room, I feel I am walking through my soul. I feel I have created a manifestation of my soul, a mirror of my inner sense of sparkle and depth.

The soul, for me, is in everything in life. It is in all the beauty as well as in all the agony. Some of the most profound "soul moments" I have experienced during my lifetime have been the most agonizing. I have sat by the bedside of a dying loved one. I have helped "midwife" a soul into the next world. I have died to this world for the days of transition. I have experienced rebirth on a new spiral in my own life.

We all experience "soul moments" in life — when we see a magnificent sunrise, hear the call of a loon, see the wrinkles in our mother's hands, or smell the sweetness of a baby. During these moments, our body, as well as our brain, resonates as we experience the glory of being a human being.

It is amazing that our souls — our eternal essences, with all their hopes and dreams and visions of an eternal world — are contained within these temporal bodies. No wonder suffering is part of the human condition.

I think of my soul as the eternal part of me that lives in my body, day in and day out. In a way, my soul is the bridge between spirit and body and, as such, is a uniter of opposites. The unity that is created by soul is crucial to my well-being. Without soul at center, I would either transcend into spirit or become mired in matter.

In my work as an analyst, I meet many people in midlife and older who are desperately searching for their souls, whether they realize it or not. They say they are seeking meaning in their lives, a sense of purpose. They have every earthly thing the world can offer, yet these objects no longer matter. They feel empty because they have lost touch with soul.

If we fail to nourish our souls, they wither, and without soul, life ceases to have meaning. Life becomes boring; it has no dimension. Without soul, we have no ears to hear great music, no perception to understand poetry or dreams, no eyes to appreciate fine art. The creative process shrivels in the absence of continual dialogue with soul. And creativity is what makes life worth living.

One of the ways I nurture my own soul is by waking every morning around four-thirty and spending two hours by myself — for myself — doing yoga, visualization, meditation, or working on dreams. If I do not give myself this time at the beginning of every day, then I feel that other people are eating me up, and I become very irritated and anxious.

Another way I nurture my soul is by keeping a daily journal. My journal is my soul book. It is my dialogues with God. Since the age of twelve, I have searched for my essence, and I have recorded my terrors, my hopes, my delights in my journal. In doing this, I have affirmed my own feelings and my own values. I have sought to discover my unique purpose. In this way, I have tried to live my own truth, which often ran counter to the culture. This is what my two solitary hours in the morning are about — experiencing the core of my soul and discovering the truth that I have to live.

I experience and nurture my soul when I'm dancing, because for me, dancing is both the flight of my body and the incarnation of my spirit. It is a union of spirit and body. My soul is the bridge.

Increasingly, I have found that growing older releases soul. It's as if I have new eyes and new ears, a new nose and new fingers. Everything has become a new experience — from an autumn walk to my grandnephew's smile. I saw these things before, but now I see them as a part of the totality I call God.

I have great friends, men and women. My friendships with women have a different dimension from my friendships with men, because we resonate with each other in a different way. Women enhance my own sense of being woman. I think most women need this type of enhancement in order to experience their full identity as women. A woman's identity is not complete so long as she depends on the approval of men. She needs to stand to her full stature in her own womanhood and so nurture her soul.

My husband and I have been married for thirty-six years. Every day we take time to talk with each other as honestly and nakedly as possible. We share soul with each other in good times and bad.

Love is energy. In meditation, I open myself to receive that energy from people, from nature, from God. I imagine myself as a musical instrument through which God plays. Sometimes I feel the masculine side energizing me, sometimes the feminine, whom I call Sophia. For me, Sophia is the manifestation of God through nature, through body, through people. One of the reasons I spend two quiet hours alone in the morning is my need to tune myself for the day, so that I will be able to see and hear and feel soul in everyone and everything I meet. I open myself to the possibility of Grace.

It is only through the Grace we receive from God that we are able to keep walking, that our souls are able not only to survive but to flourish and be filled with life and love.

2.

The
Heart of
Soul

"The world stands out on either side
No wider than the heart is wide;
Above the world is stretched the sky,
No higher than the soul is high.
The heart can push the sea and land
Farther away on either hand;
The soul can split the sky in two,
And let the face of God shine through.
But East and West will pinch the heart
That can not keep them pushed apart;
And he whose soul is flat — the sky
Will cave in on him by and by."
— EDNA ST. VINCENT MILLAY

LOVE: The WORK of the SOUL

by Bernie Siegel, M.D.

*"Every day is my best day; this is my life;
I'm not going to have this moment again."*

IN MY WORK as a physician, I've observed that people who face life-threatening illness are often able to recover the ability that most of us have lost by the time we reach adulthood — the ability to connect with the soul. The child's sense of awe and wonder is too often replaced by a preoccupation with how we look, and whether we're making enough money, and what will the neighbors think, and what do our parents think, and what did our schoolteachers tell us, and what does our religion say. In other words, our intellect controls us.

But in many cases, people who've become aware of their mortality find that they've gained the freedom to live. They are seized with an appreciation for the present: every day is my best day; this is my life; I'm not going to have this moment again. They spend more time with the things and people they

love and less time on people and pastimes that don't offer love or joy. This seems like such a simple thought —
shouldn't we all spend our lives that way? But we tend not to
make those kinds of choices until somebody says, "You have
twelve months to live."

I can walk into a group of strangers and tell who in the room
has had a serious loss or a life-threatening illness by their answers to three questions. The first is, I'm taking you all to
dinner — what do you want to eat? The second question is,
I'd like you to hold something up that will enlighten everyone
here as to what life is about — what would you hold up?
Question number three is, How would you introduce yourself
to God?

If you haven't had a life-threatening illness, you'll spend
a long time deciding how to answer question number one,
because you're worried about my paying the check and you
want to be sure you don't make an overly extravagant choice
and that I also get what *I* want when we go out. So you sit
there silently for five minutes, thinking, and never tell me what
you want to eat. But if you've had a serious illness, you'll shout
"lobster" at me, or whatever other food you love! When I ask
what you'd hold up to enlighten people about life, and you say
"a mirror" or "myself," then I know you've been through
enough to really understand your beauty and your value. And
for people who've faced their mortality, the introduction to
God is usually, "God already knows me. I'm God's child — I
don't need an introduction." But if someone plans to introduce
himself or herself by saying, "God, I'm a lawyer" — or a doctor or a mother — I suspect God's answer would be, "Come
back when you know who you are."

I believe that we're here to contribute love to the planet —
each of us in our own way. Whether you're a waiter or waitress
or manager or barber or run a gas station, if you meet other

people and are giving something to other people, then you're contributing. To nourish your soul, you've got to do what you do out of love. I am not telling you to be selfish. But to be trapped in a job you hate, or required to play a role that you don't want to play, day after day, can be deadly to the soul.

Of course, people will argue that they can't possibly change jobs because of expenses or insurance or the state of the economy, and I have two responses. The first is, find something in your life — whether it's volunteer work or painting a picture or writing a poem — about which you can say, "This is my joy." The other key is to recognize that if you don't like your life and if you can't change your external circumstances at this point, you can change your *attitude* toward your life. You can say, "All right, I choose to be happy. I choose to view what I do every day as a way of contributing love." When you go about your life with this attitude, you'll find that your circumstances *do* begin to change.

As one woman told me, "When I decided to come in to work happy, everybody around me became happy." This woman had decided to quit a job she hated, and on the last day of her two weeks' notice, she woke up happy. At the end of the day, she noticed that everybody around her was happy, too — so she didn't quit after all. She decided to come to work happy instead. Two years later, she's still on the job, radiating happiness and love.

To paraphrase something the anthropologist Ashley Montagu once said, the way I change my life is to act as if I'm the person I want to be. This is, to me, the simplest, wisest advice you can give anyone. When you wake up and act like a loving person, you realize not only that you're altered, but that the people around you are also transformed, because everybody is changed by the reception of this love. I've learned from this principle to take responsibility for what bothers me. I don't blame my wife for not turning out the lights or not living up to my expectations in some other way; and if I do something to upset her I say, "I'm sorry," and I act more loving, and of course I'm changed and she is changed, and I'm happier, and everybody around me is affected.

Part of living with love is also learning how to say "no." This may sound selfish, but in fact what it means is that we are choosing how we will love the world that day. If someone calls you up and asks you to change your plans and you don't want to, you don't need to be sick or have some other external excuse for turning the person down; you can simply say "no." Saying "yes" out of love is fine. If somebody calls you and asks, "Can you help me?," and as an expression of love for that person, you answer, "I'll drop everything right now," that's great. But to act out of need, guilt, or obligation, rather than out of love — that's not soul work. If you need help, observe your pets. Animals know their nature and live it.

Find your true path. It's so easy to become someone we don't want to be, without even realizing it's happening. We are created by the choices we make every day. And if we take action in order to please some authority figure, we'll suddenly wake up down the road and say, "This isn't me. I never wanted to be this person."

I've found that keeping a daily journal or writing a daily poem is a wonderful way to stay in touch with what's important and who I want to be. Journal and poem writing help me integrate what I'm experiencing, rather than shutting off the events in my life from my emotions. I used to be incredulous at how many gory and heartbreaking things I'd see in the hospital every day — and I couldn't even remember what they were when I got home at night. Yet I knew they were in me, because I knew how awful I was feeling. So I began to write about these things, making brief notes during the day if I needed to. Let's say I saw a terrible auto accident on the corner. I'd write "auto accident" on a piece of paper, and later, when I got home, I'd write a few paragraphs about what happened. Then I'd paint pictures for a couple of hours or write a poem about the experience, and I'd come out of that room feeling more at peace.

I've begun writing a poem each morning, and the themes that come up tell me what's going on in my life at a deep level, what I need to work on. For instance, I wrote a poem recently about silence. It began, "Fax, phone, mail, life — whose home is this? What do we all want? . . . I remember hearing nothing, surrounded by sand dunes and nature. God, how beautiful and deafening is silence . . . I need to be silent inside until I can return to the silence outside." I don't consider myself a great poet, but these lines express my reaction to coming home from a restful vacation and finding that the messages and machines and other pressures awaiting me make me feel as though I'm not in charge of my life. I've learned from this to turn my fax off when I go away — I don't want to come home to ten feet of paper. And you know, the world doesn't end.

But even when you can't turn off the phone or fax, there are ways to bring quiet to your world every day. The phone can be a bell of mindfulness, reminding you to breathe "peace" when it rings. We need to be attentive to ways of building this kind of respite into our lives, so that outside demands and expectations don't take control.

For example, I like to go for a run every morning. I call this my "talking to God time," because I'm not in charge of my thoughts during that hour. The repetitive movement — for some people it might be riding a bike or walking — puts me in a sort of trance state, and then the lid is off and all kinds of things surface: what is bothering me, what's making me happy, whatever I need to deal with or talk about. I look around at the wonder of nature, and nature gives me lots of answers. If you watch how nature deals with adversity, continually renewing itself, you can't help but learn.

When I jog, I love to run through cemeteries, and sometimes I stop to read the headstones. I saw one on Cape Cod recently at the grave of a man who died at twenty-eight — so young! The message read, "His life taught us how to live; his death, how to die." That's what ought to be on every headstone — I'd say this boy accomplished whatever he needed to accomplish in twenty-eight years. Now, other people had on their headstones that they went to Yale or Harvard, that they were lawyers or manufacturers. But I don't think God cares where we were graduated or what we did for a living. God wants to know who we *are*. Discovering this is the work of the soul — it is our true life's work.

As a matter of fact, over God's desk are two plaques. One says, "God forgets everything you remember and God remembers everything you forget." And the other says, "Don't feel totally, eternally, irrevocably responsible for everything. That's my job. — God."

ENSOULING OURSELVES

by Joan Borysenko, Ph.D.

*"Some tension is necessary for the soul to grow, and we
can put that tension to good use. We can look for every
opportunity to give and receive love, to appreciate nature,
to heal our wounds and the wounds of others, to forgive,
and to serve."*

T
O NOURISH THE SOUL means to become kinder, more
compassionate, wiser, and more loving, often through
the making of difficult choices that foster growth rather
than safety. The nourishment and growth of the soul is the
very reason for human life. When we nourish the soul we
nourish God, increasing the abundance of the life that we can
see — our children, our society — and the levels of the life
that we don't see at all. In a larger sense, soul is the substance
of the universe, knowing itself and growing itself.

Growth of the soul is our goal, and there are many ways to
encourage that growth, such as through love, nature, healing
our wounds, forgiveness, and service. The soul grows well

when giving and receiving love. I nourish my soul daily by loving others and being vulnerable to their love. Love is, after all, a verb, an action word, not a noun. You can only experience it by receiving it or giving it away. Animals are great lovers and have always been an important part of our family life.

Nature is another important aspect of nourishing the soul. After a hike in the mountains where we live, for instance, I feel a remarkable sense of gratitude and awe. My mind quiets down and allows me to see more clearly the beauty of creation. And through that gratitude, the beauty of the universe is reflected back to the creator.

Unfortunately, not all is beauty and peace. I don't believe I've ever met a person who hasn't been challenged or wounded by something. Difficulties present choices: we can either waste away from our wounds or use them to grow our souls. My husband, for example, is a survivor of the Second World War. As a child, he suffered through six years of bombings, near-escapes, and concentration camps. Part of his soul work has been the gradual transformation of this deep well of grief and pain. As he heals himself, he also participates in healing that terrible idea of war in others. I have always said that no one heals alone — we heal through and for one another. In Judaism this is referred to as *Tikkun Olan*, the healing or restoration of the world, a kind of collective soul work.

The process of making sense of our wounds is a very personal one. But a common theme in wound healing is the universal need to forgive. If we don't forgive ourselves for our mistakes, and others for the wounds they have inflicted upon us, we end up crippled with guilt. And the soul cannot grow under a blanket of guilt, because guilt is isolating, while growth is a gradual process of reconnection to ourselves, to other people, and to a larger whole.

Soul, the basic substance of the universe, yearns for connection. The interconnectedness of our souls makes service for others a natural joy. Studies have shown that people who volunteer and serve others are healthier and happier. Some of the most peaceful and soulful people I've ever met are those in twelve-step programs who are working on the twelfth step, which is to help other people in their recoveries. Because of the interconnectedness of soul, when we help others, we are, in a sense, helping ourselves.

Years ago, an interesting study was conducted at a children's summer camp, where two opposing teams were locked in a violent conflict. The need to cope with a common threat was used to resolve the hostility. A truck bringing water for the camp was purposely knocked onto its side. The kids, not realizing this was staged, all worked together to solve the water crisis. Pulling together creates tremendous bonds between people. It nourishes our collective souls.

Today, the importance of community and service to others is echoed from every corner. Robert Keck, in his book *Sacred Eyes*, explains this by noting that in terms of the timeline of creation, human beings are now just coming out of adolescence. And it is natural to separate ourselves from others and from God during this adolescence. As we look back at the way people acted in the 1980s, we can see that there was a national topping out of greed and isolation. Now we see an end to the idea that a successful life consists of putting oneself first.

However, I don't see us coming out of our collective adolescence into "a thousand years of peace." As long as we inhabit human bodies, strife and turmoil will exist, for we live on a planet made up of opposites. We have day and night, sickness and health, good and evil, male and female, up and down. Tension is unavoidable. But some tension is necessary for the soul to grow, and we can put that tension to good use. We can look for every opportunity to give and receive love, to appreciate nature, to heal our wounds and the wounds of others, to forgive, and to serve.

Besides doing things with and for other people, we all need to take time for ourselves. Part of taking time for ourselves includes a daily spiritual routine. My routine is morning and evening prayers and meditation, sometimes for an hour and other times for just a few minutes. Tuning in to the spirit helps me live "on purpose" and bring forth my gifts, whether writing a poem, cooking a meal, planting flowers, giving a workshop, or writing a book. In taking time to open ourselves to our souls, we become better givers to others and are better able to see the love that is the universe.

Albert Einstein once said that the most important question a human being could answer is, "Is the universe a friendly place?" A spiritually optimistic point of view holds that the universe is woven out of a fabric of love. Everything that is happening is ultimately for the good if we are willing to face it head-on and use our adversities for soul growth. The opposite of spiritual optimism is religious pessimism. This view sees God as judgmental, punitive, and ready to send us to eternal damnation if we make a mistake. This kind of belief in an unfriendly universe is toxic to the soul, rather than soul-nourishing.

As soon as we begin to question toxic beliefs and open up to faith in a friendly universe, the proverbial path opens before us. The people, events, and teachings we need are supplied. This is the action of grace. When we are open to grace, we find that people appear in our lives who encourage the growth of souls.

The MINDFUL SOUL

by Stephen Levine

*"Safety is the most unsafe spiritual path you can take.
Safety keeps you numb and dead. People are caught by surprise when it is time to die. They have allowed themselves
to live so little."*

W HEN PEOPLE SPEAK of nourishing the soul,
they mean opening the heart to the subtle whis-
per in the mind. The soul, the life spark, is your
essential nature.

When the soul leaves, the body experiences death. We've
got it backward. We believe we need the body to live. The
truth is, the body needs us. The soul is the spark from the great
fire. There is nothing in Jesus or Buddha that isn't in us.

When we experience an insight, we feel a sense of calm and
of being at home. Something is triggered in the body that is
responsible for the physical experience that complements the
insight. You could say these happenings give natural reinforcement to the voice of the soul.

Some people wrongly believe karma means that if we have done bad things in the past, bad things happen to us in the present. This is just fear-mongering. Karma does not have to do with punishment. Karma is the most merciful process. It teaches us — subtly, gently, lovingly — what we need to know, and keeps amplifying it until we can hear it. What could be more exquisite than a teacher able to help us remove the obstructions to the natural brilliancy of the soul?

People ask what must they become to be loving. The answer is "nothing." It is a process of letting go of what you thought you had become and allowing your true nature to float to the surface naturally. Then there is no difference between you and God. It is like the pond becoming clear after its muddy bottom has become disturbed, and then returning to rest.

There is nothing to do but be. To nourish the soul is to rest in being. Yet when we speak of nourishing the soul, people ask, "Isn't this done by meditation, by singing, by service to others?" The answer is yes, to the extent that they nourish the mind and enable us to let go of the fear that goes by the name self-image. But we are only truly happy when our heart is opening. Our greatest unhappiness comes from our longing. Our greatest peace comes from our being.

A great block to nourishment of the soul is distrust. We don't trust ourselves, so we stay rooted in the easy and convenient. We eliminate as much pain as we can from our lives and end up painted into a corner we call safety. Safety is the most unsafe spiritual path you can take. Safety keeps you numb and dead. People are caught by surprise when it is time to die. They have allowed themselves to live so little.

When we meditate, we watch the mind, to see who we are not. We sing to expand our boundaries and find there is so much more to us. But even these scarcely allow us to touch the enormity of our great nature and that which inhabits us and whose spark gives us life. Imagine going into the spark and finding not just the fire but the source of flame.

How should we behave in everyday life? Show your heart how trustworthy you really are. We had a teacher who said it was possible to have the power of *brahmachari,* which is celibacy, with one's mate, but it is not only monogamy in a sexual sense. It is one-pointedness and focus. It is focusing, for instance, on the changing states of mind throughout the day. We come to notice the qualities that block the heart and limit the expression and experience of the soul. Monogamy allows you to love God and your true nature even more than the person you love most in the world. When you love *the* Beloved even more than *your* beloved, you become a collaborator with God and your beloved on the path to the soul.

Also, it's important in everyday life to work with kindness. Learn patience. When you stand in lines or are at a red light, soften your belly. Open your body and your mind to the subtler levels of experience, letting go of your attempt to control, to be right, not worrying about appearances, not trying to be safe.

Someone asked one of our teachers why he smiled all the time. He said, "Because I have nothing, because I am nothing." He was experiencing his boundless nature. Everything that goes beyond "I am" is a limitation. I am a man. I am a woman. I am a mother. I am a father. I am a carpenter. I am a good person. I am a bad person. I am a poet. I am a mechanic. I am a doctor. I am a janitor. All these are names for your suffering, for what you fear you will lose when you die. These are limitations to your soul, blockages to your heart, measurements of your distance from God.

You lessen your distance to God by monogamy. You watch your mind to see who you are not. I watch my mind to gain a sense of its content, which has always been *my* pain. As I watch

The Mindful Soul

it, I get a sense of its impermanence. Thoughts come and go as part of a process. I see how content dissolves into process and begin to see the patterns in the process. Realizing it isn't *my* suffering, *my* pain, it becomes *the* pain. I've gone from the tiny, the small, and the the individual to the universal. I feel *our* pain. When we do, we go from fear to compassion. Fear is *my* pain, compassion is *the* pain.

Watching my mind, I can see that anger is made up of multiple states, including fear and hope and dismay. You go inside yourself, and that which was hidden in the subconscious begins to reveal itself. The mercy you feel is astounding. I know people who have been doing this for twenty years, and still they shake their heads and say, "I can't believe how well this stuff really works."

You begin to get a sense of the space that the process floats in. You have, in a sense, gone from the mind to the soul and to God itself. The space is the universal, and essence of being. You begin in the first stages to be kind and loving, you try to slow the mind down, to make it less self-centered and egotistic. Then you become aware that this is what *the* mind does. When you stop taking *the* mind so personally and become aware of the process, you see that the mind is actually just a level. It's not who you are, it's an aspect of what you are. You go into the enormous space of beingness, of suchness. You understand God is much too small a word to express the enormity of its reality. You cannot know God. You can only be God. Knowing implies boundaries. But how can you define something that is literally indefinable because it has no boundaries?

The path of the soul is from the individual to the universal, and beyond and to Itself, essential suchness, formless Being. Happiness is a superstition, but joy is your birthright. We think that by working in our everyday, busy mind and polishing the personality and letting its best aspects express themselves, we can make ourselves perfect. But even enlightenment does not perfect the personality — only the point of view. We are enlightened out of the personality, the individual and separate, into the soul, the universal inseparable.

LOVE VITAMINS for YOUR SOUL

by John Gray, Ph.D.

"I believe that to nurture my soul and to fulfill my soul's purpose, I must learn from every event in my life. I must come to realize that every experience has within it a seed of a tremendous gift — a soul gift."

EACH DAY YOU are faced with opportunities to help others, to forgive them, to have compassion for them, to be tolerant of them. Do you seize these opportunities, or do you let them slip by?

Though seemingly inconsequential, these everyday decisions have direct impact on the state of your soul, for you nurture your soul by giving of yourself to others in a loving way. And each time you choose to help others, your soul grows and flourishes.

We all have many God-given gifts. The challenge with which we are each faced is to discover these gifts and then make full use of them by serving others. That is how our soul grows, in the highest sense: the soul stretches itself and fulfills its purpose.

But though our soul thrives when we give of ourselves, we must realize that we cannot give love unless we can receive love. Our ability to receive love is based upon our ability to feel, because it is through our feelings that we are able to receive support and then be motivated to give support.

In order to give of ourselves, we must nurture ourselves. One of the ways we receive this nurturing is through having a good relationship. This gives us the opportunity to serve our partner — and serving others is intrinsic in nurturing our own souls.

Men and women receive love differently. This is because men and women are basically different and do not approach life in the same way. Because most of us do not understand these differences, we rarely get what we need from the opposite sex.

Let me give you an example: Men are often described as being unfeeling or out of touch with their feelings, and therefore in need of massive doses of therapy to "get in touch with their feelings." But if you go to a football game, you will find men who are very much in touch with their feelings. They are very alive and enthusiastic. Whenever a man does anything, there is a feeling behind it, a feeling that motivated him to take action.

The primary way to love a man and help him get in touch with his feelings is to appreciate him for what he does. To nurture a man's soul, you must repeatedly send him the message that he makes a difference, that his actions are worthwhile. You must also let him know that when his actions are mistakes, they are forgivable. You must assure him that he is accepted just the way he is. If you try to correct him or tell him what to do, he will only resist. And if he does not resist he will weaken; he will lose touch with the inner guidance within him that needs to be in control of his actions.

Women often need to feel in control of their feelings. The way to nurture a woman's soul is to give her the support she needs to freely express herself, to talk about her feelings, her wants and wishes. You must not attempt to correct her feelings or talk her out of her feelings. If she is feeling bad or afraid or angry, do not be critical of that. This is a huge task, but it is of immense importance.

Once we have learned how to nurture our partners, we can then go out and make a difference in the world. Parents, for example, can begin by making a difference for their children. As their children grow, the parents can move beyond the family to the community, then outside the community to the world at large.

This process of giving unconditional love nurtures us and fulfills our purpose in life. Whenever you are able to give of yourself without expecting anything in return, you become a bigger person.

Just as unconditional love is one of the manifestations of soul growth, there are other attributes as well: forgiveness, courage, patience, faith, compassion, generosity, wisdom. An evolved soul requires all of these qualities, in proper balance.

Let me give you a personal example. I believe that to nurture my soul and to fulfill my soul's purpose, I must learn from every event in my life. I must come to realize that every experience has within it a seed of a tremendous gift — a soul gift — some new strength.

When I feel betrayed by someone, instead of sulking, clinging to my resentment and playing the role of victim, I am challenged to strengthen my soul through forgiveness. By forgiving the person who hurt me, I strengthen my soul.

The Heart of Soul

So you can see that forgiveness is one of the attributes of soul growth. And each time we are called upon to forgive, we nourish our souls and learn more about who we are and what we have to share in this world. This is also an example of unconditional love.

Sometimes life frightens me and I'm tempted to retreat instead of risking failure. But when I challenge this fear and choose to take a risk, this stretches my soul. By forging ahead and trying something new — even when I am scared — I perform an act of courage. And this act of courage strengthens my soul and strengthens my character.

So you can see that forgiveness and courage are two intrinsic virtues of the soul. But there are more.

Patience is one. Within our hearts, each of us has dreams, like seeds waiting to sprout and grow into beautiful flowers. We are anxious for all these dreams to come about; we long for something we can't have at this moment. In order to nurture your soul, you need to realize this and accept the fact that all things come in time. You must learn to be patient and yet to persist.

Faith is yet another quality of the soul. All of us are confused and ambivalent at times. We don't know the answer to a problem, or we are faced with conflicting answers. Instead of giving up, instead of drowning in doubt, soul growth requires that we forge ahead, that we continue to ask questions and look for answers — all the while having faith that everything is unfolding in the right manner.

I draw upon all these qualities of my soul during times of trial and tribulation, during times of suffering. I dig deep within myself to draw out the best of myself — and, miraculously, the suffering goes away. Because forgiveness takes away suffering; patience and tolerance take away suffering; faith takes away suffering. All adversity is really an opportunity for our souls to grow; all adversity is really a form of growing pains.

Compassion is another virtue capable of neutralizing suffering. Compassion also motivates us to give service in this world. When we experience the pain of another person, we instinctively want to take away that pain. But by taking away the other person's pain, we also take away his or her opportunity to grow. To be truly compassionate, we must be able to share another person's suffering and pain — knowing there is nothing we can do to relieve it and that we are not responsible for it, and yet knowing and understanding what that pain feels like.

Generosity is another virtue of the soul, and it goes hand in hand with compassion. If you have no compassion, you cannot have generosity. Let me give you an example: Think of the many poor and homeless people in our country. People who are lacking in compassion cope with the sight of a poor person by eliminating that person from their awareness. They ignore the situation because they can't deal with it. They look the other way instead of extending their understanding and generosity.

However, if these same people had compassion, the compassion would motivate them to act in a generous manner. Generosity manifests itself when we are motivated by compassion.

Sometimes little can be done, but we do what we can. And this is an example of how compassion brings out another attribute of the soul — wisdom. Too often, when people start to feel compassion for another human being, they also feel compelled to change the other person, rather than simply empathizing in a compassionate manner. They want to offer advice. A truly wise person will have the wisdom to know what he can do, accept what he can't do, and have the generosity of spirit to extend himself in ways that can make a difference.

Each of these attributes leads into the other, almost like the rungs on a ladder. Each is an expression of the soul.

What is critical is to realize how interrelated all these virtues are, and how they should be balanced.

Consider a woman who is full of compassion yet meddles too much in other people's lives. She takes too much responsibility for them instead of helping them in a way that helps them help themselves. She has compassion, but she lacks wisdom.

When you choose to give to others, your generosity must be unconditional. Consider the case of the generous person who gives too much and later resents it because he feels unappreciated.

Serving others can be very difficult, especially if we feel unfulfilled as individuals, if we have little support in our lives, or if we have not taken care of ourselves. You have to give to yourself first; then you can mature into the highest level of soul growth, which is service to others.

A relationship with God — or a higher power — is vital to nurturing and tending one's soul. Without it, you will encounter a variety of troubles: you'll expect your partner to be perfect, because you don't have a relationship with perfection. Or you'll expect your partner to be your higher power. This is a big mistake.

In order to nurture our souls, we must also come to understand what I call "love vitamins." These are basically the different types of love that we require for spiritual health. We must realize that we all need a balanced combination of love vitamins. If you expect to receive all your love from your partner, for instance, it will never be enough. You need a balance.

Vitamin S is love of self. Vitamin O stands for love received from the opposite sex. Vitamin F is love from friends and family. Vitamin P is love from parents.

If one of your relationships isn't working, it could be that you are deficient in another love vitamin. For example, let's say you have unresolved issues with your mother or father. Did you realize that these neglected issues could block your partner from providing you with love and support? If you felt ignored as a child and your partner ignores you a bit, you'll probably overreact and blow the situation out of proportion when, in reality, he or she was just preoccupied. See? You tend to project onto your relationship with your partner the unresolved issues in other aspects of your being — your relationships with your parents, your family, your friends, yourself, your buddies, and your peers.

A need for a relationship with God is the critically important vitamin G. This is actually broken down into vitamin G_1, which is our most immature relationship with God, our most dependent relationship, and vitamin G_2, which is our most mature state, when we are serving God. Vitamin G_1 is the basis of vitamin G_2, but neither one is superior, neither is better than the other.

In our first, most immature relationship with God, we perceive God as the big parent in the sky, the omnipresent, omnipotent flock of angels that supports us. Based on this relationship, we grow and come to know ourselves and our abilities. We begin to use the support we have received in our life to serve. And as we serve our children, as we serve society, as we serve the world, as we serve our soul, we gradually discover ourselves to be pure instruments in the service of God.

3.

Journey
of
the Soul

———

"I've known rivers:
I've known rivers ancient as the world
and older than the
flow of human blood in human veins.

My soul has grown deep like the rivers."
— LANGSTON HUGHES

The SOUL'S LEGACY

by Brian Weiss, M.D.

"My work is a daily reminder that we are not our bodies or our brains, but our souls. That's the part of us that is eternal. Our souls keep returning, as though we were in a large school, until we are able to understand and to graduate."

THE FIRST STEP in nourishing your soul is to realize that it exists. I always thought of myself as a body and a brain. Through working with patients using regression therapy, I have discovered that this was a misconception. We're far more than that. We're souls having a human experience.

I'm reminded every day of the power of finding one's soul. I work with patients who, under hypnosis, go back to other lifetimes. I have had so many experiences with people healing grief. Sometimes it's funny; sometimes it's touching and moving.

An example of one of my experiences is when Joan Rivers asked to be regressed on her television show. I agreed to work in a private setting, but not on the show, because this is a very serious form of therapy to me, not a game. A few days before the show, I met with her and helped her remember two lifetimes. The more important one for her was in the 1820s in England. She began to cry, because her daughter in that lifetime was dying very young. She quickly recognized that girl as her mother from this lifetime, who had died several years earlier and for whom she was still grieving. As she saw the connection, she began healing her grief. She could see the continuity of the soul. Her mother and daughter had never really died, because she was with them in both lifetimes. She could see that she would be again.

My work is a daily reminder that we are not our bodies or our brains, but our souls. That's the part of us that is eternal. Our souls keep returning, as though we were in a large school, until we are able to understand and to graduate.

I don't think the nature of the soul changes very much from one lifetime to the next. What changes is one's awareness. At the level of the soul, we know everything we need to know. For some reason, we have to experience physical lifetimes to learn in a different way. This is the only place where we have physical bodies and emotions. Our task here is to become more Godlike, to recognize the divine and spiritual nature of our soul. To do that, we need to unlearn rather than learn. When we unlearn fear, violence, greed, ego, and power, then kindness, joy, love, and spiritual wisdom are all there. We are constantly progressing through many spiritual dimensions. When we have finally progressed to the level of complete integration with our soul, we find God.

We all have a tendency to slip back into the three-dimensional world. There are several things we can do to stay in touch with our soul. The most important thing is to go within. This doesn't have to be formal Eastern meditation. You can meditate with your eyes open. You can meditate while walking or being close to nature. The purpose is to remind yourself of your true nature, which is that of a spiritual being. You are not your body. The body is like a car, and you're the driver. As you find your true nature, you find that you are really a being of love. And when you think about it, you see that everyone else is, too. So besides meditating, practice acts of love. Reach out to others. Don't worry so much about the end results. As you do this, you recognize the unity and universality of our nature. Souls don't have races or sexes or religions. They are beyond artificial divisions.

The more you go within, the more you understand your true nature, and the more joy and happiness you feel in your life. That is very motivating. It's so pleasant that it inspires us to increase the time spent meditating or helping others or giving and receiving love. For that reason, the process of rediscovering the soul gets easier as you go along. On the other hand, we work on different traits at different times. In one series of lifetimes, you may be working on greed; in another, lust; and in another, violence. As you conquer one negative trait, you may go back to the beginning with another. There are starts and stops. As you come into a new lifetime, you may have forgotten some of the joy of finding the soul. But there will be reminders to lead you along the way. We are all heading in the same direction, but perhaps at different speeds.

Often, when a traumatic or catastrophic event occurs, we don't understand the significance. But with time and understanding, we see how that event caused our soul to grow. When we view the event with a different perspective, we see that it was necessary for our spiritual growth, even though it was painful at the time.

Sometimes, as I work with lifetimes, I find that the most traumatic ones are where the most growth has occurred. Sometimes an easy lifetime, where everything is smooth, means

we're resting and not really learning as much as quickly. Sometimes a person might choose to do two or three lifetimes in one
because the progress is so rapid. We're allowed to do that.

A good metaphor for our progress is to think of ourselves
as multifaceted diamonds. Some of us have facets that are cov-
ered with dirt and tar, which stands for ignorance. All of us are
the same under the dirt and tar, but some have many clean
facets; others, just a few. When all the facets are clean and the
diamond is gleaming beautifully, the solid form is transformed
into light. That is our soul.

I believe we are all part of a universal soul. At some level,
we are all the same. We are all connected. Everyone in our
drama is a facet of ourselves, and we are a facet of them. We
are all facets of the same energy — an energy possessing incredible wisdom and love. We all have God within us.

The PILGRIMAGE of AWARENESS

by Ram Dass

*"Be patient. You'll know when it's time for you to wake
up and move ahead. Just by picking up this book, you've
acknowledged your interest. That very acknowledgment will
prompt change and carry you to the next step
in the journey."*

I T'S INTERESTING TO HAVE a conception of the soul, a way
of thinking about it. But to ask how I cultivate the "relationship" with my soul implies that my soul and I are different, separate from each other, and I don't think that's true.
So before discussing how one *nourishes* the soul, I'd like to talk
a little bit about the soul itself.

Perhaps the best way to describe my understanding of the
soul is to imagine it as having a story line. Although the "soul
story" has no beginning and no end, I'll arbitrarily start it by
saying that in the beginning we are simply pure awareness. It's
hard to talk about pure awareness, because there are no words
in the English language — or in any language — that can

adequately describe it. The best I can do is to say that it is simultaneously everything and nothing; it is nowhere and it is everywhere; it has no form, yet it contains all forms. Pure awareness transcends soul, yet all souls are part of it. It can be called God. It can also be called "the immanent manifest," the thing that has not yet taken form on the physical plane.

At some point, pure awareness begins to divide — and that's when we move into the domain of soul. We could say that, in a sense, a little piece of pure awareness begins to bud off from the larger entity. Although it is preparing to manifest itself on the physical plane, this new entity hasn't yet taken incarnation or physical form. It is unique and separate from pure awareness, and it has, for example, "John-ness" within it, but it is not yet "John." Rather, it is the soul that will soon be identified as "John."

Then, finally, the soul takes incarnation on the physical plane, takes on the body and personality known as "John." So when we talk about "nourishing the soul," we're really talking about nourishing ourselves. We and our souls are the same thing.

But becoming John, reaching the physical plane, isn't the culmination of the story. At the end of John's lifetime — or perhaps at the end of many lifetimes — the soul that was John returns to the pure awareness where it began. All of us souls are on a circular journey, from beginning to beginning. Nourishing the soul helps move us through the physical incarnation — the "John" part of the journey – and bring us back to the state of pure awareness again.

When the soul is part of the pure awareness, it doesn't need any nourishing. But as it buds off and takes form as an individual entity, as it becomes separate from the pure awareness, it develops uniqueness. Along with the uniqueness comes a set of attachments, of clingings and aversions and predispositions, which we call karma. Now the soul is faced with a predicament: the predicament of being an individual who desires to be unique and separate from everyone and everything, and yet who also yearns to return to the undifferentiated pure awareness from which it came. It can only return by increasing its unity with the oneness, yet its very individuality and the separate actions it takes push it further and further away from the unity. And the separation creates suffering. So as we become aware of that predicament, we begin to nourish the soul in ways that help it work through the problems of separation and attachment, so it can move ahead to the beginning. What an interesting journey!

Now, there are many, many different ways to nourish the soul and decrease the separation. Positive experiences, such as compassion, love, and resonance with another soul, decrease our separateness. A moment's meditation into the deeper, undifferentiated awareness in ourselves brings us back into the unity. Anything at all that makes us aware of our identity with the larger consciousness can be positive — even trauma or a near-death experience. Through study and spiritual practices we can overcome the mind's natural desire to be separate and reclaim our connection to pure awareness. But though intellect can take us to the end of the diving board, it's faith that gives us the courage to leap.

As we look more deeply at our lives, we become more and more aware of the relationship between separation and suffering. We see that we nourish the soul by understanding that we are not merely "John" and that John is not a completely separate entity. The soul is nourished by the realization that we are all part of everything and that we are all forever journeying back toward pure awareness.

One powerful technique for awakening ourselves to that awareness is to set aside a quiet time each day — a time when we can go deep inside ourselves. Through contemplation, meditation, or reflection, we can loosen the hold of the social identity we've learned for ourselves. Weakening the notion that we're only and irrevocably "John" helps us reach out toward the unity. From a quiet place, I can begin to see "John" as an object, a role, rather than as what I am. I can learn that "John" is part of me, but not the sum total.

Think of the sum total — the awareness, the "I" — as a flashlight shining on all the different parts of John. I see the various pieces and shadows illuminated by the light, and I believe those pieces to be what I am. But I am really the flashlight — not just what the light shines on. The *flashlight* is the true entity, not the incarnation we call "John." In the process of becoming our separate somebodies, we've focused on the little parts of John we can see. The flashlight, the real John, stays hidden in shadow.

Anything that quiets us down, that connects us with the flashlight rather than with what the light is shining on, makes us aware of our unity with everything else. And that's what nourishes the soul. Once you connect with your own flashlight, you begin to look for the flashlight in other people. You begin to see them as fellow souls who have taken form as "Fred" and "Doris," rather than as totally separate entities named Fred and Doris.

Awakening our awareness to the unity nourishes the soul. So does balancing within ourselves the three stages or aspects of our being — pure awareness, soul, and incarnation. I've spent perhaps twenty-five years now learning how to be in all three planes simultaneously, how to be balanced in them. When we first begin to awaken, we see that we've been trapped in our incarnations, in our "John-ness." So we often use spiritual techniques as a way of resisting the predicament of our incarnation, to try to increase our identity with the soul. But there's the trap! The desire to flee your incarnation is based on an aversion to something, which means it's rooted in separateness and longing. And longing, desire, is just what keeps you stuck in incarnation.

So eventually you begin to realize that you can't push away your incarnation. And that's the beginning of progress. Instead of pushing it away, you look for ways to regain the balance, to come back into your incarnation without forgetting about your soul. You begin to learn how to integrate the two planes, to keep your awareness open to your incarnation and your soul at the same time.

Of course, the ego isn't ready to give up without a struggle. The purely "John" part of me doesn't want my soul to wake up. The ego has a long history of controlling my life, and it enjoys the role. Ramakrishna had a wonderful image of that tension between ego and soul: There is a horse-drawn carriage, he said, the kind with a driver up on top. The driver, who has been guiding the carriage all throughout a long trip, gets to thinking that the carriage belongs to him. Suddenly the person inside the carriage knocks his cane against the roof and says, "Stop here." The driver says, "Who do you think you are?" The man answers, "I own this carriage." But the driver says, "Don't be silly — this is *my* carriage." The driver, the ego, has been having too much fun guiding the carriage to surrender control to the real owner, the soul. But once the soul has awakened and established its control, the ego can begin to play its role as a wonderful servant.

There are many methods we can use in our lives to stay connected across planes of consciousness. For example, I usually carry a *return* with me — a string of beads. In a checkout line at the supermarket, I'll have my beads going in my hand. The beads are a device for reminding me that I am a soul, at play in a supermarket checkout line. Just feeling the beads in my fingers can change my whole consciousness. Or the breath — often a simple breath will awaken and balance me. So will seeing the Beloved in other people: suddenly I'll find myself looking through the veil to see what's hidden, to see another soul that's taken incarnation in a different form.

Being part of a community is another wonderful device for staying conscious. My guru and the Buddha and my friends are all my family. They are all *satsang* (the sharing of wisdom and teachings). They bust me when I lose the balance. That's part of the fun of having good friends around you who are on the same journey. They bust you, but they do it in a loving way.

You've picked up this book, so you already know what the issue is. I can't tell you specifically what *you* should do to nurture and balance your soul, because it's different for each one of us. Singing in the church choir may be one person's way of touching the soul. For another, it's doing tai chi. For someone else, it may be solving a difficult problem or cooking a bouillabaisse. The specific practices don't matter, so long as they open you to an appreciation of the relative nature of reality, to the multilayered levels on which we live. That knowledge alone will motivate you and guide you to what you need to do next.

You can decide how long to remain asleep as "John" and when to wake up to the journey. Many of us are like the abbot who admired the desert fathers. He said he wanted to be more like those renunciates in the cave, but he didn't want what he wanted just yet. And that's exactly where most people are at. They say, "Yes, I understand that suffering comes from the clinging of my mind, and I want to wake up. But I'm getting such a rush off my trip that I don't want to give it up just yet."

Be patient. You'll know when it's time for you to wake up and move ahead. Just by picking up this book, you've acknowledged your interest. That very acknowledgment will prompt change and carry you to the next step in the journey.

CLEANING OUT the CLUTTER

by Sydney Banks

*"When you aren't distracted by your own negative thinking,
when you don't allow yourself to get lost in moments that
are gone or yet to come, you are left with this moment."*

T HE SOUL IS THE only true source of spiritual nourishment. There are many ways to connect with and rekindle your relationship with your soul, but the most
effective way is to rid yourself of the obstacles that come between you and your purity of thought.

When our channel to the soul is open, we live in a more
harmonious reality. Such a state involves no effort and nothing we *have* to do. We simply go about our everyday business
of living, our actions stemming from compassion, love, and
wisdom.

This soul thinking is always present when we aren't engaged
in other types of thinking. Often our negative thinking gets in
the way, and we are pulled away from this pure state of
thought. It's almost as if a second type of thought is available

to us. I call it "analytical thinking." Obviously, we need our analytical thinking in order to live an effective life. However, this capacity for analytical thinking can be both a blessing and a curse, especially when we get caught up in negative and fearful thoughts. We are very apt to take these thoughts too seriously and stray from our inner serenity. When our thoughts are in such an impure state, a sort of darkness descends upon us, closing us off to messages from the soul. In this darkness, we forget that the only way to experience happiness, contentment, and joy is to be connected to our own inner wisdom. At times, we lose our positive feelings about life — so, naturally, we turn to our analytical thinking to find out what's wrong. But, like a hamster on a wheel, our minds go faster and faster without getting anywhere. We don't see that it is our negative thinking that took us away from our purity of thought in the first place, and we soon find out that the more we think negatively, the worse things get.

Let me give you an example of how our own thoughts can trick us, pulling us away from our true state of consciousness. Suppose Martin had a hard day and he's tired. He's on the bus, going home from work. Fifteen minutes from now, he'll be with his wife for a quiet evening at home. As he is riding home, a few stray negative thoughts start drifting through his mind. "I hope my wife remembered to pick up my dry cleaning. Last week she forgot. I hope she doesn't forget this week. She forgets to do her share of the work a lot of the time. It's really not fair." And on and on his thoughts go, until Martin has just about guaranteed himself a miserable night.

In fact, such thinking is the only thing getting in the way of a lovely time. Our soul or consciousness thrives on quiet, gratitude, and inner peace. Martin didn't realize he was in an ideal position to engage in all three. He was all alone on a dark, quiet bus, on his way to be with the person he loves more than anyone else in life. He could have been basking in gratitude, enjoying the moment and the quiet ride home. If he were thinking at all, it could have been about how lucky he was to be on his way to a quiet evening alone at home with his wife. This nourishing mind-set would have resulted in a rich, positive feeling.

If Martin had recognized what was happening, he could have dropped the negative thinking and brought himself back to a state of gratitude. He would have found himself reconnected to a truer state of consciousness. Sound simple? It is — but it's not always that easy!

What we are talking about is learning to live in the present moment, in the now. When you aren't distracted by your own negative thinking, when you don't allow yourself to get lost in moments that are gone or yet to come, you are left with this moment. This moment — now — truly is the only moment you have. It is beautiful and special. Life is simply a series of such moments to be experienced one right after another. If you attend to the moment you are in and stay connected to your soul and remain happy, you will find that your heart is filled with positive feelings.

Many of us adopt practices that keep us spiritually nourished. I myself am nourished when I spend time in solitude. I enjoy being alone, in the quietness of my mind. Many others throughout the world use the practice of meditation to attain such a marvelous and unending source of wisdom, which comes from the inner self. Such a state fills one up with strength, harmony, and peace.

Does this mean we never need to use our more analytical mode of thought? Of course not. It merely suggests that we stay aware that our soul is always with us, waiting to nourish us, and that the connection to our inner peace is never more than a moment away. Once a person realizes that the brain sends conditioned and habitual messages that needn't be taken too seriously, he or she is free to go back to soul thinking.

One nice by-product of understanding the distinction between our natural, effortless soul thinking and our habitual analytical thinking is that a feeling of forgiveness will follow. We can stop analyzing our past, our childhood, anything and everything bad that has ever happened to us, and realize that now is really the only moment that exists. As we dismiss our thoughts about who did what to us in the past, we free ourselves from the slavery of our negative history.

If we can forgive everyone, regardless of what he or she may have done, we nourish the soul and allow our whole being to feel good. To hold a grudge against anyone is like carrying the devil on your shoulders. It is our willingness to forgive and forget that casts away such a burden and brings light into our hearts, freeing us from many ill feelings against our fellow human beings.

You can begin the process of nourishing the soul by living in the present moment, in the now. And if your mind wanders, don't take these thoughts too seriously. Just let them go, realize that they are nothing more than fleeting thoughts, and you will soon be on your way to finding the peace of mind you seek, with loving feelings for yourself and others bringing joy and contentment to your life.

SEASONS
of the SOUL

by Linda Leonard, Ph.D.

*"Getting in touch with one's soul means going through
one's own struggle and despair and also realizing that it is
working through those wounds that helps unite you with
other people."*

THE JOURNEY OF the soul is a continual cycle, somewhat like the seasons. In spring, things open. In summer, they come to great fruition. In fall, things go out
in a blaze of glory. In winter, the seed is in the dark ground
and can't be seen.

At different points of our journey, throughout our whole
life, we are in one of these cycles. Winter is often experienced
as a period of despair. At the same time, it is a period of creative hibernation and development. When we get sunk down
in the dark night of the soul, it helps to remember this is just
one phase that will change into something else. We will come

out of the darkness with something that will help us and help other people. It is actually a kind of purification phase.

When we are in the light, we also have to accept that we will be going back into the dark again. The aspen tree is a good example. In summer, the leaves are green, lush with chlorophyll. In autumn, the leaves are at their greatest beauty, a blaze of gold. Yet this is a time of their greatest pain, since they are becoming depleted of the chlorophyll that helps them breathe. When they are in their last phase, the golden leaves tremble in the wind and then drop off the trees. But they come back again. It is that way in our own lives also.

Perhaps that's why I find nature so nurturing. I love to hike, especially in the mountains. When I'm walking in nature, I feel in awe of the wonder of creation. Nature is full of surprises, always changing, and we must change with it. In nature, the soul is renewed and called to open and grow. In the wilderness, you're up against whatever nature brings you — the dangers as well as the beauty.

I was raised in a big city. We were poor and didn't have a car, so we had little access to nature. At the row house where I grew up, there were very few trees or even greenery. But my grandmother used to tell me stories about her life on a farm. She read Walt Whitman, Emerson, and Thoreau to me. Sitting on her lap as a young girl, I was given the gift of a greater reality than the big cement city that was my world.

I grew up in an alcoholic family where there was a lot of pain and violence. It was a traumatic, disruptive life. I was plunged into darkness as a child, but at the same time I felt love from my family — even from my father, who was drinking. When he was sober, he took me on walks around the city. My father loved animals and would introduce me to the dogs in different neighborhoods. I got a sense of adventure from my father. From my mother, who supported the family, I got a sense of incredible stability and loyalty. My relationship with my grandmother gave me security and tenderness. Both she and my father introduced me to the world of books.

Reading has been very important to me on my soul's journey. Reading Dostoyevsky and Rilke and participating in their souls' journeys has given me hope and encouragement. It helped me touch the really dark sides of myself, as well as the joyous and redeeming sides. Because I was somewhat isolated in my family environment, a lot of my hope for change came from books. I'm very grateful to the authors who helped me along the way, because without their books, I don't know what would have happened to me.

For me, reading poetry and literature is always nurturing, because it puts me in touch with myself and with other people, especially people in other countries. Films do that also. I see the soul's journey as one that's both unique and universal at the same time. Each time I read a great book or go to a great film or listen to a symphony, it opens my heart and puts me in touch with someone else's journey and the soul's journey that we all share.

I do a lot of traveling and trekking all over the world. These outer journeys help me experience and understand other ways of life and receive wisdom from other cultures. Recently, I took several trips to the Arctic, to try to learn more about the nomads who follow the reindeer. I stayed with a Siberian group of reindeer people, the Evens, in the wilderness of Yakutia, a place near the Arctic Circle, which is very far from everything. The Even people believe the reindeer is the messenger that carries their souls to the other world.

A dream led me to that experience. Dreams have been essential to my soul's journey. When I went to search for the nomadic people, I was following the dream of my soul mate,

Keith. About ten years ago, he shared a dream about a reindeer woman, and it really touched my soul. I decided I wanted to write about her, since she embodied feminine spirituality, which our Western culture needs. When we traveled to Lapland and Siberia to try to understand the soul of the reindeer and the people who live with it, we discovered that many of the ancient Arctic peoples honored a reindeer goddess still revered by the Even people with whom we stayed. The loving looks of the people with those animals is a healing image that is always with me. My new book, *Creation's Heartbeat: Following the Reindeer Spirit*, tells that story.

I began following my dreams as a way of healing the wounds of my childhood. It was through a dream that I was called to write about my relationship with my father and to put that knowledge into a book called *The Wounded Woman*. In the book, not only do I share what I have learned, but other women tell about their particular journeys. When you share your own personal story, you find it isn't just your story; it is so many other people's stories. That's the power of the twelve-step movement. A group of what I call "wounded healers" shares their stories and helps heal each other. In sharing each other's stories, we feel the common human bonds that unite us.

For me, writing is essential. That's the way I'm able to process my own struggle and transformation and share it with other people. In the process, I stay in touch with myself and with others. The most grounding and loving thing in my childhood was sitting on my grandmother's lap while she read poetry to me. From her, I developed a love of reading and writing. I also inherited her desire to teach. Originally, I wanted to teach high school, but instead went into journalism. I worked as a journalist on a small daily newspaper in Colorado, until I realized I didn't have enough deep understanding from my education. I went back to school to study philosophy, and then taught it in college. Although I enjoyed teaching — introducing people to new ideas and other viewpoints — I also wanted to work in a deep, intimate way with other people, and that's what directed me into therapy. After studying at the Jung Institute in Zurich, I became a therapist working with people's dreams. I came back to writing because I realized that that was the broadest way to share whatever it is I have to offer.

As a Jungian analyst, I feel that healing is feeling and understanding one's own individual part of the common universal journey. For transformation, you have to be in touch with your own personal struggles but at the same time able to go beyond them. Sometimes people who grow up in a sheltered environment think life should be easy. They don't reflect about themselves or others. Kierkegaard said such people lead a life of "unconscious despair." They are as wounded in their own way as people who grow up in a dysfunctional family, but they don't know it. On the other hand, people who are too caught up in their own personal despair are also cut off from helping. Getting in touch with one's soul means going through one's own struggle and despair and also realizing that it is working through those wounds that helps unite you with other people.

By watching films about Vietnamese children or Maori women or native American people — people all over the world — we learn more about the human condition and can share in the grace of healing the wound and touching the spirit.

Everyone gets thrown off balance. What keeps me centered is walking in nature. I find a balance and sense of serenity there. While I am walking, I often say the Serenity Prayer.[1] I also say it before I lecture or anytime I need to center myself.

---

[1] "God, give us grace to accept with serenity the things that cannot be changed, courage to change the things which should be changed, and the wisdom to distinguish the one from the other." — Reinhold Niebuhr

Being with friends and in relationship with others is central to nourishing my life. When we are feeling overwhelmed and stuck in our own despair, we need to reach out to other people. Sometimes you think it's only you. It's important to gather something in yourself to give to somebody else. That helps you connect and unite with somebody else, and it takes the focus off your own pain. Dreams sometimes come to help us in those situations. If we're open to what's going on inside and outside us, we can see a connection. It might be a chance encounter with a person, or seeing a flower. It could be anything. That's why I love the films of Krystov Kieslovski, the Polish director. They show the mysterious connections among people, animals, and the moods of Nature, and how our souls' paths are mysteriously interwoven.

If you can offer yourself as a channel for creation who nourishes both yourself and others, I think that in the process you find a community of travelers on the soul's journey.

4.

Rekindling Your Soul

"You know of the disease in Central Africa called sleeping sickness. . . . There also exists a sleeping sickness of the soul. Its most dangerous aspect is that one is unaware of its coming. That is why you have to be careful. As soon as you notice the slightest sign of indifference, the moment you become aware of the loss of a certain seriousness, of longing, of enthusiasm and zest, take it as a warning. You should realize your soul suffers if you live superficially."

— ALBERT SCHWEITZER

REKINDLING the FIRES of YOUR SOUL

by Jack Canfield

"After all, can a martini or thirty minutes of Married with Children *make you feel truly, deeply joyful, nourished, unconflicted, and peaceful? Probably not! So, while it can be difficult to find the time for activities like meditation, it is worth it."*

LET ME BEGIN by saying that I think there is a big difference between "nourishing your soul" and "being nourished by your soul." We don't nourish our soul. Our soul nourishes us. We don't do something to our soul so much as have our soul do something for us. Our challenge as human beings is to open ourselves to receive this nourishment — to rekindle our connection with our spirit, the spirit that is always there waiting to nurture, heal, and direct our lives.

To bring out the best in yourself and enjoy your life to the fullest, nothing is more important than learning to open to, and accept, the nourishment of your soul. As you open yourself to your soul, a calming sense of peace and connectedness develops within you. This peaceful feeling deepens your levels of thought, releases the innate healing powers of your body, reminds you to be grateful for all the gifts of life, and broadens your perspective, so that you can be at peace with the way things are.

When I take time to meditate, the energies of the soul take me to a higher viewing place, where I can see different aspects of issues that are often invisible to me when I am caught up in my fear or ego. As I open to my soul, I become much more compassionate in my relationships with other people and more loving and accepting of myself. If my body is sick or injured, I begin to feel better. If I am emotionally upset, my soul energy helps my emotions level out. I feel a sense of inner peace — a level of contentment that I believe is impossible to obtain without connecting to one's spiritual self. It allows me to come at life from a place of intention and creativity instead of fear and reactivity. In short, as I rekindle my relationship with my soul, my entire life becomes greatly enriched.

Many ways and paths are available to reconnect with one's soul. I like to practice a number of different disciplines, such as meditation, yoga, tai chi, participating in a sweat lodge, Sufi dancing, or chanting with a group of monks. These activities all allow me to slow down and refocus, so that the "opening" to spirit can begin to occur and deepen. As I participate in these activities, I begin to feel at a conscious level what I call "soul energy" and "soul awareness." I am flooded with peace, relaxation, insights, and a sense of oneness with all things.

I believe that if people would do some form of physical and mental relaxation every day, all the conflicts we take for granted as a normal part of life would eventually disappear. When you set aside time for peace and tranquility — a massage from a loved one, a yoga class, thirty minutes of deep meditation, or the like — it's hard to stay in a conflicted state of mind.

When the benefits are so consistent and reliable, one has to wonder why so few people engage in these soul-energizing practices on a regular basis. Perhaps it's because so many people are still unaware of the personal and social benefits to be gained. People in my seminars often tell me, "I don't have time to meditate," when, in fact, they really don't have time not to meditate. When you set aside the time in a disciplined way, wonderful things begin to happen in your life. You no longer need to spend a great part of your day consistently stressed out, frustrated, engaged in conflict, or "putting out fires." You spend far less time — if any! — in these energy-draining states.

An investment of thirty minutes of meditation will indeed take thirty minutes of your day — but you will receive a happier, more peaceful, and productive day in return: you will actually increase your capacity to "get things done." You'll be far more creative in problem-solving, and you'll truly work much smarter on everything you engage in. You'll live in greater harmony with everyone and everything. In short, every aspect of your life will work better — all from a few minutes a day to quiet your mind and body! When you consider that the average American watches six hours of television a day, thirty minutes can't be that difficult to find!

Most of us, myself included, live a very fast-paced life, which can fool us into believing we don't have time for meditation or quiet time. My wife and I have a four-year-old child to love, spend time with, and care for, in addition to very hectic work schedules. Often, the only time I have to practice my own spiritual disciplines is late in the evening, after our son is asleep. My wife, on the other hand, meditates early in the morning, before the rest of us wake up.

Our cultural conditioning makes such discipline and effort very difficult. Society says, "If you're stressed, have a drink, take a drug, or bury yourself in front of the television. That will help you relax." If you're honest with yourself, however, you know in your heart that these techniques aren't the real answer. After all, can a martini or thirty minutes of *Married with Children* make you feel truly, deeply joyful, nourished, unconflicted, and peaceful? Probably not! So, while it can be difficult to find the time for activities like meditation, it is worth it. In fact, without it, life can seem meaningless and overwhelming, even like a battlefield.

Given the dominant Christian context of our culture, I've often felt that one way to transform America in a positive direction would be to have a respected Christian leader come out and say, "Christ has told me that the way to save the world is for everyone to dedicate thirty minutes a day to meditation!" If people would do it, the result would be a "kinder, gentler nation" of people living the life that Christ promised us was possible.

I just received a letter from a woman who attended one of my seminars. "I started with just ten or twenty minutes of meditation a day," she wrote. "I could barely find the time and it was difficult. Now, several months later, I can't get enough of it! I'm up to forty minutes a day and my entire life is better — my job, my relationships, everything! There is no other effort involved other than the meditation itself."

As you take a few minutes each day to quiet your mind, you will discover another nice benefit: your everyday, "ordinary" life will begin to seem far more extraordinary. Little things that previously went unnoticed will begin to please you. You'll be more easily satisfied, and happier all around. Rather than focusing on what's wrong with your life, you'll find yourself thinking about and more fully enjoying what's right with your life. The world won't change, but your perception of it will. You'll start to notice the little acts of kindness and caring from other people rather than the negativity and anger.

In addition to meditation, many other important vehicles can be utilized to open yourself to the nourishment of your soul: visiting holy places and putting yourself in the presence of spiritual people; attending a special church or other place of worship; chanting alone or with a group; or repeating affirmations such as "I have a body, I am not my body" or "I am a source of love and peace." My wife and I have a few unusual but useful practices that help us reconnect and feel nourished. The most important two are that we do regular meditation retreats, and we also have what we call our "annual day of silence." During this day, we each spend the whole day alone in a room — away from each other. For twenty-four hours we don't talk, read, write, or watch television. We meditate, do yoga, think, rest, and simply "be" by ourselves. It's amazing what this twenty-four-hour period of solitude does for our sense of well-being. It opens the channels, so that our souls can get through to us. When we come out of this day of silence, we always feel as though the entire world is moving twenty miles an hour too fast. We realize how overstimulated we have become and how difficult it is to feel connected to our souls with so much stimulation in the air. (I recently read that we are exposed to more information in one Sunday newspaper than the average person was exposed to in an entire year in the late 1700s!)

I believe that we are all different and that we each have to find our own path. The best way to learn what specific soul-nourishing techniques are right for you is to experiment. Start somewhere. Be willing to try different things. If you happen to be kinesthetic by nature, try tai chi, yoga, Sufi dancing, or something else physical. If you're more of a mental type, try some form of contemplative meditation. Or if you're emotional, try something celebrative, such as singing praise to God or chanting in a group. Many, many techniques are available. There is something for everyone. The point is, do something, anything, to reconnect with your soul energy! If you trust in yourself and fully immerse yourself in some sort of spiritual discipline, I can assure you from my own experience and the lives of thousands of my students that your entire life will begin to transform.

Let me end by saying that one very powerful way to connect with spirit, to lift yourself, and to make a difference is to engage in some kind of selfless service, such as feeding the homeless, teaching the illiterate to read, tutoring in an inner-city school, or volunteering at church. I used to think that we had to save the entire world and we needed to do it fast. I would get frustrated by being attached to the result, rather than experiencing the act of loving and being nurtured by it. The story that changed all that for me was so powerful that Mark Victor Hansen and I included it in our book *Chicken Soup for the Soul*. It is called "One at a Time":

A friend of ours was walking down a deserted Mexican beach at sunset. As he walked along, he began to see another man in the distance. As he grew nearer, he noticed that the local native kept leaning down, picking something up, and throwing it out into the water. Time and again he kept hurling things out into the ocean.

As our friend approached even closer, he noticed that the man was picking up starfish that had been washed up on the beach and, one at a time, he was throwing them back into the water.

Our friend was puzzled. He approached the man and said, "Good evening, friend. I was wondering what you are doing."

"I'm throwing these starfish back into the ocean. You see, it's low tide right now and all of these starfish have been washed up onto the shore. If I don't throw them back into the sea, they'll die up here from lack of oxygen."

"I understand," our friend replied, "but there must be thousands of starfish on this beach. You can't possibly get to all of them. There are simply too many. And don't you realize it is probably happening on hundreds of beaches all up and down the coast. Can't you see that you can't possibly make a difference?"

The local native smiled, bent down, and picked up yet another starfish, and as he threw it back into the sea, he replied, "Made a difference to that one!"

As you start on or continue along your path, be gentle with yourself and remember this story. We don't have to save everyone with our actions. Neither do we have to achieve all our spiritual growth in one day. Begin slowly, focus on each small step, and be concerned only with today, with right now. Don't try to become like the Dalai Lama or Mother Teresa in one day. You can't do it, and even if you could, you'd miss the incredible journey along the way. There is so much joy to be found on the journey itself! Do what you can do today, just a little bit, "One Day at a Time." The days will quickly merge into weeks, then years. And over this time, little by little, you'll be nourished by your soul and you will deeply nourish others in the process. Do all of this in love, and your life will truly become a miracle.

Earth, Body, and Spirit

by Lynn Andrews

"Unfortunately, society does not generally allow us to express the wilder, instinctual side of our natures — our soulful and spiritual selves. Neither does society encourage us to explore the possibilities of body-spirit unity. As a result, frustrated and negative forms of our spiritual forces may begin to build up within us."

MANY OF US hurry through life, filled with drive and ambition. We eagerly gather material rewards, neglecting the nourishment and integrity of our souls. But all our rushing around cannot help us escape that deep, often unrecognized need within ourselves to feel the comfort of the soul.

As individuals and as a society, we must dig deep enough to once again touch the rich earth beneath — deep enough to find the manifestations of nature within our own souls. To do that, it is imperative to find our way into natural settings, into the wilderness. It's there that the soul is healed. It's there that we can begin to unite body and soul.

Unfortunately, society does not generally allow us to express the wilder, instinctual side of our natures — our soulful and spiritual selves. Neither does society encourage us to explore the possibilities of body-spirit unity. As a result, frustrated and negative forms of our spiritual forces may begin to build up within us. This spiritual frustration sometimes shows up as illness. Disease is the body's way of trying to tell us something. When we manifest a disease, the body is saying, "You are not listening. You are not paying attention. You are not learning the lessons that you came here to learn. So I'm going to help you learn those lessons."

If such a person comes to me for healing, I look for the "disease" within his or her soul. You see, a healer never actually heals someone: a healer helps people heal themselves. A true healer learns to hold up mirrors. And if people choose to look in those mirrors, they may begin to speak from the self-wound instead of just from the mind. They may begin to shift, to change, growing away from the illness that they have unknowingly created within themselves.

I believe we all contain the keys to wholeness and health within ourselves, within our subconscious minds. These keys allow us to access the collective consciousness and the absolute truth. We can become enlightened within a lifetime, if we choose. The choice is difficult, however, for it means facing great fears.

Fortunately, many tools are available to help us reach the collective consciousness, to assist us as we dig beyond the trivialities of life to the truth. Prayer is one of those tools. Prayer helps give us the courage and wisdom to access the spirit, day by day. Prayer comes in many different forms, including meditation. I meditate every day, to center and to reacquaint myself with a sense of the soul. By meditation, I mean simply sitting quietly, away from the usual distractions, letting ideas pass gently through the mind without grabbing on to them, until you get to a place of silence inside yourself. Though simple in concept, this is hard to do; it takes practice. But if you have the tenacity to get to that quiet place and embrace the stillness, you will be meeting with your own soul.

Books such as this one can teach us much about using meditation and other tools to access and nourish the soul. But learning about the spiritual journey of life is not enough; we must integrate that knowledge into our lives. Societies have amassed an enormous amount of borrowed knowledge. We tend to sit in class, listening to others, impressed by their magnificent learning. But how do we make the facts and the truths that others have learned part of our own lives? We must physically do something. One of the most important things my teachers ever taught me was that we need to experience teachings about truth and higher consciousness in a physical way in order to make them part of our own circle of truth.

An activity like drumming, for instance, can bridge the gap between the inspiration that comes from a higher consciousness and the reality of daily life. Drumming helps us manifest that inspiration as something real and tangible, something that can be felt and shared with other people. It doesn't make any difference if you're a Catholic, or a shaman, or a Buddhist; you can sit down with a circle of people and just start to drum. And if you do this, not worrying about how you sound, not worrying about the fact that you have never played a drum in your entire life, you will realize that the first music any of us ever heard was the heartbeat of our mother when we were in her womb. Drumming reminds us of our original nature. Through drumming, we begin to remember who we are.

Ceremony is another way to make inspiration real. By ceremony, I mean creating a circle of activity that brings us closer to the great spirit, to our God. Unlike ritual, which is activity performed by rote, ceremony is different every time we do it. It may have the same boundaries each time, but there's always an aspect of us within that ceremony. Every time we perform the ceremony, both we and the ceremony will be a little bit different.

Ceremony can be very simple. It does not require memorizing a set of rules and parameters. Ceremony can be done alone or with a group of people availing themselves of each other's energy with the intention of approaching a higher consciousness. The goal of ceremony is to make the spirits of place (the spirits that live in all the named and nameless places throughout our universe) stand up, listen, and help us with their energy and their power.

Ceremony can easily be performed through prayer. We may do this by sitting on a lawn with our back against a tree, or down at the ocean, or at the base or the top of a mountain, or in a park. Listening to the heartbeat of Mother Earth, we move into that place of stillness and bliss within our own hearts. At that point, we are performing our own ceremonies. Reaching deep into the Earth, we bring our souls into a place of comfort and peace.

PASSION and SOULFULNESS

by Nathaniel Branden, Ph.D.

*"Even when our life is most difficult, it is important to
remember that something within us is keeping us alive —
the life force — that lifts us, energizes us, pulls us back
sometimes from the abyss of despair. True spirituality does
not exist without love of life."*

WHEN I THINK of nourishing the soul, I think of
nurturing the ability to respond positively to
life — that is, the ability to sustain passion for
our interests, values, and projects. I believe that the worst of
all spiritual defeats is to lose enthusiasm for life's possibilities.

Every life has its share of setbacks and disappointments —
of tragedy and loss. So the question we all confront, in the face
of negatives that may assail us, is: How do we keep our inner
fire alive?

Two things, at minimum, are needed: an ability to appreciate the positives in our life — and a commitment to action.

Every day, it's important to ask and answer these questions: "What's good in my life?" and "What needs to be done?"

The first question keeps us focused on positives; the second keeps us proactive and reminds us that we are responsible for our own happiness and well-being.

Another aspect of focusing on the positive, and thereby nourishing the soul, is to stay focused on the inquiry "What in my life do I most enjoy? What most stimulates me?" Someone once said that you can know who a man is if you know what wakes him up.

The pleasures that nurture me personally may be as simple as enjoying the view of the city and the ocean from the window of my living room, or spending time in the garden, or appreciating good health. Of course, one of the greatest joys that nurtures me is having a loving relationship with my wife. In addition, when I think of nurturing the soul, I think of listening to music and rereading books that have meant a lot to me. I also think of the act of writing. When I spend time at my computer, writing, I almost invariably experience a tremendous sense of appreciation of how wonderful it is to be alive. If I am away from writing too long, I feel discouraged, or at least dispirited. Writing takes energy, and it also creates energy.

For all of us, the key is to pay close attention to which activities make us feel most alive and in love with life — and then try to spend as much time as possible engaged in those activities.

Even when our life is most difficult, it is important to remember that something within us is keeping us alive — the life force — that lifts us, energizes us, pulls us back sometimes from the abyss of despair. True spirituality does not exist without love of life. If we feel unhappy or unfulfilled, the most urgent question is, "What needs to be done?" Or one might say, "What's missing in my life — and what can I do about it?" The sin is to suffer passively. We must never forget that we have the capacity to act. So we must always be concerned to know "What avenues of action are possible to me? What can I do to make my life better?"

If we stay oriented to the two basic questions — "What's good in my life?" and "What needs to be done?" — and strive to respond to those questions appropriately, the predictable result is that we will be happier human beings and get far more of whatever it is that we want in life.

Some writers — Erich Fromm, for one — contrast a so-called "being" orientation with a "doing" orientation. The implication is that being and doing are in some sense antithetical. Of course they are not. Doing and being, action and stillness, are dependent on one another. Without action, we would cease to exist, and without stillness, we would neither be able to appreciate our existence nor have a foundation from which to act. We need stillness, we need the pure experience of being, in order to fully realize ourselves. Out of that stillness can come the motivation to act and also the awareness we need to act wisely, not to lose perspective.

When being and doing are in harmony, when stillness and action are friends to each other, we create an integrated, satisfied soul. We are then in the best position to truly enjoy and appreciate life and not be destroyed by adversity.

Another aspect of nourishing the soul is the ability to stay focused on the present, to live in the present. Many years ago, in the 1960s, I was writing a book called *The Psychology of Self-Esteem*. I was a young man at the time, in my thirties, and one day I was sitting at my typewriter, impatient for the book to be finished, thinking that my life would really begin to unfold only when this book was finished. Yet I intuitively knew that something was wrong with this line of thought. So I asked myself what I thought I would be doing when the book was finished, and I immediately answered, "Planning the next book." And when the next book was finished? "Planning the book after that." I saw that my life, first and foremost, was about writing: that was and is my passion. So, in the middle of writing *The Psychology of Self-Esteem*, I finally realized "This is it. This is my life. If I can't enjoy it now, every day, there is no reason to believe I'll be better able to enjoy it in the future, after the seventh, eighth, or ninth book."

That realization was a turning point for me. The impulse to focus on the future can be quite strong. It's natural to look ahead. Yet I realized that the key to happiness lay in enjoying the process, not just the final result — because the greater part of my life was going to be spent at the level of process and not at the stage of contemplating the finished product. So now I bless each day I can get up and go to my computer and sit down to write and know and love the fact that this is what my life is about.

I believe that earning your living doing something you enjoy is one of the very best ways to nourish yourself. But even if you are employed at something that is not your ideal work, it is important to find ways to take as much pleasure in it as possible. Living in the present moment can make ordinary activities more interesting and joyful; you may be surprised, if you only look, at what you will find. If you try to stay connected with why you are doing what you are doing, for example, then even the parts of your life that aren't especially interesting can become more meaningful.

Sometimes I have to go to an event that doesn't especially interest me. I've learned to tell myself, Make this experience as happy for yourself as you possibly can. Once that becomes a conscious purpose, it's amazing how imaginative one can become. Life becomes infinitely more interesting.

Rekindling Your Soul

Nothing I am saying about the importance of living in the present denies the value of being concerned with the future. We want to keep in mind our goals, what we're moving toward, and to see the progression and direction that underlie our activities. We need to be able to plan for the future without sacrificing the present, and enjoy the present without making ourselves oblivious to the future. Obviously, we cannot control every single aspect of our life. We are not omnipotent. But we do have an enormous degree of responsibility for the shape our life takes. We have many options about how we will respond to events. We are not passive spectators, but active contestants in the drama of our existence. We need to take responsibility for the kind of life we create for ourselves.

How do we nurture the soul? By revering our own life. By treating it as supremely important. By reaching for the best within ourselves. By learning to love it all, not only the joys and the victories, but also the pain and the struggles.

LOVE IS
the ANSWER

by Gerald Jampolsky, M.D.

"We nourish the soul when we find value in the stillness of the moment, recognizing that the present time is the only time there is."

W E LIVE IN a world of illusion, where fears and thoughts can sometimes bring a darkness that blinds us to what our soul is. Our souls hunger and thirst for recognition. We nourish our soul when we give our love away unconditionally to all others. To nourish the soul, we need to learn to rid ourselves of the defenses of the ego that keep us from the soul — to let go of guilt, blame, fear, and negativity.

In nourishing my soul, it has been essential to discipline my mind so that the peace of God is my only goal. At home, we try to do this by simplifying our lives and bringing balance. My wife, Diane, and I begin each day at 4:30 in the morning with a ritual. While still in bed, imagining light from above and within, we remind ourselves that we are the light of the world. The whole world becomes light. Then we say a prayer from *A Course in Miracles* to remind us who and what we are and what our purpose is: "I am not a body; I am free, for I am still as God created me." We say a blessing to bring all people into that light. Then we take a walk around the wonderful place where we live. It is a very holy place on forty acres, with a beautiful lake and animals of all kinds.

This silent walk is really a meditation that allows us to get in touch with nature. It reminds us of our inner connection: that we are the grass, the deer, the trees; we are not separate. Upon returning, we sit on a bench five minutes from our front door, looking out on the trees, and meditate for another twenty minutes. After that, we shower, eat a light breakfast, and start our day.

I find gardening a creative way to nourish my soul. About two years ago, I was on retreat in Australia, and when I returned home, I felt strong guidance to become a gardener. For nine months, I worked in the garden at least nine hours a day. We nourish the soul when we continue to plant seeds of love wherever we go. When we let go of our negative thoughts and forgive ourselves and other people, that's like taking the weeds out of the garden and letting love bloom.

This past year, I've also nourished my soul by doing something I thought was impossible. I've always been told and always believed that I had no artistic ability. When I allowed myself to begin working with clay, I found it was creative and fun and opened up another part of me to love.

Another example of how one can open to love and happiness was shown to us when we were in Guadalajara. A woman named Pilar traveled all the way from Buenos Aires to see us. She was born without any arms. For many years she was full of anger and felt that her parents had rejected her. After reading some of our books on attitudinal healing, she went through an amazing spiritual transformation. She has become an artist and has learned to draw with her toes. When she heard we were coming, she made an effort to come that far to be with us. She was a witness that these spiritual principles work. She was a wonderful miracle in our lives, with a wonderful bright light, reminding us that our happiness has nothing to do with our bodies.

When we're helping other people, we're nourishing our soul. Depression or unhappiness means we've got the wrong goal. We have forgotten that peace of mind is our only goal. By concentrating on helping another person, we renew contact with our soul and with God. We can feel peaceful again. A sense of joy surrounds us and all the frustration, agitation, and self-anger disappears.

Peace of mind has nothing to do with the external world; it has only to do with our connection with God. Love really is the answer. We're here only to teach love. When we're doing that, our souls are singing and dancing. When we remind ourselves that we are spiritual beings, that life and love are the flame eternal, that's when our soul is nourished.

In our attitudinal healing workshops, we often ask, "If this is your last day on earth, how would you want to be described?" Ninety-nine percent of the time, the reply is, "I did my best to love other people and to make a difference by being caring and compassionate." And yet, when most of us look at our day-to-day lives and our style of loving, it wouldn't look that way at all. We mistakenly think making money or driving a fancy car will make us happy. Instead of living in the present, we are thinking more of the next moment. Nourishing our soul is the recognition of what our purpose is: to love and forgive.

It may sound simple, but it isn't easy. Simplicity is very difficult for a confused mind to understand. The ego wants to make everything very complex. It wants to make the intellect our God.

We nourish the soul when we find value in the stillness of the moment, recognizing that the present time is the only time there is. The essence of our being is *love,* and *forgiveness* is the key to our happiness.

SOUL WORK

by Jon Kabat-Zinn, Ph.D.

"When experience is viewed in a certain way, it presents nothing but doorways into the domain of the soul, and they are all found in the present moment."

IN TERMS OF my own development, I finally began to understand something of the difference between soul and spirit, and the meaning of both, through the teachings of people like Robert Bly and his sometime colleague, James Hillman. They make a Jungian distinction between *soul work*, which involves a downward movement in the psyche — a willingness to connect with what is dark, moist, deep, and not necessarily pleasant or uplifting — and the movement of *spirit*, which has a quality of moving toward the light — upward, ascending.

When we talk about a soul feeling, it really has to do with a sense of depth and recognition, and frequently a soul feeling may not be all sweetness and light. Soul can have a lot of heat and pain associated with it.

I think, when you come right down to it, one might ask, Well, what isn't soulful? For me, soul really has to do with a sense of the heart being touched by feelings. It also has to do with the overall journey of life as a story, as myth, as a representation of deep inner meaning.

I try to stay away from the word "spiritual" entirely. One reason is that I need to frame my medical work in a vocabulary that does not sound religious or mystical. Another reason is that the word is often used as a New Age cliché — something one talks about or pretends to be, rather than a commitment to integrity beyond form and surface appearance.

Instead of the word "spiritual," I prefer to speak in terms of being truly human. In that sense, is being a father or mother spiritual? It depends on how you relate to it. Is being a scientist spiritual? Einstein spoke of a "cosmic religious feeling" when penetrating a secret of nature and finally seeing the beauty, order, and connectedness. It takes your breath away!

Is that spiritual or soulful? I would say both. But the insight doesn't just come — it takes a lot of groping around in the dark, much of the time feeling completely lost.

So the question is, What nourishes the soul? We might also turn the question around and ask, Whether and how does the soul nourish us? Soul or heart or a deep connectedness is always present, but we are not always in touch with it. Nourishing the soul is the process of drinking at the life stream, coming back to one's true self, embracing the whole of one's experience — good, bad, or ugly; painful or exalted; dull or boring.

At the Stress Reduction Clinic of the University of Massachusetts Medical Center, we train people in formal and informal ways to cultivate greater nonreactive, nonjudgmental, moment-to-moment awareness — what the Buddhists call *mindfulness*. The entire focus of the clinic's program is training mainstream Americans — referred by their doctors with a vast range of stress- and pain-related and other medical problems — in mindfulness. Mindfulness is vast, because it is fundamentally about wakefulness, about paying attention in one's life — all of it. It is often spoken of as the heart of Buddhist meditative practice. We teach it without the Buddhist vocabulary and cultural/religious accoutrements. In our program, it is simply a universal vehicle with which to explore deep inner connectedness — to access one's own resources for growing, healing, and self-compassion. We use meditation to help nourish the whole of us, both human and divine.

Mindfulness can be one reliable door into the domain of soul. There are others. For some people, music might be one, or poetry. Dance might serve, or physical exercise. Parenting is certainly a gigantic doorway into the domain of the soul. In fact, any experience can be. When experience is viewed in a certain way, it presents nothing but doorways into the domain of the soul, and they are all found in the present moment. However, we often find ourselves functioning in a kind of automatic-pilot mode. We're not really in touch with the subterranean spring, the inner fountain, the water of life that myths and fairy tales speak of. A mountain or river is always there, waiting to be seen. But if you're not holding your experience in your awareness, its power is not available to you. We are easily caught up in emotional storms that cloud the heart and harm ourselves and others without our really knowing what we're doing or seeing things as they are. Part of soul work is to honor the pain and grief we all carry and not to think it is a door to someplace else. It's a doorway to right here, right now, this moment. Suffering is part of the human condition. It needs to be held in the same way that joy and uplift need to be held — wakefully, as a mature adult.

One of the main reasons we use intensive training in mindfulness meditation at the clinic is that most of the time, most people are unaware they are not in *this* moment — and that learning, growth, healing, and the shaping of new directions always come out of *this* moment. Nor are they aware that they are thinking constantly and that our behavior is virtually dictated by our reactions to our own thought content — which we misperceive as being true. We believe our thoughts unquestioningly and react to them emotionally, although they are mostly inaccurate.

Let's take a thought that's not necessarily a fact, like the thought "I'm over the hill; it's all downhill from here." Many people believe this when they reach a certain point in their lives. They feel they didn't get where they were "supposed" to get. They look in the mirror and realize, "My God, I'm not going to achieve those things." And then the thought comes up, "It's all over for me," or "I've wasted my life." In such moments, you might not realize that that's just a thought. You instinctively believe it. That collapse can spiral you into depression, overwhelming you with feelings of hopelessness or helplessness.

Now, our thoughts are forming maybe a thousand times a second, so they have a very powerful way of coloring our lives — our views, our relationships, the feelings we experience, the things we take on or don't take on, the choices we make, and everything else. Usually we have no idea this is being driven by inaccurate, reactive thinking.

Meanwhile, here we are, missing the fullness of the present moment, which is where the soul resides. It's not like you have to go someplace else to get it. So the challenge here is, Can we live this moment fully? When you ask a group of people to spend five minutes watching their own breaths moving in and out of their bodies, just as an experiment, with people who have never meditated before (you don't even have to call it meditation), they discover, often with great surprise, that their

Soul Work

minds are like bubbling vats, and it's not so easy to stay on the breath. The mind has a life of its own. It carries you away. Over a lifetime, you may wind up in the situation where you are never actually where you find yourself. You're always someplace else, lost, in your head, and therefore in a kind of dysfunctional or nonoptimal state. Why dysfunctional? Because the only time you ever have in which to learn anything or see anything or feel anything, or express any feeling or emotion, or respond to an event, or grow, or heal, is this moment, because this is the only moment any of us ever gets. You're only here now; you're only alive in this moment.

When people make this discovery, it is an experience of waking up to a realization, a reality, they did not know before: most of the time, we're operating in an automatic-pilot mode that is more asleep than awake. When you have that realization, you begin to see differently and then act differently.

The past is gone, and I don't know what's coming in the future. It's obvious that if I want my life to be whole, to resonate with feeling and integrity and value and health, there's only one way I can influence the future: by owning the present. If I can relate to *this moment* with integrity, and then *this moment* with integrity, and then *this moment* with integrity, wakefully, then the sum of that is going to be very different over time, over mind moments that stretch out into what we call a life, than a life that is lived mostly on automatic pilot, where we are reacting and being mechanical and are therefore somewhat numb.

The autopilot mode switches on in virtually every domain in life. It happens at work, it happens at home, it happens in the family, it happens in the car, it happens when you're alone. Most of the time, if you're not really paying attention, you're someplace else. So your child might say, "Daddy, I want this," and you might say, "Just a minute, I'm busy." Now, that's no big deal — we all get busy, and kids frequently ask for attention. But over your child's entire youth, you may have an enormous number of such moments to be really, fully present, but because you *thought* you were busy, you didn't see the opportunities these moments presented. And then thirty years later, your child comes back to you and says, "You were never there for me." "What do you mean? I was home — I was home a lot." "Yeah, you were home, but you weren't *home*." People carry around an enormous amount of grief because they missed the little things.

It's important to practice mindfulness, because most of the time we are practicing the opposite. Every time we react with frustration, sadness, or anger and we don't hold that reaction in our awareness, it takes on a life of its own — it "does us" instead of us doing it, whatever *it* is. The result of continually letting mindless reactions envelop you is that you're going to get better and better at making fists and clenching your jaw, at hunkering down and contracting, at withdrawing and being emotionally diminished. Over time, what you're doing is *practicing* mindlessness. By not being fully awake in each moment, you are getting better and better at reacting, or going numb. As you get older, a lifetime of not paying attention and not nourishing what is deepest and most important has profound consequences. The details and excitement of youth, work, ego gratification, the pursuit of name and fame, all fall away. What you're left with is the fundamentals you have been practicing. If you've been practicing resentment for fifty years, if you've been practicing not being sensitive to other people's feelings, if you've been practicing being on some colossal ego trip, it doesn't just stay the same — that would be bad enough. It builds. It ends up imprisoning you. You get more and more locked into that behavior.

Whereas, if you're practicing mindfulness, it doesn't matter if you get angry or depressed or irritated or contracted. The eddy or whirlpool in the mind or heart becomes the object of your attention *because* it's as worthy of attention as anything else. You're not editing your life; you're not saying, "*This* is good and *this* is bad, *this* is soulful, *this* is spiritual, I want this, I don't want that." You're saying, "The whole of it is my life as long as I'm willing to hold it in awareness." Even depression and anxiety have enormous energy to propel us into greater states of insight, awareness, compassion, and, ultimately, wisdom — the wisdom of not getting caught up in the "I" thought, the "me," and "my" thoughts.

This may sound like an interesting theory. But I'm not talking about a theory. I'm talking about a *way of being*. An *intentional* way of being. You give some care and attention to your life as it unfolds in actuality. Thoreau called it the greatest practice in life: "To affect the quality of the day, that is the highest of arts." One could, and usually does, think, "Well, days just unfold, kids just grow up, work just happens, relationships just happen, old age just happens." But nothing "just happens." It only "just happens" if you're not paying attention to it. Then you're not a player; you're just a passive bystander — or worse, a victim. If you choose to be a player, that doesn't mean you magically control the whole thing, or even anything. Earthquakes happen, floods happen. Storms come up in the mind. But that's all okay if you can embrace it in awareness.

Meditation isn't the answer to all of life's problems, nor is "just" giving credence to the soul. There's no "answer" to life's problems.

Zen has an expression, "nothing special." When you understand "nothing special," you realize that everything is special. Everything's special and nothing's special. Everything's spiritual and nothing's spiritual. It's how you see, it's what eyes you're looking through, that matters. Are you looking through eyes of wholeness, or are you looking through eyes of fragmentation? Are you looking through eyes of compassion and self-compassion, or are you looking through eyes of greed and hatred? Are the veils of ignorance so great that your eyes are clouded all the time, seeing only vague shadows on the wall of Plato's cave and living your whole life in a reflected dream? Life is an adventure. I'm not saying that any of us has arrived anywhere. It's obvious we haven't. The question is, are we willing to continually dance with life? For me, that is what nourishes. Everything else is — as Kabir, the fifteenth-century Sufi master, put it — "an apartment in the city of death." The thirteenth-century philosopher Jalal ud-din Rumi put it this way: "There are hundreds of ways to kneel and kiss the earth."

5.

Lessons
of the Soul

———— ·••· ————

*"For what shall it profit a man, if he shall gain
the whole world, and lose his own soul? Or what
shall a man give in exchange for his soul?"*

— MARK 8:36–7

Becoming a
Waking Dreamer

by Wayne Dyer, Ph.D.

*"To nourish the soul means to participate in the very
mechanics of creation — to become a co-creator of your life
and of the world as you want it to be."*

T HE GREATEST SENSE of happiness and contentment
possible can be achieved with relative ease. Unfortunately, many of us suffer the sadness of feeling separated from ourselves, from others, or from life itself. Carl Jung
once said, "In about one-third of my cases, the patients are
suffering from no clinically definable neurosis, but from the
senselessness and emptiness of their lives."

Jung writes of the four stages that people go through in their
development as human beings. In the lowest stage, which he
calls the "Athlete," the emphasis is almost entirely on the
physical body. In the second stage, the "Adventurer" or "Warrior" stage, physical prowess is extended outward. From there,
progressing to the "Statesman" or "Wisdom" stage, the physical exploits are left behind and energy is primarily channeled

into wisdom. At the fourth and highest stage of maturation, the "Spiritualist" stage, the emphasis is on the spirit, rather than the body or the mind.

To nourish the soul is to nourish this "Spiritualist," this highest part of yourself. Doing so means that our vision of life becomes more expansive. We find that the things that preoccupied us, such as the emphasis on the body — on what it can accomplish, what it looks like, how it compares to others, whether it smells right, whether it's insured, whether it's balding, what color its hair is and whether or not it's falling out, how wrinkled the skin is — become less important.

As you begin to leave these concerns behind, you are able to cultivate a part of yourself that I call the "Witness." As a Witness, you begin to discover that you are not that which you have been observing; you are not those things that you have been noticing about your body. Instead, you are the noticer.

As you notice that you are the noticer, you begin to understand the mechanics of creation — you learn that what you want to create in your life or on the planet is not determined by what you do with your body. Instead, your ability to create is determined by where you put your attention — and where you leave your attention. As a Witness, you can begin to participate in the "quantum mechanics of creation." You become a creator because everything that you observe is affected by the fact that you are observing it. The act of witnessing becomes a creative act.

You witness with your soul, not your eyes, for the soul is the divine part of you that observes everything. As you begin putting much more attention and energy into your soul, you begin to discover the "divineness" that is within you and everything else. To nourish the soul means to participate in the very mechanics of creation — to become a co-creator of your life and of the world as you want it to be.

Lessons of the Soul

Those people who are still in the "Athlete" or "Warrior" stages or are preoccupied with their minds consider the idea of "nourishing the soul" something other folks do. But when you leave those stages behind — or, as Jung puts it, "mature through those stages" — all those things that were so important at the lower stages now seem meaningless. They become simply things you are noticing. The soul becomes paramount.

You can move through the stages to become a Witness by learning how to nourish the soul. Nourishing the soul involves issues of the ego, and dealing with the ego can be confusing. In my book *Your Sacred Self*, I attempt to answer questions such as "How do I know whether it's my ego or my higher self at work?" "Is this idea of who I am really who I am?" and "Am I the noticer or that which is being noticed?"

There are differences between the ego and the higher self, differences that can be observed and used as guides in answering these questions. The ego is concerned with questions such as "How do I do it?" and "What are the rules?" and "What techniques can you offer me?" The higher self, however, says, "Just pay attention, be at peace, and trust." As one of my favorite lines from *A Course in Miracles* points out, "If you *knew* who walked beside you at all times on this path that you have chosen, you could never experience fear again." The higher part of yourself has a "knowing" that you're not alone, that you go where you're sent, that you'll be guided, that you can surrender, and that it's going to work out. The higher self helps you look at yourself and at others from the perspective of love rather than fear. If you listen carefully, you'll hear the difference between the ego and the higher self. You'll know how to nourish the soul with the energy of attention.

That's really all there is to nourishing the soul! You could, of course, master a thousand techniques of meditation, prayer, and chanting. You could read and talk to wise people. However, all that you must *essentially* do is place your primary emphasis on the higher part of yourself, that part which is doing the observing, and create that "knowing" that you are being guided in a divine direction. Through this process, which I call "intention," you will begin to see your ordinary life becoming extraordinary.

To illustrate the concept of "intention," I ask you to think about what happens when you dream at night. If, in a dream, you want to walk across the room, you don't have to tell your dream self to get up and begin moving. You don't have to do that while you're in your dream; you simply bring the desired action or thing to yourself through the power of your own intention. You can bring whatever you want into your dreams; you can make anything happen through the power of your intention. It all happens as you desire, because you have no doubt that it will happen exactly as you wish. But then, when most people wake up, they nourish the doubting aspect of themselves by saying, "I don't have the power to do that in my waking state."

Who says you don't have the power to bring to yourself that which you desire? Who says you cannot master "intention"? I'm suggesting that you can become a "waking dreamer," that you can do in your normal waking state everything you do in a dream state. The only difference between the two states of consciousness is that you don't doubt your ability when you are sleeping and are in a dream state, as you do when you are awake.

One of the reasons you do not doubt in the dream state is that you can erase your past when you are dreaming. In a dream state, you don't have a "story." If you don't have a story, there is nothing for you to live up to. You let go of all of that and free yourself. When you rid yourself of your past, when you are in your present moment, and when you get rid of all of the doubt, you'll know what Jung meant when he used the word "synchronicity." You will begin to collaborate with fate. You will start to see exactly what you need in this moment manifesting itself in your life. At first you may think, "Wow, how is this happening?" But after a while, you will see that you can truly manage the coincidences of your life through this state of higher consciousness. All you have to do is become a waking dreamer.

One of my favorite metaphors illustrates the importance of recognizing the past for what it is. Imagine that you are on a boat heading north at around forty knots. As you stand on the stern, looking down into the water, three questions come to mind. First, you ask yourself, "What is the wake?" The answer is that the wake is nothing more than the trail left behind. The second question is, "What is driving the ship?" The answer is that the Present Moment Energy that you are generating through the engine is driving the ship. Finally, you ask yourself the most important question: "Is it possible for the wake to drive the ship?" The answer is "no," of course, for the wake is just a trail that is left behind. It can never drive the boat!

Now imagine that the boat is your life, and the wake is all the things that have happened in the past: what your body is like, what your parents were like, where you were in the birth order, how your mother treated you, whether your father was an alcoholic, and anything else. Most people live with the illusion that their wakes are "driving" their lives — which is absolutely impossible. In order to nourish your soul, you must be able to "get out of the wake." And when you get out of the wake, you manage your doubts as you "cultivate the Witness." You become the Witness, instead of that which is being witnessed.

One way to nourish the soul, and thus to become a Witness, is to shut down the inner dialogue and learn to become quiet.

You must have quiet in order to know your soul. As Melville said, "God's one and only voice is silence."

Even after you've filtered out much of the extraneous noise and are listening to your inner voice, you may wonder whether you are hearing your higher voice or your ego. If you're not sure which is speaking to you, ask yourself whether or not this inner voice promotes peace. If it promotes peace, it's your higher voice. If it promotes turmoil in any way, it's your ego. If your higher voice is speaking, you must listen. If not, ignore it!

For example, there is no peace in "more is better" messages, in thoughts of competition, of having to defeat someone else, or of consumption. As you go inward and shut down the inner dialogue, you will become increasingly quiet. You will hear your higher voice, and you will find peace. The fact that you are meditating is not as important as what you bring back from your meditation. The goal is to bring back a sense of knowing that you're not alone. The goal is getting to that place where you know that, as St. Matthew has said, "With God, all things are possible." Notice that this statement leaves nothing out! This is the infinite field of all possibilities. You can only reach this place by allowing yourself to become silent, by removing all the chatter and disturbances.

This process of quieting all the noise will put you into the state called "flow." When you're in flow, all the distractions are gone. Your overriding spiritual objective is to tune in to the ecstasy of the moment. The difference between being in and out of flow is the difference between knowing God and knowing *about* God. Knowing about God does not nourish the soul; it is simply practicing someone else's orthodoxy. Everything that comes from "out there," regardless of whether you like it or not, comes with doubt attached. Doubt is attached to everything because it's someone else's point of view.

"To know about" is to doubt. When you know, however, there is no doubt. Knowing God comes from within. The way you ultimately know God or your soul is to abolish all doubt, cultivate the Witness, erase your past, shut down the inner dialogue, and tame the ego.

The ego isn't real; it doesn't exist. The ego is not the self. Rather, it is the idea we have about the self as being separate, being special and important, needing to consume, being offended, and so forth. The ego is just an idea that we carry around with us. In fact, if you think about it, the ego is insane. After all, insanity is defined as believing that you are something that you're not, and the ego has you convinced you are something you're not. It has you believing that you are your body, that you are your accomplishments, and that competition or being better than other people is important.

You're not your ego. You are really a divine and eternal spirit. You are a soulful being who is never born and never dies, having a human experience. And when you know God, when you are part of the mechanics of creation, you have achieved the highest stage in life.

SOUL INTENTION

by Richard Carlson, Ph.D.

*"Less effort is sometimes better. This is true with respect to
observing our thoughts and our connection with the Soul.
The less significance we give our thoughts, the easier it will
be to connect with the deeper parts of ourselves."*

ONE OF THE MOST thought-provoking questions I've
ever heard was asked by Stephen Levine. He asks,
"If you had one hour to live and could make only
one call, who would it be to, what would you say, and why are
you waiting?" A similar question could be asked of our relationship to our Soul: Why wait a moment longer to connect
with and nourish the Soul?

Our connectedness to our Soul is critical to our ability to
feel peace and love, to act in kindness toward others, and to
feel a sense of gratitude and wonder for life. To nourish the
Soul means to attend to and care for the parts of ourselves that
make us happy and that enable us to become kinder, gentler,
more compassionate and loving. As we get into the habit of

nourishing the Soul, we move to an entirely different level of life. Many of the "external" aspects of life that were so important and meaningful will seem insignificant, even silly. Everyday, ordinary life will take on new meaning and richness. As we begin to sense the divine in the "ordinary," our "ordinary" lives will become quite extraordinary. Our need to be special and different will diminish, and we will be more easily satisfied. We'll be happier!

Where we choose to place our primary attention has a great deal to do with our ability to open ourselves to the Soul's nourishment. Is my attention on my external life — what my body looks like, whether or not I'm achieving my goals, what others think of me, how much money I'm making, how I stack up against others, whether or not I'm stylishly slim, and so forth — or is my attention on my inner world, the world of the Soul? I have often been tempted to focus on my personal ambitions and goals. Over the years, however, I have noticed that when my attention is on these outer or external aspects of my life, it matters not how well things are going, because deep down, inside my being, there is an emptiness. No matter how much money I make or how great my body looks, I still feel a sense of shallowness.

When I remember that the primary purpose of life is to feel and appreciate the presence of God, to live from a state of love and compassion, and to be of service to others, then instantly, like magic, I begin to feel at peace. And, just as magically, when I transfer my energy from my external circumstances to my inner knowing, to my "Soul energy," my external circumstances usually work out terrifically. In fact, as I work with clients, parent my children, grow with my wife, write a book, wash dishes, or attempt to solve a problem from a place of peace and wisdom rather than one of fear and reaction, my life seems easier, quieter, and more satisfying.

Soul Intention

There is something in life more important, more beautiful, and more satisfying than what we "think" is important. That "something" is an internal place beyond thought, beyond form. Our thoughts about what we want, what we wish were different, and where we would rather be will come and go. But behind these thoughts, before their very formation, a deeper level of life is waiting for our attention. This is the realm of the Soul. The Soul is the part of us that watches our thoughts come and go. It is not the thoughts themselves.

For most of us — certainly for me — thoughts are extremely compelling. As the thought "I'm really mad at her" enters the mind, we're tempted to latch on to it, pay attention to it, see where it goes, give it significance. In short, we're tempted to take the thought far too seriously. As we do so, thousands of times every day, we feel anything *but* nourished by the Soul. Instead, we feel angry, jealous, hurt, or frightened, depending on the content of our thoughts. We think; we feel; then we think some more. We want to believe that if we could just think through our dissatisfactions or analyze our problems, we would somehow feel better. But that never works, because nourishment for the Soul comes not from the intellect but from the heart. We can't think our way to happiness. Instead, we must open ourselves to our true nature, which *is* happiness.

Behind thoughts such as "I'm really mad at her" lies a spaciousness, a constant hum of quietness and self-confidence, a feeling of nourishment that comes from the Soul. If our thoughts "come and go," if indeed we "let them go," we will discover this source of quiet and peace within ourselves. If we treat our thoughts as what they really are — simply thoughts — instead of believing that they are all that there is, we can give them less significance. When a disturbing thought enters the mind, as so often happens, rather than panicking and reacting, we can say to ourselves, "Ah, there's another one,"

Lessons of the Soul

and then let it go. When we trust in the Soul, when we know there is something else, something deeper and more important than the content of our own thoughts, it becomes possible to step back, relax, and become the observer of those thoughts.

A simple Zen statement reminds us that "Spring comes, and the grass grows all by itself." In other words, less effort is sometimes better. This is true with respect to observing our thoughts and our connection with the Soul. The less significance we give our thoughts, the easier it will be to connect with the deeper parts of ourselves. This isn't to say that what we think about isn't important — just that it isn't everything there is. If we overanalyze our thoughts and become overly concerned with them, we find ourselves caught up in our thinking, struggling to find answers, trapped in what I call "analysis paralysis." But as we simply "let go," noticing our thoughts and allowing our wisdom to surface, we will find a new sense of ease and comfort. Life will seem less like an emergency!

It always helps me to remember that I am the thinker of my own thoughts. Thinking isn't something that happens *to* me, as it often seems to be. Rather, thinking is something that I am doing on a moment-to-moment basis. I wouldn't become insulted by reading a nasty letter I had written to myself — neither should I allow my own thoughts to upset me. I can "think my thoughts" without becoming overly concerned by their content, without overreacting with a "thought attack." I know that as I quiet my thinking and connect with my Soul, my love and wisdom will surface and my fear will fade away.

For as long as I can remember, I have heard that you must "turn inward" to discover happiness and peace, to feel nourished. It wasn't until fairly recently, however, that I actually trusted that this would work. Although I don't always "walk the talk" as well as I would like, I have come to see that my inner life, my connection to my Soul, meaningfully affects what happens in my life. If I'm feeling angry and frustrated, every aspect of my life seems overwhelming and stressful. When I'm feeling fearful, I attract fear. But when I'm feeling contented and peaceful, my life seems to flow. Everything falls into place and makes sense, as if it all has a purpose. In a sense, our lives are like automobiles, meant to be driven from inside.

I find that practicing the art of love in my day-to-day life is among the most helpful ways for me to feel nourished by my Soul. Everything begins with an intention. Although it isn't always easy, I find that when I set my intention on feeling love, I often get exactly that feeling. And when I do, I connect with that place inside myself where peace exists. Every day, I find many opportunities to practice love — at work, with my wife and daughters, through an unfulfilled dream, with a stranger who is acting in a way I don't care for, even with a problem or disappointment.

An excellent way to practice love is to set your intention on seeing beyond someone's behavior or personality. Try to realize that beneath the surface insecurity, negative thinking, and poor behavior, everyone is connected to God. Just as you wouldn't get angry at someone simply because he or she is in a wheelchair, you need not be angry because a person hasn't yet opened his heart to the nourishment of his Soul. When people act in *un*loving ways, it only means they are out of touch with their Souls and aren't feeling spiritually nourished. When that happens, there is no need to panic. The best we can do for ourselves is nourish our own Soul by looking beyond the behavior we don't care for, thus practicing the art of love.

We may have more than an hour to live, but why wait a moment longer to connect with our Souls and begin practicing love?

SOUL GIFTS
in DISGUISE

by Elisabeth Kübler-Ross, M.D.

"If we could see that everything, even tragedy, is a gift in disguise, we would then find the best way to nourish the soul."

OVER THE YEARS, I have learned that every life circumstance, even a crisis, can nourish your soul. Recently, the farm and home that I have loved so much for so many years burned down in a horrible fire. Everything that I owned, without exception, was lost. There was even speculation that foul play was involved.

At moments like this, we stand at a fork in the road. If we take the fork most commonly traveled, we collapse, we give up, feeling hopeless and defeated. We focus on the negatives, losing ourselves in the "problem." We point to our unhappy circumstances to rationalize our negative feelings. This is the easy way out. It takes, after all, very little effort to feel victimized.

We can, however, take the other fork. We can view the un-happy experience as an opportunity for a new beginning. We can keep our perspective, look for the growth opportunities, and find an inner reservoir of strength.

By simply deciding to see the possibilities rather than the pain, I was able to come through the loss of my home with more strength and contentment than I had before the fire. Viewing the situation in perspective, I realized that most of the things I had collected over my lifetime were, in fact, just things. I didn't need them anymore. No longer tied to my house, I decided to move to Arizona, to be closer to my son. I love my new surroundings as much as I did my previous environment. There are trees, coyotes, and too much beauty to describe.

Had I taken the fork of despair, I would have remained an-gry and depressed over the fire, missing a golden opportunity to move west. Looking back, I see that I was too attached to my old environment to make the move on my own. In a sense, I needed the tragedy to push me onward. I don't mean to trivi-alize the difficulty of certain aspects of life. It is important to look for the larger picture. Only then can we nurture the Soul with our experiences. If we could see that everything, even tragedy, is a gift in disguise, we would then find the best way to nourish the soul.

We are all so bent and determined to get what we want, we miss the lessons that could be learned from life's experiences. Many of my AIDS patients discovered that the last year of their lives was by far their best. Many have said they wouldn't have traded the rich quality of that last year of life for a healthier body. Sadly, it is only when tragedy strikes that most of us begin attending to the deeper aspects of life. It is only then that we attempt to go beyond surface concerns — what we look like, how much money we make, and so forth — to discover what's really important.

Lessons of the Soul

One of the first things most AIDS patients learn is who their true friends are, who really loves them, and who will be with them until the end. Most of us will never know who really loves us; not at that same, very deep level. It may be that we cannot receive the "gift" of knowing without the "curse" of a dread disease.

"Crises" can help us discover much about ourselves and enrich our lives. Another wonderful experience that can grow out of a seeming disaster is the joy of appreciation. AIDS patients who relearn how to walk, for example, are often delighted at being able to take two or ten steps again. They appreciate tremendously something that they took for granted their entire lives. How many "healthy" or "normal" people are grateful that they can walk or talk? My guess is, very few. But how much value is there in something taken entirely for granted? If "disaster" enriches our lives with gifts that would otherwise have been taken for granted, is it really a disaster? Or is it a gift in disguise?

Perhaps one of trouble's greatest "side effects" is that it teaches us that life is rarely the way we want it to be; rather, life is simply the way it is. And we are simply the way we are. What we need is the desire to look for the gifts in ordinary and extraordinary experiences — and the wisdom to accept ourselves as we are. With this more expansive perspective of life, we begin to accept things and people for the way they are. We become less judgmental, more kind and loving. By accepting ourselves, others, and life as not being entirely okay, we become more okay than ever. (I once considered writing a book called *I'm Not OK and You're Not OK, and That's OK*.)

Nurturing the Soul means opening our hearts to the lessons of life and surrendering to what we have learned. One of the best ways of doing this is always to do what feels right to you, to follow your "gut reactions." I remember, as a young woman, challenging my father's insistence that I work in his office. My father was a powerful man; people did not cross him lightly. He nearly had a heart attack when I told him that I wanted to be a doctor, but I stood firm, because my heart and Soul were telling me to go into medicine. I knew that I would be unhappy for the rest of my life if I didn't listen to my inner calling. Rather than nurturing my Soul, I would be living my life solely to gain his approval. And I couldn't do this to my Soul.

I spent years working as a lab technician while attending medical school, each week getting closer to my goal. Although it was difficult, I was happy every single day of the journey.

When you spend your life doing what you love to do, you are nourishing your Soul. It matters not what you do, only that you love whatever you happen to do. Some of the happiest people I've known have been nannies, gardeners, and housekeepers. They put their hearts into their work, and they used the work itself as a vehicle to nourish their Souls. I've known other people with more prestigious professions who absolutely hated their jobs. What good is it to be a doctor or a professional if you do not genuinely love what you do? Working in a job you do not love does nothing to nourish your Soul.

I often hear people say, "I couldn't do what I wanted to do because I didn't have enough money for school," or give some other excuse. To them I reply, "Nonsense." You can do whatever you want to do when you put your mind to it. It all goes back to where you place your attention. Are you stuck on how difficult the task will be — on all the obstacles to overcome? Or is your entire heart and Soul focused on doing whatever is necessary to carry you toward your goal? I've known many people who had nothing but a dream. Without any outside support or money or education — with nothing but a dream — they persisted and succeeded.

Lessons of the Soul

Ultimately, when you listen to your inner callings, when you "follow your bliss," you are practicing the art of self-love. Many of us have been taught that self-love is negative, narcissistic, and selfish. In fact, self-love is just the opposite. People with genuine self-love feel nurtured and complete: they have something left over for other people. When you look for the best, when you love yourself fully, and when you know that "you're not fully OK, but that's OK," you are nurturing your Soul on a daily basis. The Soul accepts you as you are — and you and the Soul are one. How can you not love that which the Soul loves?

Whether you know it or not, one of the most important relationships in your life is with your Soul. Will you be kind and loving to your Soul, or will you be harsh and difficult? Many of us unknowingly damage our Souls with our negative attitudes and actions or by simple neglect. By making the relationship with your Soul an important part of your life, however, by honoring it in your daily routine, you give your life greater meaning and substance. Use your experiences — all of them — as opportunities to nourish your Soul!

SOULFUL LIVING

by Anne Wilson Schaef, Ph.D.

*"I find that in participating fully in my life, I am nudging
my soul all the time, every day, and that life
is very, very easy."*

T
O ME, NURTURING the soul is a simple matter of honoring my process, of trusting in and turning my life over to what the Higher Power has in mind for me. Whenever I fight my process, I'm miserable. Instead of struggling, I need to ask every day, "What do You have in mind for me today?" Then I accept the answer, trusting it, rather than fighting to control my life.

In his book *To Be Human Against All Odds*, Frederick Franck argues that our task is not to be gods, but solely to be human. As human beings, we are part of the created order, and we need to participate, to play our parts. For me, participation is soul-nourishing. Unfortunately, our society tends to pull us out of participation, so that we may be "objective," so that we can manipulate and control our environment. In the process of seizing control, however, we lose the ability to participate in our lives, to participate in the ongoing process of the universe. I think this is one of the reasons we feel so free to destroy the environment. We don't realize that we're destroying ourselves when we destroy the planet. When we understand that *we* are the rain forest, then there's a possibility we can save it.

In everyday life, we participate in the created order by focusing on ourselves rather than on other people. For example, if we have rough interactions with others, instead of analyzing and blaming the others, we need to stay with our own feelings and needs. We need to let ourselves feel the hurt but not focus on the other people. Unfortunately, Western culture teaches us to focus on the external and on others. (I think of Western culture as a virtual reality that we've constructed and then forgotten is not real.) We do the same thing with ourselves, focusing on ourselves as "the other." In so doing, we lose the ability to participate in our own lives. But life *is* participation. Life is doing it. When we think about doing it, we're no longer doing it. It is really very simple. We can't will or control life; we have to let it go. *Then* we can do it.

Several things help us let go and live, including honesty and openness. I am totally honest in the way I live. I can't control what someone else does; I can't make him or her change. All I can create is my own behavior. I can say that someone did something that made me feel uncomfortable, but then I let it go. I also think that it's important to be ruthlessly honest in relationships. Whenever a fear, a thought, or even a dream about a relationship comes up, instead of feeling "That's too silly" or "I can't really think that," I say what has come to mind. This really results in stress-free living, which is nourishing to the soul.

I also find it soul-nourishing to be around people who are willing to explore their habits and change if necessary. Willing, open self-searching is very important. I find it too exhausting to be around people who aren't at least open to change, so I avoid them as much as possible. I also want to surround myself with loving, "fun" people. Last year, I decided I would only spend time with people who delighted in my company and in whose company I delighted. Otherwise, I didn't want to be around them. It was too draining. Being in cities is also very draining to me now. I prefer being in the country — Hawaii or Montana — where I can connect with nature and realize that we're all one.

Native people seem to know this instinctively. In the past few years, I've spent a lot of time with native elders throughout the world. It has been a time of listening, healing, and revelations. At a family reunion last year, I learned that my father was American Indian. I never knew my father or much about him. Upon learning who he was, my life seemed to fall into place. I suddenly knew why it was not possible for me to nurture my soul without nature. You see, I need to continually reconnect with my own awareness that I am part of a larger process, a larger universe. I need to remind myself that I am not dominating it, nor am I necessarily dominated by it. Instead, I am a participant. Somehow, this realization becomes clearer to me when I'm in nature.

I'm doing so many things in my life that I love. I'm writing poetry and children's stories. I've started a new novel. I find that in participating fully in my life, I am nudging my soul all the time, every day, and that life is very, very easy. Although I do many things, I live quite simply and love doing so. When I teach, I share my own awareness. I share what I have learned about myself from the man I love, from my children, from my dog. When I share what I have learned about myself, I connect with others.

Right now, I'm living with a group of people. We've decided to stay together for at least five years, in order to share what we've learned and to do living-process work. My friends are rich and poor and from all walks of life. I see the change in them, and I feel tearful. I'm grateful to have been given the gift of being a part of their lives. It's a great gift, a great honor.

I have a responsibility to live this life with the talents I was given. It's my responsibility to do it. Not to think about it; just to do it. That's why I'm here. It's really that simple. The rest is up to the Creator.

6.

Soul
Communion

———•—•——

"A soul friend is someone with whom we can share our greatest joys and deepest fears, confess our worst sins and most persistent faults, clarify our highest hopes and perhaps most unarticulated dreams."

— EDWARD C. SELLNER

The GUIDING CONSCIENCE

by Stephen R. Covey, Ph.D.

"I think that the most significant work we ever do, in our whole world, in our whole life, is done within the four walls of our own home. All mothers and fathers, whatever their stations in life, can make the most significant of contributions by imprinting the spirit of service on the souls of their children, so that the children grow up committed to making a difference."

TO ME, THE ESSENCE of keeping the soul nourished is obedience to one's conscience. I don't think that the soul can be nourished unless people have a strong sense of conscience that they have educated and developed and soaked in the universal and timeless principles of integrity and service. This way, the individual's soul becomes part of the universal soul of service, contribution, and making a difference.

You need to take your private victories and make them public. Much of the self-esteem literature has created a kind of narcissism of taking care of the self, loving the self, and nurturing the self and has neglected the next step: service. If you don't have a public challenge, then your private victory may be just a lot of heart massage. You think you're nurturing your soul because it feels warm and cozy, like you're taking care of yourself. You may be good, but what are you good for? You've got to be good for something. You've got to be about some project, some task that requires you to be humble and obedient to the universal principles of service. You've got to live a life of complete and total integrity in order to give this kind of service. This integrity enables you to love other people unconditionally, to be courageous and kind at the same time, because you have integratedness inside your own soul. Most often, a major external challenge or project — some Mother Teresa kind of project — is necessary to bring this integration.

What does this integration involve? I see the soul as the primary essence of our true nature, our spirit self. When all the parts of the self — the intuitive system, the feeling system, the senses, the conscience system, the value system, the habit system — are in sync, then the soul becomes the dominant force in your life. When this happens, you start to see the potential in other people. You affirm them and you help them see that they can make a major contribution, and so the goodness starts to spread, one person to another.

Our firm, Covey Leadership Center, just produced a little film on a young man in Uganda by the name of Stone, who was a great soccer player. Someone purposely blew out his knee in a soccer game, ending his professional career. He could have chosen bitterness. But instead, he began to help other young men who were aimless and without direction, who were on drugs, in gangs, doing nothing. First he gave himself to building them up by teaching them to be soccer players. Once that relationship was established, he helped them develop skills and crafts, so that they could make a living and then become responsible fathers and community contributors.

What he has done is truly inspirational. You could see how his own soul was nurtured by his desire to contribute, to focus outside himself. This kind of soul development comes after you have acknowledged some great need that is external to yourself. Then, in order to respond effectively to that need, you find yourself needing to go within and nurture and develop your soul.

Then a beautiful process begins. Responding from the soul, you become truly empathic and sensitive — very patient and very aware of the reality of the other person's need. The other person begins to get a sense of your vision for his or her possibility, and you affirm his goodness, her potential. An inside-out growth process begins for both of you.

One soul can be an island of excellence in a sea of mediocrity this way. And that one soul can change the whole sea. One soul can stop the transmission of bad tendencies from one generation to the next. One soul, let's say, was abused as a child. But she doesn't have to abuse her child, because there has been a reconstitution of the soul. This comes through tapping into four unique human endowments, which all people have. The first of these is self-awareness — the ability to examine your own life, to stand apart from it and study the scripting inside you. The second is your power of imagination — your vision of how you can create a better situation for people, for yourself and society. The third endowment is your conscience, a deep moral sense of what is right and wrong. And finally, you have independent will, which you can exercise to act on the other three endowments.

It is when these four endowments are exercised on a regular basis that the soul develops deeply and starts to reach out to influence other people. A person who chooses this path is literally a change catalyst. I call them the trim-tabbers, because they are like the little trim-tab on the rudder that moves the rudder, which in turn moves the big ship. One soul can make a whale of a difference in any environment that person is in. Look at Viktor Frankl's (German psychiatrist and author) experience as a prisoner in the death camps of Nazi Germany. Look what Nelson Mandela has done for South Africa — twenty-seven years in prison, and now he forgives and has become a charismatic, mature man. He's another Gandhi. People like these inspire the Gandhi in all of us.

This work can begin no matter where you are. I think that the most significant work we ever do, in our whole world, in our whole life, is done within the four walls of our own home. All mothers and fathers, whatever their stations in life, can make the most significant of contributions by imprinting the spirit of service on the souls of their children, so that the children grow up committed to making a difference.

For myself, the key thing, again, is the education of the conscience. Personally, I choose to prayerfully study the scriptures every morning and every night. I get up early so I can be alone, to have what I call a private victory, a moment of clear understanding of what my life is about. As I exercise on my stationary bike, I study and plan my day of service and contribution; then I try to put that plan into action during the day. At night, I try to have some meaningful, rich time with the family. I help my children with homework, or go to their basketball games or whatever they're involved in, and spend time with them. I listen to them. We have our scripture reading at night. Then we pray, because we rely so much on God and on the power that comes from Him and the way He can nurture our conscience. We are also very active in our church on Sunday; we renew our covenants with God through our church program and with our involvement in service projects.

Often, people get pulled away from the soul's guiding principles. We're living in a hurried world, in which instant success is the watchword of the day. A sense of urgency develops, and we often develop an addiction to the intensity and pressure. Much in our lives seems urgent, yet is not important.

I believe that if you build up the important areas of your life, the urgency will pull at you less and less, and your life will feel more focused and purposeful. To me, the things that are truly important include building relationships, empowering other people, developing a vision, and nurturing the soul. I call the process of developing these important areas sharpening the saw, and we do it in four areas: the physical, the mental, the social, and the spiritual. Focusing on these four areas will eventually let you see how much in your life is irrelevant, how much you can say no to.

The transition to emphasizing the important over the urgent is a difficult process. People seem to have withdrawal pains as part of moving away from the pressure. But once you get into focusing on importance over urgency, the benefits are enormous and satisfying. If the people I work with move to this way of thinking, they'll start talking to other interested people, beginning with their families, then work groups, and so forth. We have seen entire organizations move to this kind of thinking in just this way.

In fact, real benefits to the marketplace come through this process. The pragmatic fruits are becoming increasingly obvious. I think it's primarily because you cannot survive in a global economy with low quality. And you cannot produce high quality unless you have high trust. So it is also impossible to have high, sustainable trust unless you have deep trustworthiness in the people of that culture. Now, getting people to focus upon nurturing the organization's soul brings about this sort of deep character development.

The Guiding Conscience

Everything is driven by these values, and by this truth: humility is the mother of all virtues. When you are humble, you accept that there are certain principles that are external to self, that we must align ourselves with. Each person is not a law unto himself. Natural laws define how we nurture our souls. These laws are universal, covering cultures and religions and nationalities. As people cultivate these principles inside themselves and develop the service ethic, the desire to make a difference, to help the dispossessed and disadvantaged, grows.

These natural laws and the logical outcome of obeying them reflect how we belong to each other. We're sisters and brothers in the family of God, and therefore we are of each other's nature. So even though I don't know you in an earthly way, in a deeper sense I do know you and care for you, and you for me. This is where we meet and where our connectedness nurtures our souls.

I am convinced that soul nurturance depends on our having a vision for ourselves and our world. I think that the recovery literature has focused too much on understanding the scarring of our souls from abuses of childhood, and not enough on vision. I'm convinced that vision is infinitely greater than baggage. We have within us tremendous capability and potential for actualizing that vision and eclipsing the baggage. Mind you, I am not against the self-awareness that comes from talk and insight therapies. I just don't think it's sufficient; it's not transcendent enough. We can't think small. We have to think about outside contribution. That is what changes and heals people.

An internal structure within us supports this process. I think of it as a little family: the mother of the little family is humility, which says, I am not in charge; I must submit myself to the governing principles. The father of the family is courage, because it takes tremendous courage to overcome the deep psychic scarring and scripting of your own nature, to overcome the powerful social forces that aren't aligned with the governing principles. The child of that union is called integrity. That is the place where our soul is rooted around a set of balanced, timeless, universal principles. Finally, there are two grandchildren. The first is wisdom, meaning that you see the larger picture; how things are related to one another. The second is abundance mentality, which says that you know your security comes from within, not without — that life includes ever-increasing resources.

Our service to others, then, opens the soul. When other people suffer from soul sickness, we can seek to build relationships by understanding their world and their feelings, so that they feel deeply understood. Then we begin to affirm them — their potential, their innate power and goodness. And then they might be open to being taught to be independent, and so the student becomes the teacher, and more souls are touched.

Several dimensions are critical to our capacity to do this work, to develop our capacity for soul. Leaving out one dimension has a domino effect upon the others. We need to balance these dimensions. There is the physical: people who don't have control over their flesh will eventually find that they won't be able to get control over their spirit. Their minds, their passions, their appetites will control instead. Then there is the mental: we need constant development of the mind — including professional development — so that we continually improve our ability to think deeply, analytically, creatively, conceptually, and abstractly. And then, of course, there is the spirit — the whole cultivation of one's conscience and spiritual sense.

I had an experience in Mexico that dramatically illustrated how the process of maintaining soul connectedness works. I don't speak Spanish, so at this event I had on earphones with simultaneous translations of the speeches. I could hear the

English translation through the earphones while at the same time hearing the speaker. And I thought, this is how it works with the soul. You are experiencing the sensate world outside yourself. But if you have cultivated the soul, you also hear a small, deep, inner voice that helps you understand and interpret your world, that directs you so that your conscience — not external social mores — becomes your guide. Just as I could shift my consciousness between the Spanish voice, which I didn't understand, and the English voice, which I did, we can shift our consciousness from the confusing externals to the clear directives from within. As long as there is this balance between the inner and the outer, our soul is nourished, and we can live a life of service.

SOUL CREATION

by Matthew Fox, Ph.D.

*"Soul is our appetite, driving us to eat from the banquet
of life. People filled with the hunger of soul take food from
every dish before them, whether it be sweet or bitter."*

W E ARE NOT born with guarantees that we will
have strong souls. No, we must work on our
souls, enlarging and expanding them. We do so
by experiencing all of life — the beauty and the joy as well as
the grief and pain. Soul work requires paying attention to life,
to the laughter and the sorrow, the enlightening and the frightening, the inspiring and the silly. It's been said that "God delights to watch the soul grow." Perhaps we were put here to
expand our souls through the experiences of life.

Silence and emptiness nourish the soul. So does meditation — being empty and letting go. Being still. Laughing. Putting oneself in the presence of beauty, grace, or empathy. Being
with people who are at the edge, who are giving birth or dying,
nourishes the soul. When we are grieving, we are living life,

although many of us shy away from the pain. That's why grief work is a big part of soul work — it helps us accept all our emotions and feelings, including anger and sorrow. I recently spoke with a fellow who has AIDS. He told me that the day he found out he was going to die was the day he began to live.

Nourishing the soul means throwing ourselves into our yearning for beauty and goodness, for community and connection with others. It also means struggling, standing up to injustice and paying whatever price is necessary to right a wrong. Everything that is encouraging, no matter how difficult or trying, nourishes the soul.

And we must nourish the soul, for without a strong soul, we would stumble through life at a superficial level. Without the passion that soul gives, we would not be living life. Instead, we would simply be waiting to die. In a sense, soul is our appetite, driving us to eat from the banquet of life. People filled with the hunger of soul take food from every dish before them, whether it be sweet or bitter.

The ways that individuals may nourish their souls will vary a great deal, according to their stories and interests. For people who do not know how to live all the experiences of life, I would suggest that they begin by looking for something that gives them joy, then spending more time with that.

Many people in our culture seem to feel that they have no right to joy, that they're lucky if they can grab a little happiness once in a while. These people must give themselves permission to find and take time for joy, to structure space for joy in their lives.

Seekers of soul nourishment may also look for ways to be with the great mystery, however they define it. Becoming involved with the community and with ritual are excellent ways to nourish the soul. I think that one of our problems as a people is that we lack common rituals. These missing rituals could expand our souls through the power of the rituals themselves, as well as by connecting us with others.

I'm currently working with a group of young people from Sheffield, England. They are reinventing a mass using techno-music, multimedia, rap, and rave dancing. We performed the mass at the base of Grace Cathedral in San Francisco in late October 1994. The ritual and community, along with the music and creativity, and yes, even the struggle to put it all together, was exhilarating and nourishing.

People looking for a way to nourish their souls may want to make creativity a part of their everyday lives. The universe is creative. When we are creative, we are giving birth, as the universe gave birth to stars, planets, microbes, plants, birds, animals, and humans. When we create ideas or love or humor, we multiply the opportunities for ourselves and for others to experience life, thus nourishing many souls at once.

Looking for and enjoying beauty is another way to nourish the soul. The universe is in the habit of making beauty. There are flowers and songs, snowflakes and smiles, acts of great courage, laughter between friends, a job well done, the smell of fresh-baked bread. Beauty is everywhere, ready to nourish the soul. It must only be seen to begin helping us.

Humor is wonderful food for the soul. Too much serious-ness violates the laws of nature. Living a humorless life, turn-ing a blind eye to the paradoxes around and within us, or never even laughing at ourselves shrinks the soul.

Work nourishes the soul. All the creatures of the universe are busy doing work, and we honor life when we work. The type of work is not important: the fact of work is. All work feeds the soul if it is honest and done to the best of our abilities and if it brings joy to others.

Working, creating, enjoying humor, righting a wrong, fac-ing a sorrow head on: every aspect of life can be nourishing to

Soul Creation

the soul if we take it into our lives. Meditation and prayer take us to the quiet places of soul. Shouting against injustice or noisily celebrating a holiday take us to the noisy places of soul. What we choose to do is not as important as that we choose to live and to do.

Many paths lead to our soul. Four in particular correspond to what I call in theology the "Four Paths of Creation Spirituality" that help name the soul journey for us. The first path, the Via Positiva, or the experience of divinity as the blessing of creation, is our experience of awe, wonder, joy, and delight. The second path, the Via Negativa, is that of darkness, pain, emptiness, nothingness, and letting go. The third path, the Via Creativa, or the Creative Way, is our experience of giving birth and creating. The fourth path, the Via Transformativa, or the Transformative Way, is our experience of compassion, struggle, doing justice, ablution, and imagination.

There are no set rules for nourishing the soul, no "three steps to guaranteed soulfulness." Loving, laughing, crying, creating, praying, tilting with windmills, raising a child, saying good-bye to a departed loved one — it's all living, if we're aware of what we're doing. Some embrace life naturally; others have to learn. Some readily open themselves to life; others can only do so after a breakdown or calamity. For all of us, however, it is a question of living, of being alive and aware of what's really going on. Living life is nourishing to the soul — and there's a lot of living to do.

The SACRED IMPULSE

by Jacob Needleman, Ph.D.

"You can't experience the truth of another person without feeling love. Understanding and love go together. When we nourish the soul, we automatically nourish our capacity to love another person."

A YEARNING EXISTS within the human psyche that has not been acknowledged by modern psychology or supported or nurtured by our culture. Plato called this yearning "eros." We have limited this word mainly to the sexual side of life, but Plato emphasized it as a yearning to participate in the greatness of being, both in the universal order and within ourselves. The way he put it was "the human being is pregnant with the soul."

Since the beginning of the century, modern psychology and psychiatry have tended to think of human beings mainly as animals with an especially complicated brain. The spiritual element in human nature tended to be regarded as secondary or reducible to sociobiological desires. This has led to a metaphysical repression far more deadly, more dangerous, and more destructive than sexual repression — the repression of the sacred impulse that is at least as essential to us as sexual desire and as much a part of us as the desire for food and shelter.

That need is now trying to reclaim its own in our culture. Many of the things we're seeing today are signs that eros is bursting through again. People are turning to new religious movements and spiritual ideas of many kinds. There is a disillusionment with science. People are getting all the money and possessions they want and are still questioning how to have a meaningful life. Widespread signs throughout the world indicate that our modern culture has left something out. That "something" is the soul.

Some years ago, I taught a course in philosophy to high school students. These young people told me there was no place in their environment — with their families, their friends, psychologists, or their churches — where they could simply ask the questions of the heart: Who am I? Why are we here? What are we meant to serve? Does God exist? All the questions that are what I call the heart of philosophy. These are the real questions that come with the search for the soul. These students were enthralled to find a setting where they could ask these questions, instead of being ashamed of them. One student said to me, "If I had known about this sort of thing, I never would have tried drugs." This made me realize that these essential needs have to be honored and nurtured.

The search for the soul is part of human nature. It's as basic as wanting to eat or have clothes or marry and have children. The Koran tells extraordinary stories on this subject. So do Jewish folktales. One tells of God about to create mankind by mixing clay and spirit. The angels, who were watching, said, "God, why are you creating such a being? You know what

kind of trouble this is going to be?" The angels are pure spirits. They don't understand what God is doing. God's answer
in the Koran is simply, "I know what you don't know." This is
the unique creation that we are. We have an animal, earthly,
worldly nature in us as well as a sacred possibility. We're
meant, as I see it, to live in relation to both aspects as long as
we're on earth, to give each aspect its due. It's a very difficult
thing, but until we're able to at least approach that, we are
never going to be happy or fulfilled. If we try to satisfy just the
horizontal side of our nature, the sociobiological side, we'll get
a lot of desires satisfied and a lot of physical pleasure, but we'll
find no real happiness or meaning. A lot of anxiety will go with
it. If we try to be just pure spiritual beings, we'll be denying
this other part of ourselves. That will not bring us meaning
and fulfillment either.

So this search for the soul is just part of our natures. The
question is, why is it happening now? We are coming to the
end of decades and decades of a society that has been able to
give us what we want in certain respects and discovering that
it's just not what we need. It may be more than happenstance
that as we approach the year 2000, we are seeing that we've
lost the meaning of the foundation of our Western civilization. That foundation needs to be rediscovered. Part of that
foundation is the notion of the soul and the spirit within each
of us. It's happening in the '90s in a dramatic way, because
what's gotten us through up until now is being shown to be
inadequate.

How do we go about nurturing our soul on a day-to-day
basis? A soul is an embryo in us that needs to be nurtured and
nourished. The soul in its young and embryonic form — and
in all of its stages — needs and desires something very different from what the sociobiological self needs. It has a different
set of values. It doesn't want the pleasures and satisfactions that

The Sacred Impulse

we as an ego want. It wants something that the ego finds mysterious and incomprehensible. What it needs, at least partly, is experiences of truth.

The soul needs to take in, like food, experiences of truth about oneself and the world. When we allow in the experiences of ourselves and others as they really are, the soul is being nourished. One of the most important things is to find other people who have the same kind of aim and associate with them. I don't think we can follow this path alone. The first thing to do is to find what I call a philosophical friend — someone who has these values too. Together, you support the search for nourishing the soul. Sooner or later, experiences of truth are inseparably connected with helping others. Truth always goes with love. You can't experience the truth of another person without feeling love. Understanding and love go together. When we nourish the soul, we automatically nourish our capacity to love another person.

Another word for philosophical friend is soul mate, not in a sentimental way, but meaning another person whose main interest in the relationship is truth. That is sometimes hard, because we often turn to friends to support our illusions. If they don't support our egoistic illusions, we get angry with them. Soul mates sometimes look like enemies. But they're enemies of the false. Soul mates don't always have to be people you like. They're just people whose values are a search for truth and service.

Rightly conducted meditation is very good for the soul. Human beings are meditating animals. Everyone has to meditate in one way or another, but forms of meditation vary. Teachers vary. Like every spiritual practice, it helps to have support and guidance from people who know something.

Music and reading can greatly support the movement toward oneself. It's a kind of silence the soul desperately needs in order to grow. The soul cannot grow unless there's silence in some sense. For me, it's very important to realize that it's my attitude toward the life I've been given each day that really determines whether my soul will be nourished. All the books and music in the world are not going to do much if I don't have an inner intention to receive the truth. And on the other hand, even a lot of distractions and unpleasantness won't really hurt me if it is my intention that my relationship to my own mind be focused. It is possible to have a meditative life even in the midst of activity and distraction. We can't get rid of distractions in order to get on with living. These difficulties *are* living. They're never going to go away. It is therefore important for our soul growth that we have some intentional relation to them.

Attitude is probably the most important thing, but it's not easy. It's difficult to have an attitude toward life that no matter what happens, all we experience is for our inner growth. But it's the *sine qua non* — the most important thing to have. We can't depend on external things to give what can only come from inside. It's a form of idolatry in the ancient sense of the term to expect the outer to bring what only the inner can bring. Viktor Frankl managed to nourish his soul even under the hellish conditions of Nazi concentration camps. That's a shining example of what's possible in terms of inner attitude.

SOULFULNESS IS a VERB

by Phil Cousineau

"In a world moving at hyperspeed, where so many of us are anxious because of the rate of change, the soulful move is the move toward contemplating the source of things deeply rooted in eternity, the things that always are."

WHEN I HEAR someone say, "I've lost my soul," what I hear is, "I've lost my connection to life" or "I've lost my deep meaning" or "I've lost my imagination." I'm reminded of the belief that since the dawn of human history, the search for soul has circled around the issue of immortality — in other words, the mystery of continuity and the inscrutable *depths* of life.

With the birth of science, many people stopped believing in immortality, which suggests that they also stopped believing in the soul. So if someone says, "I'm here only once, and when I die, that's all there is," it's highly unlikely this person is going to believe in the soul or take a discussion of the soul seriously.

Yet the word itself is still so combustible. Even if you're a card-carrying atheist, if someone tells you that you sold your soul to get that real estate deal, or you turned in a soulless performance last night at the Hollywood Bowl, the phrase stings. But if someone says, "You're looking particularly soulful tonight," that language hums in us. It seems to me soul is still our touchstone word for what's authentic and vital. So if someone says, "I've lost my soul," what I hear is, "I've lost my authenticity. I've lost my spark. I've lost my connection to the sacred."

If it's lost, the question becomes, how do you get it back? There is no one path. One way I think we spontaneously try to retrieve our souls is by being around soulful people. Another way is by going to soulful places, either in nature or by way of a pilgrimage to places like Chartres Cathedral or the Wailing Wall of Jerusalem, or even Yankee Stadium. Find those places that are charged with the sacred — places in the world that are actually holy to us.

We can also retrieve soul by attending something soulful — an art exhibit, a music performance, a poetry reading. If we hear soulful language, something is sparked in us, and, like a flint that is sparked, our soul can be sparked again. To me, that's the power of religion and ritual and art — to help wake us up, to stir the vital force within us and remind us of the depths.

For some contemporary people it's extremely difficult to think about soul, so to talk about *soulfulness* seems to be more acceptable, especially soul moments — for example, the moment of writing a letter, as in that wonderful phrase by the poet John Donne, where "Letters mingle souls."

When you write a letter, you are giving attention to life. You are giving attention to paper and pen and ink. You've slowed down your thoughts. You're contemplating one other soul in the world. And when you do that, your soul mingles with someone else's. Writing a letter by hand is a soulful moment in today's world. My view on soul, then, is that it has a lot to do with attentiveness, thoughtfulness, mindfulness. Soul is a measure of the depths of our lives — "the divine spark" in us, as Meister Eckhart said.

Other sources of soul in ordinary life might be storytelling, prayer, intimate relationships, or having a communal meal. A lot of us eat most of our meals alone at a desk or standing up at a counter somewhere. And I think at some level we realize this is a kind of soulless way to feed ourselves. Eating together, a communal meal, is a soul moment. Teaching somebody something, if you're a teacher or a coach or a mentor, is a soul moment. When you are passing on your knowledge or your wisdom, there is soul. These little moments quicken the soul because they all involve the catalyst of *love*. As the ancients said, the soul is realized in love.

In contrast, a lot of movement in today's life is away from others. That's part of the American myth of individualism. We are lone wolves, us against the world — individually, or sometimes as a small, nuclear family. But I think we've paid a high price for that in this country. There's tremendous solitude and isolation. Perhaps this revival of interest in soul is reflecting a slight turn away from the isolation of individualism back to the cohesion of community. Soulful life nudges us toward reconnecting ourselves to the neighborhood, toward community action, political activity, reattaching with our family, our past, our ancestors, and revitalizing our spiritual lives. For me, it's a curious notion that soulful life tends not to be too consumed with future or evolution; instead, soul moves us backward, where we begin to contemplate the past.

I've recently finished writing a film called *Ecological Design*.

It explores the inspiring movement in architecture right now toward green design, in which architects and designers are re-considering the materials they use for buildings, the longevity of buildings, how buildings fit in with the landscape, the community, the spirit of the place. This attitude nurtures the soulful essence of contemporary life by re-minding people of their connectedness to the rest of life. I think this is another way that contemporary America is ensouling itself.

Jamaka Highwater, the Native American writer, makes a distinction that would be helpful for those of us today mired in the cult of individualism. He says that in Native American tra-dition (except for the Plains Indians, who were robustly indi-vidualistic), they didn't so much believe in the individual soul as they did in the collective soul. The word he uses is *orenda*. This can mean either of two things: the tribal soul or the tribal flame, which goes back to an image that a lot of the mystics used — the flame for soul. Native tribes and also some African tribes believed that the soul of a clan, a tribe, or a village is flamelike, and it rises and falls. It's at its strongest when people are living for a common cause. When they are performing ritu-als together and praying together and hunting and dreaming together, the flame is at its strongest. That way of life is called "the red road." But if you turn away from the collective and you're only interested in yourself or the few souls around you, it's called walking "the black road," which is the road of self-ishness and, often, violence.

That road is one we've gotten stuck on here in contempo-rary America. A belief in only the individual soul closes in on itself and arrives at a selfishness that is fracturing us. If we opened up our very concept of soul to include the community, the soul of nature, the soul of the world, we might begin to imagine our lives as having something to do with that flame that burns all around us.

Soulfulness Is a Verb

163

In Davis, California, local planners have a community in which they've replaced yards with gardens and orchards and thrown away the whole notion of straight streets. They saw that children are often killed in American neighborhoods because the straight streets encourage young guys to drive eighty miles an hour in a twenty-five-mile-an-hour zone. I think it is easier to bring soul into your everyday life if you actually have ensouled the design of your neighborhood, the design of your house with care and a concern for beauty.

We can spend a lot of time working on our private individual souls, but if we then walk out into the world in which our buildings are soulless, where the community is soulless, then the individual soul can be overwhelmed, forced into retreat. How can we become "soulful" people if we're ignoring the safety of our streets, the soul of the environment, and the quality of our educational system?

Recently, I was rereading Martin Luther King's "I Have a Dream" speech. I was stunned by his prophetic phrase, "We must rise to the majestic heights of meeting physical force with soul force." Believing that our souls can have a cumulative effect that goes out and meets the world is another way for us to look at the nobility of soul, rather than as just an outdated theological notion.

I've had friends in foreign countries tell me that they have heard King's speech and not understood all the language, but understood the soul in his voice, and wept because of it. Here is a beautiful echo of what the poet Longfellow meant when he said that the soul is invisible but audible. Soul is in the voice.

Or, in another venerable tradition, the fingertips. According to the craftsmen of the Middle Ages, that's why we have spiral patterns on our fingertips. They thought the whorls there are the marks left by the soul entering or leaving the body. In this imaginative way of thinking, we infuse the people and things we touch in the world with soul by the care and attention of our touch. Our soul emerges from this mysterious place inside us and out through our fingertips, ensouling the wood we carve, the gardens we cultivate, the children and animals and lovers we touch. To me, this is a poetic way of imagining how we bring soul back into our personal lives — by paying attention to the very way we touch, as with the way we prepare food or the care we give our work or the manner in which we touch the earth.

Perhaps the fascination with soul is a reflection of the desire for continuity of life. To me, continuity is at the heart of this whole discussion of soul. We know very well how fast things change around us, from the buildings and businesses in our neighborhood to the friends who come and go to the people who die every day and night around us. Change is constant. Accompanying change, however, is a mystery I like to call the strange persistence of life. Something irrepressible seems to last in the midst of all of this change.

It can be something as simple as the gleam in the eye of your grandfather in the photograph you've seen of him from 1915, as with my grandfather, Horace Cousineau. If I contemplate that, I'm contemplating the mystery of soul. If I put my hand on the stones of Chartres Cathedral and actually take in the mystery of that continuity — how a cathedral could last and move people for seven hundred years — I'm contemplating the mysterious continuity of things. And that's a contemplation of soul, the depth dimension of life.

In a world moving at hyperspeed, where so many of us are anxious because of the rate of change, the soulful move is the move toward contemplating the source of things deeply rooted in eternity, the things that always are. The reading of a fairy tale, the journey to an ancient sacred site, the cultivation of true friendship are all ways to contemplate the things that last, that are continuous. When we touch that mystery, we're nourished in a profound way. If we're not touching the eternals — if we're not in touch with mythic stories, with ancient sites, with old family scrapbooks and heirlooms and deeply probing relationships — then we're lost. If all we're trying to do is keep up with change, I think we lose the momentum of our soul's journey. But once you touch an old story, a true mentor, or the mysterious powers of nature, somehow your soul is nourished and, by a movement that still mystifies me, you find the courage to go on.

7.

A Return
to Soul

———— ⋅⋅◆⋅⋅ ————

"The new work of art does not consist of making a living or producing an objet d'art or in self-therapy, but in finding a new soul. The new era is the era of spiritual creativity . . . and soul-making."

— HENRY MILLER

LETTING GO
of the MOUNTAIN

by *Benjamin Shield, Ph.D.*

*"Soul is where the fires of our passions burn. It is where our
love is most alive. The soul longs for this deeper love,
for a connection between form and formlessness, for a continuum between the earth and the divine."*

ONE AFTERNOON, A MAN named Harry went mountain climbing. All in all, things were going very
well. Then suddenly, the path he was walking on
gave way, taking Harry with it. With flailing arms, Harry managed to grab a small branch on the side of the mountain. Holding on for dear life, he screamed, "Help! Help! Is anybody up
there?"

Miraculously, the clouds parted, and a beam of light illuminated Harry as he hung tenuously from the branch. A voice —
clearly the voice of God — spoke directly to Harry and said:
"Harry, I will save you. I am all that is good, all that is
true, and all that has meaning. Let go, Harry; I will save you.
Let go."

Harry thought hard about this. Then, with a sudden burst of conviction, he looked up the mountain and shouted, "Is anybody *else* up there?"

How often we find ourselves in Harry's position. Do we find ways to hold on tighter and tighter to what we know won't support us, or do we learn to let go, into the realm of soul?

Letting go is one of the most difficult challenges human beings ever face. I've always pictured letting go as transformation — moving from a closed fist to an open hand. As we take an open-handed attitude toward life, we can be free of the self-made obstructions that litter our path. This process requires a willingness to shed our persona — those inauthentic trappings we hold onto for identity but that no longer serve us. Like Harry, each of us is faced with these choices every day. The choice to let go frees us to follow the pathway to our soul.

And when we embark on our journey to soul, what then? Is the soul a fragile piece of art, like some holy chalice that we now safely and adoringly preserve in a glass box? Or is the soul the way we view our world — seeing the best and most authentic elements in everyone in our lives and everything around us?

The soul can be experienced by releasing the familiar and safe, by the constant renewal and expression of our presence in the world, and by the moment-to-moment attention we give to daily life. Then the relationship we have with our soul becomes the model for the relationship we have with our world.

Our soul's journey is not about acquiring more and more knowledge. It is a journey of re-minding ourselves of those precious truths we have long known. It is not a process of gathering enough data to eventually achieve the "Big 'Ah-ha!'" Instead, our soul's journey is a process of freeing ourselves to the newness of each moment, constantly clearing away those thoughts and fears that have obstructed access to our soul and, equally, our soul's access to us. As Robert Frost said, "Something we were withholding made us weak / Until we found it was ourselves."

We might think of soul making as the same process by which Michelangelo created his sculptures. He believed that a statue's completed form already existed in the marble. All he needed to do was chisel away everything that was *not* the completed sculpture, and it would appear. This is the nature of the soul — perfect, yet hidden. Our "marble" can be chiseled away by the passionate desire to know our soul as well as its obstructions.

Experiencing the soul is like the magic you feel when falling in love. This is a time when our ego boundaries — those defensive walls we build around ourselves to keep us separate from one another — crumble. This is a time of soul nourishment. Remember the feelings that infuse our souls when we sing and dance with abandonment? Witness a birth? Hear Schubert's "Ave Maria"? Become lost in another's eyes? Ironically, we often describe these special moments as "losing ourselves." In the "losing," we are actually finding ourselves. Letting go, then, becomes the gateway to creation, to generating soul.

In our search for soul, it is important to bring along two things: humility and "unknowing." This means being completely present with an open heart and open mind. This openness is not an absence of thought but, rather, a clear attentiveness to the moment. It is achieved not by effort but by letting go — giving up the need to be in control and dissolving our preconceptions of the way things "should be." All experiences that bring our minds into attentiveness, into the present, guide us on the path to our soul. When I am in doubt as to how to begin, I try to allow myself the time to clear my mind and open my heart. Sometimes I might focus on my breathing—

Letting Go of the Mountain

feeling the breath travel up my hands, arms, and shoulders toward my head on the inhalation, then slowly down toward my feet on the exhalation. Or I might be transported by feelings of being in love, or by watching my dog, Annie, play with her friends.

Negative thoughts and the powerfully dramatic feelings associated with them often get in the way of experiencing wholeness. As though they rested on opposite sides of a balance, when negativity goes up, soul goes down — as do intelligence, perspective, and almost any possibility for a genuine moment in life. When I am coming from a place of negativity, especially directed at myself, my tendency is to "react" toward life, and the present moment becomes diverted by past remorse or future insecurity. It feels as if I have one foot on the gas and one foot on the brake! This dichotomy wears on my soul, my mind, and my body. When I come from a place of letting go, from the closed fist to the open hand, I am infinitely more present, loving, intelligent, and peaceful.

When we choose to let go of self-judgment, we create greater access to the wisdom of the body. We experience a new comfort and a greater love for ourselves and others. A new vision dawns, and we become more capable of experiencing our soul's birthright. It is in the domain of soul that we have the most perspective, intelligence, and love. In this nonjudgmental place, we can bring forward new paradigms and visions. The soul is where self-judgment is transformed into self-compassion, where the self-inflicted wounds can heal. Viewing the world through the experience of negativity is like looking at the world through a pinhole. When we view the world through the eyes of soul, every day is as if we were seeing the Grand Canyon for the first time.

Our body is our most sacred resource available to experience soul. For centuries, many of the world's theologies have exhorted us to transcend the body in order to achieve higher soul consciousness. The body was viewed as an outright obstacle to our soul's growth. To me, being in one's body is an essential component of soulfulness. In a passage from *Ulysses*, James Joyce tells of a man "who lived just a short distance away from his body." Ignoring the innate wisdom of our bodies prevents us from accessing all our resources and diminishes our perception of soul to a cerebral experience. At times like these, I look at a beautiful painting and think to myself, "This is beautiful," rather than *feeling* its beauty in every cell of my body. We have entered a time that is beginning to accept what William Blake said long ago: "Man has no Body distinct from his Soul; for that called Body is a portion of Soul discerned by the five Senses, the chief inlets of Soul."

My work as a therapist has confirmed for me that the body is a crucible where our thoughts, actions, and emotions are transformed into soul. The body continues to guide us as we wend along our soul path. For example, when I wander from my soul path, my body signals me with strong physical messages, such as headaches, illness, or fatigue. They are like voices warning me I have strayed. If I ignore these voices, they become louder and more adamant. These divergences from our path show up as physical and emotional "dis-eases."

Soul is where the fires of our passions burn. It is where our love is most alive. The soul longs for this deeper love, for a connection between form and formlessness, for a continuum between the earth and the divine.

Don't be fooled into thinking you are alone on your journey. You're not. Your struggle is everyone's struggle. Your pain is everyone's pain. Your power is everyone's power. It is simply that we take different paths along our collective journey toward the same destination.

I do not believe that any technique, secret knowledge, or

mystical practice to "find" soul is more effective than the simple practice of letting go. When we focus the power of our attention on the present, the full measure of our soul is available to each of us at every moment.

Remember that soul is not a destination but a journey. The journey of the soul sends us through burning stars, out beyond the dark, icy planets. This journey takes us through the knowing and the unknowing, the discovery and the recovery, the letting go. And best of all, the journey always returns us to our true selves.

GATEWAY
to the SOUL

by Angeles Arrien

"When we go to a medicine person or healer because we are feeling disheartened, dispirited, or depressed, he or she might ask questions like, 'When did you stop singing? When did you stop dancing? When did you stop being enchanted by stories? When did you begin finding discomfort in the sweet territory of silence?'"

O NE DAY, A WOMAN found herself standing at Heaven's gate. The angels' only question to her was, "Zusai, why weren't you Zusai?" Within that simple question lies the heart of all our soul work. If you are David, why aren't you fully David? If you are Susan, why aren't you completely Susan? We are here on Earth to become who we are meant to be. Being who we are is the heart of soul work, for a two-way relationship between soul and personality lights the path to becoming fully ourselves.

The need to be who we are always brings us back to soul. I don't believe we're ever disconnected from the soul. I think that it's always there, waiting to be recognized, even though we may have turned a blind eye to the soul or stopped paying attention to our inner guidance. Sometimes people become instinct-injured and can no longer trust their intuition, their souls. That is unfortunate, for the real value of being connected to soul is that it's literally the basis for trust. The opposite of trust is control; control is an announcement that we do not trust. But when we are in touch with our souls, we can trust, and when we can trust, we feel our bond with that which remains a mystery, which is outside nature or deep within one's nature, which has yet to be explored or even discovered. Opening a connection to our souls opens so many gates in life.

Sometimes, the soul is temporarily forgotten because of ego needs or stages. But even then, we always remember what once was, or feel what might be. That remembering or feeling is usually marked by pangs of separation, isolation, loneliness, and meaninglessness. Boredom, vulnerability, dissatisfaction, disorientation, and dis-integration of the mind/body connection are often signals, too, that a profound need must be addressed. When these feelings come up, we are standing at the soul's gate. This is our opportunity to enter the realm of the soul.

Many people mistakenly think of the gateway to the soul as a hole to be filled, not knowing it is an opportunity. And so they look for something to plug the hole, rather than going through the gate to reconnect with their souls. They fill this hole with diversionary addictions that keep them looking outward for satisfaction. The answer, however, is never in "the outer." The outer is simply a mirror of what is working or not working inside. Focusing on the outer keeps us from going through the soul's gate. But when we're right *at* the soul's gate, and when we *see* it as a gate, we can surf right through it, beginning the process of reconnection.

A Return to Soul

To help me stay connected to my soul, I begin each day by spending an hour in nature. Every day I give gratitude; every day I pray; every day I meditate. One day a month I devote to silence and reflection. Usually I fast on this day; it's a whole day of being, and of listening to my inner guidance. On my monthly silent day I'm not involved in any activity at all. There's no doing. There are no telephones or faxes, no writing or working on projects. I literally either walk in silence or sit in silence, listening. And it's amazing what comes through when I just take the time to listen. These practices help open my creative fires to the mysteries of the soul and to what wants to come through. The soul should not be separated from life or saved for Sundays — the soul is for every day, for every moment. And being alive to every moment of every day is a way of listening to the inner guidance and accessing the mysteries of our soul.

Of course, silence isn't the only way of connecting to the soul. When we go to a medicine person or healer because we are feeling disheartened, dispirited, or depressed, he or she might ask questions like, "When did you stop singing? When did you stop dancing? When did you stop being enchanted by stories? When did you begin finding discomfort in the sweet territory of silence?" I believe that singing and dancing and being enchanted with stories (particularly my own) are ways of surfing through the gateway of the soul. And so I sing every day. I make sure to include dancing in my life, because spontaneity connects me to my soul. I love stories and I love poetry; they are part of my creative work and play. I feel that poetry and play and creativity and friendships are all ways of nurturing the soul.

So many windows lead to the soul, and personality is one of the most important. In fact, personality is a crucible for soul work. One of the illusions that harm us so is the notion that ego and soul are adversaries. We need to recognize that the ego-soul partnership is one of the greatest teams going. Each nurtures and feeds the other. Of course, the ego-soul partnership can become unbalanced, but that's no reason for alarm. When my personality manifests itself too strongly, I simply need to get out of my own way and say, "Okay, here we go, let's work on this together." When we team up with the soul this way, the personality learns that it's not alone but is a member of the team journeying through life.

Many other windows lead to the soul. A lot of things we consider interference or irritants along our paths to the soul are actually part of the paths themselves. We can look at these obstacles as invitations to grow again, to move beyond the familiar and knowable. As it says in the *I Ching*, the ancient Chinese book of wisdom, the event is not important, but the response to the event is everything. Our response to events can turn rutted paths into a great adventure filled with wonder, awe, curiosity, discovery, and exploration.

Another important part of soul work is to examine what keeps coming to our gates. What positives and negatives have come to us three times or more? In the past year, what consistently positive feedback has mirrored our gifts, talents, and resources? What consistently challenging feedback about stubbornness and willfulness have we heard from three or more people? By showing us aspects of ourselves, these messages may open the way to the next lesson. Sometimes the messages are troubling to receive; we tend to resist seeing our dark side. But we must learn to embrace both the beauty and the beast within our nature. Both good and bad must go into our learning crucible, so that we learn not only how to manifest our gifts but also how to tame and reign in and tickle our beasts. Everything that's presented to us is a learning tool, another way to contact our soul.

So many gateways lead to the soul, so many states of being, so many voices wanting to be heard. I know I am in the realm of internal guidance when I hear the clear, nonjudgmental voice that neither denies nor indulges. In that quiet place, when the chatter stops, we can receive the messages that guide us on our own true life's path. And we can surf through the gateway to the soul, to become who we are meant to be.

The DIVINE

SPIRIT

by Betty Eadie

"Faith is not complacent; faith is action. You don't have faith and wait. When you have faith, you move."

I N EACH OF US is a sheltered place from which our spirit stems. Our spirit is the pure part of us. When we are born to this earth, we often lose contact with that spiritual part, the divine self. When we lose the awareness of our divinity, we become disconnected and depressed. To feel whole, we need to reconnect with our divinity. Since we are all at various levels of spirituality, people reach this understanding in their own unique ways.

My spiritual understanding was transformed when I had my near-death experience; that is, when I was first brought in contact with my higher self, the divine part of me. I came to recognize that this divine part is connected with the flesh for only a short period of time, the time that we are here on Earth. It's easier for me to live in the world knowing that divine part of me. Too often, the flesh seems to be in conflict with the spirit rather than in unison with it. The flesh squelches and diminishes the spirit. During those periods when the transitory needs and desires of the flesh are being satisfied at the expense of the spirit, which may be much of our waking lives, I don't feel complete or serene.

I believe that seeking a balance between body, mind, and spirit is essential. When I am in this balanced state, my spirit is no longer at the mercy of the body. The spirit can control the flesh and it can raise temporal desires to a higher level. It is when we achieve that kind of balance that we function most creatively, spiritually, and naturally while we are here on Earth.

When I feel the separation or lack of balance between flesh and spirit, I need to enter a quiet place within myself and reflect on my spiritual needs. Everyone has a different way of reaching that quiet place. Some people get in touch with the inner self by using incense, music, or other aids. What works best for me is simply to allow myself to become very still — something I can do anywhere, at any time. Then I contemplate the unseen spiritual part of me, and I allow that part to be the greater part, rather than tensing up and allowing the ego to dominate. When I release myself from the ego and allow the spirit to prevail, I am calm again. I return to a deep sense of peace and knowing that can be felt only when the spirit is in tune with God.

To be able to understand this, I first needed to understand some greater truths. The most profound of these is an awareness of the existence of God, not just as an idea, but as a being: a Spiritual Father. The many religious faiths have different ways of experiencing God. Each person becomes aware of a sense of God's presence and the spirit's divinity in his or her

The Divine Spirit

own way. I believe that caring for the spirit is something that cannot be done just through rituals. When we are too deeply involved with rituals, we tend to become focused upon the rituals and not upon the spirit.

Being in tune with the divine self is something we should be aware of always. Of course, this is a process that has to be developed, but it can become as natural as breathing. We don't ask ourselves to breathe in, breathe out; it just happens. Through prayer and stillness we can develop the same ability to be naturally in touch with the spirit. In my own life, an important part of this process is expanding myself to the concepts of love. This openness encompasses not only love for other people, but the love of everything I see, and appreciation for the beauty around me.

When I awaken in the morning, I am thankful for a new day. I am thankful for everything that I have materially. I am thankful for everything I have spiritually. I thank God for allowing me to experience these things, even the experiences that may not seem so positive, such as developing an illness. I may not understand why I have the illness, but I sense that it is there for a purpose, and so I thank God for it. I ask Him to allow me to expand beyond my narrow-mindedness and self-centeredness so that I can see the good that comes from everything.

The spirit is constantly being challenged. As we grow and become stronger, the spirit becomes stronger too. Then our challenges also become greater. We may see people facing one challenge upon the other, and we wonder how they can take one more thing. Yet these individuals continue to grow and expand. Their growth is enhanced by their willingness to take what appear to be negative events and turn them into something very positive.

Our relationships with other people can also help us grow in spiritual understanding. I believe that the people we need come into our lives at the right time. These may be people with whom we connect deeply, such as spiritual sisters and brothers, who touch us and help us move on to even greater heights. There may also be people who, at the time, seemed not to be in tune with us at all, and who pass on out of our lives (an ex-spouse, for example), yet who may have acted as a bridge for us, enabling us to move from one level of awareness to another.

Clergy, therapists, and counselors can also be a part of this network of spiritual sisters and brothers. So many people, when they were born into this physical world, were born into dysfunctional families, and they still see themselves as dysfunctional . . . as less than they are. Sometimes, to develop a clearer vision, we need someone else to lean on for a short period of time — someone who will help us see ourselves in a different light. It's important not to get stuck in the belief that only one person can touch and help us. I've always encouraged people who are in counseling to move on if they feel they are not progressing, because the right person, the one they need to be working with, *is* out there.

It often seems easier *not* to move on; even the muck and mire in which we're stuck seems less fearful and less challenging than the unknown path ahead. Some people use faith as a reason to remain stuck. They often say, "I have faith, so I'm waiting." But faith is not complacent; faith is action. You don't have faith and wait. When you have faith, you move. Complacency actually shows a lack of faith. When it's time to move in a new direction in order to progress, the right people will come to us.

We are responsible for one another. Collectively so. The world is a joint effort. We might say it is like a giant puzzle, and each one of us is a very important and unique part of it. Collectively, we can unite and bring about a powerful change in the world. By working to raise our awareness to the highest possible level of spiritual understanding, we can begin to heal ourselves, then each other and the world.

LESSONS of LOVE, LESSONS of HOPE

by Melody Beattie

"Often it is at our lowest points in life that we learn the most. We say, 'God, this is too much. Life has disappointed me beyond all belief.' . . . Those low moments are the magical moments. They are the beginning stages of our journey."

S O MUCH OF our journey is learning about and removing the barriers between us and our soul. As long as people have been on this planet, we have been striving to live in connection with soul, to go forward with an open heart.

I wish there were a book I could read each day to tell me exactly what to do to live consciously from my heart and soul. But part of the mystery and magic, part of the reason I'm here, is to try to stumble through and hear what the soul has to say about what it needs at each moment — whether it is to work through an emotional block, discover what the next lesson is, meet the next soul mate, or finish my business with the one I'm with now. Ultimately, for most of us, the journey comes down to the same issue: learning to love freely. First ourselves, then other people.

Sometimes I'm amazed that it's so simple to free my soul on any given day. It can be as easy as walking on the beach or touching a tree. It could come from taking a break to get a cup of coffee with a friend. It could be window-shopping in a favorite mall. Taking care of one's soul could be calling a friend, taking a hot bath, reading a story to a little child, or writing a letter saying how very, very angry I am.

First, we need to get in touch with ourselves. We need to express and feel the blocks to soul — whether anger, disappointment, or grief — and release them. Then we come to understand that this is part of our own process. It moves us to the next place in our journey.

We are all at different stages of growth, so we each need different things to trigger that connection to the soul. What works for me on any given day might not work for someone else, or for me on another day. Often, it is basic things. I live ten feet from the ocean, in a small cottage. I need to be by the water; I've spent a lot of my journey getting closer and closer to this water. I need to remember, to get up in the morning and watch the sunrise and take a moment at night to see and feel the sunset. I need to see the colors of the sky; I need to feel the colors. I need to surround myself with music, because my soul resonates to music. I've decorated my home with the colors of the universe — bright colors. Color is light. Colors help me feel alive, help me feel passionate, help me remember that I'm here to be an alive, passionate human being.

I need friends around me, people to laugh with, to be myself with. This is especially true for me now. Sometimes people expect you — and you begin to expect yourself — to be something you're not. Being with friends gives me the space, when I feel sad or happy or giggly or giddy, just to be in that place.

A Return to Soul

It's essential for me to have people around that I can be myself with, laugh with, struggle with, be crazy with, cry with.

That's what nurtures my soul.

I've learned that my life has cycles and seasons, just as nature does, and that I can't get too comfortable in any one season, because it isn't forever. I used to think that change is part of life; everyone says that. Now I believe more deeply than that. Evolution is part of life, and we're always evolving into a new cycle, learning something, going into the next time. We learn to ride freely with that flow. When I hang on and don't go for the ride, I start getting all blocked up in my soul. I don't mean to suggest that going with the flow is easy. It isn't, because when we do that, our conscious mind doesn't know the plan. There is no rule book. That means we have to not only connect with our soul but also trust where it's leading us. I think that's a big part of the journey for many of us. Trust.

Sometimes it seems much easier for me to go on automatic pilot, to give in to fear and limitation. Fear is my biggest challenge — not just fear by itself, because we all have fear. I get into trouble when I refuse to acknowledge the fear. I call it something else, deceive myself about why I don't want to move forward. Sometimes I find that I am paying more attention to other people's processes. I come back to my own journey when I remember that *nothing* is really about the other person. What I see in them, as I stand and stare, is actually something I need to learn about me. I am *always* being taught what I need to know for *my* journey.

Frankly, the last four years of my life have been the hardest of my forty-six in terms of the lessons I've had to face and the pain I've had to live with. But I've also learned that the journey is absolutely magical and that not only do we live, we live in a vibrant universe that really will dance with us, that will teach us wonderful things. It will take us to wonderful places every morning that we're willing to get up, look at the sunrise, and say, Yes, a new day. Every day that we're willing to sit with and through the pain until we get to the other side.

I am often asked whether I believe such things as soul mates exist. I do, but my definition of that has changed, too. When I started thinking about it, I naively thought, Oh, that means there is one person out there for me. And then there was also the misconception that when I found this soul mate, it would be a euphoric experience — no challenges, no triggers, a heaven-on-earth kind of thing. Wrong. At least, in my life that wasn't the case. I've learned that I have many, many soul mates here, and they come to me at the right time and in the right place. They come to help me when I'm lost, and each comes with different sets of lessons for me — usually, *always*, my most intense lessons — the ones my soul came here to learn.

I absolutely believe that my children are soul mates. My friends are soul mates. And of course, there is a special romantic relationship. The people I work with are often soul mates. They are all my teachers; I believe that we have tasks to accomplish on a spiritual level and on the physical level on this planet. I never know what the next lesson is going to be, because we're not supposed to know; we're supposed to trust ourselves to discover it.

My view of why we are brought to this planet has also changed dramatically over the years. I used to think we came here to get it all together, quickly, have it all together, keep it all together, and live happily ever after. I don't believe that any longer. We came here because the earth is abundant and alive — a rich, rich field of lessons for us to learn. The lessons are not comfortable, because if we weren't challenged, it would mean that we didn't need to learn these lessons of the soul: courage, patience, faith, learning to love, embracing eternal life, and the most magical lesson of all: It's not what I do, it's knowing I am. We are here to learn about love, to let others love us, to discover that love is a living force — real, broad, encompassing. I have also learned that universal love is there for me, and will be there for me, if I'm open to it and believe in it.

Often it's at our lowest points in life that we learn the most. We say, God, this is too much. Life has disappointed me beyond all belief. Or, My life just isn't what I wanted it to be. Or, I've really been missing the boat. Those low moments are also the magical moments — the turning points and junctures of our journey. So often we think, Okay, now I've got to run around to get what I need. I've got to go to the mountains of Tibet or to a magical island in Hawaii. I've got to go *someplace* to begin this spiritual journey. But the fact is, the moment we say we want to go on that journey, we've begun it — right where we are. I trust so much in the power of the heart and the soul; I know that the answer to what we need to do next is in our own hearts. All we have to do is listen, then take that one step further and trust what we hear. We will be taught what we need to learn.

Some activities help bring the lessons to the fore. Meditation works for many people. Some people find formalized religion helpful. I live in an area where Buddhism is very popular, where many people find Buddhist chants take them where they need to go. But more important than a particular technique or practice is the need to listen and tune in to the cycles of the soul. When you are ready, you will be led right into the next level of your journey, to soul connectedness. The universe will provide your options.

Often the humblest acts, done with soul-awareness, can help take us where we need to go. I discovered this recently. I used to be extremely poor financially, and I did all my own work myself. When I got successful, I had more money, and I paid to get a lot of things done. That help was important at the time; I was busy, and it gave me more freedom and more time with my children. But I've also found that I miss a lot in life by not doing my own dishes, washing my own laundry, raking the yard myself. Those simple, almost Zen-like acts are important. They keep me in touch with how the world and my life work.

For anyone trying to get in touch with the soul, I want to say, It's an alive journey. The minute you ask a question and look for the answer, it will be right there, if only you let yourself see. The awareness is your soul *announcing* the lesson. It may be that you're walking through a bookstore and a particular book holds your answer. Someone may bring your answer in an innocent, everyday conversation. We can even get some of our answers from movies. A friend may have the answer. A new job, an old job, taking a class, spending more time with nature, learning to connect with the cycles of the seasons — all these are our teachers. If you can really trust that the answer is right there in your heart, it will be.

Nurturing my soul makes a difference. Whether we are aware of it or not, we are all on — and part of — an incredible journey. Something about consciously moving into it makes it a magical experience. I've gone through more pain in the last four years than I ever thought possible: my son died, my family became shattered. I had to begin again, one more time, and I wasn't sure I wanted to. But I've also learned more about life and my soul and heart than I ever dreamed possible. In doing so, I've discovered the most ancient message of all: even when people tell you there isn't any hope, there is. There is always hope, purpose, and a new magical lesson.

Afterword

"So is our task ended, and an anthology compiled plentiful as the floods fed by the unfailing waters of the hills, rich in examples as the seashore in grains of sand; may its reception meet with none that bar the stream of Asuka, and the joys it shall afford accumulate, as dust and pebbles gather together to form a high mountain, into a boulder of delight."

— KI NO TSURAYUKI
(Tenth-century editor of
poetry anthology)

We hope in our hearts that you have treasured the experience of reading this book as much as we have its creation. The completion represents not an ending but a continuation of a journey.

This book is a handbook. It is meant to be used, to be read and reread, to be the subject of debate. It is our wish that some of the thoughts, voices, and wisdom in these pages may remain with you. Let these thoughts resonate in your mind and spirit. Play with them. Shape-shift them into your own experience.

Again, we want to extend our deepest gratitude to the contributors of this book. What we have gleaned from their words has been life-changing. Yet, as important as their words is the privilege of having seen firsthand what lives look like when they are expressions of soul. For this, we will always remain grateful.

The contributors of this book share the conviction that a relationship with the soul can be cultivated through understanding, insight, care, attentiveness, and love. They share the belief that nourishing our relationship with our soul isn't something merely to read about and forget, or to think about when it's convenient. Nourishing the soul is a lifelong journey, traveled day by day, that is worth making the most important focus of our lives.

Soul is like any other aspect of ourselves: the more we contact it and use it, even challenge it, the stronger and more accessible it becomes. Do things that touch your soul, from the silly to the profound. We can judge the quality of our experience by the degree to which it touches our soul.

We did not begin this book in an effort to come up with definitions and answers. It was our intention to facilitate the intimate and collective exploration of soul. We hope that this book has helped you remember those things deeply held but forgotten. As the poet Rainer Maria Rilke wrote, "Have patience with everything that remains unsolved in your heart. Try to love the *questions themselves*."

The fact that this book caught your attention says a great deal about you. It says you are well along your journey of enriching your relationship with soul. It says you are willing to cultivate and cherish those elemental aspects of that which is important in your life.

The sacred quality of our soul's being touched, of soul connection, brings meaning and fulfillment to our lives. Honor the process. Together, we can make the world a better place.

With respect and friendship,

BENJAMIN SHIELD, PH.D.

RICHARD CARLSON, PH.D.

FOR FURTHER INFORMATION

Benjamin Shield and Richard Carlson are available for public speaking engagements. They may be contacted at the addresses listed below:

To contact Richard Carlson regarding audiotapes, other books, or his newsletter, *The Soul Times*, send a legal-sized SASE to Richard Carlson, Ph.D., P.O. Box 1196, Orinda, CA 94563

OR

To contact Benjamin Shield, Ph.D., write to 2118 Wilshire Blvd., Suite 741, Santa Monica, CA 90403.

About the Contributors

LYNN ANDREWS

Since the publication of her first book, *Medicine Woman* (1981), Lynn Andrews has chronicled her explorations into feminine spirituality in eight books, three of which have been *New York Times* nonfiction bestsellers. Her previous titles include *Jaguar Woman* and *Shakkai: Woman of the Sacred Garden,* as well as *The Power Deck,* a series of meditation cards containing affirmations of self, and four workbooks, including *Teachings around the Sacred Wheel, The Mask of Power,* and *Walk in Balance.*

Ms. Andrews's recent work, *Woman at the Edge of Two Worlds: The Spiritual Journey through Menopause,* is perhaps her most self-revelatory book to date. She has gained a worldwide following and is considered a preeminent teacher in the field of personal development.

ANGELES ARRIEN

Angeles Arrien is an anthropologist, educator, award-winning author, and corporate consultant. She lectures nationally and internationally and conducts workshops that bridge cultural anthropology, psychology, and religions. Her research and teaching have focused on beliefs shared by all humanity and on the integration of ancient tradition and modern times.

She is the author of *The Four-Fold Way: Walking the Paths of the Warrior, Teacher, Healer, and Visionary* and *Signs of Life: The Five Universal Shapes and How to Use Them*, which won the 1993 Benjamin Franklin Award.

SYDNEY BANKS

Syd Banks has been lecturing internationally for over twenty years on consciousness, psychology, and spirituality. He is credited with the original insights for the psychology of mind, a concept that is providing hope and new life to thousands of people from all walks of life.

He is known and loved for his insistence that the secrets of life are simple and straightforward rather than complicated and analytical. He believes that all people have the potential for a joyful, grateful life. His books include *In Quest of the Pearl* and *Second Chance*. Mr. Banks lives on an island in Canada.

MELODY BEATTIE

Melody Beattie's first book, *Codependent No More*, has sold over 4 million copies and was on the *New York Times* bestseller list for 115 weeks. Her other bestsellers include *Beyond Codependency* and *The Language of Letting Go*, each of which has sold over 600,000 copies. *The Lessons of Love* is her sixth book.

Helping readers tackle their problems by drawing from her own experiences is Beattie's forte. It was her own realization that she was a codependent — "someone who allows another person to affect him or her and is also obsessed with controlling that person's behavior" — that led to *Codependent No More*.

Beattie's literary career began after she graduated from high school in her hometown of St. Paul, when her job as secretary at an advertising department inspired her to become a writer. For years, while she was a counselor for spouses of alcoholics, she sold her stories to local newspapers for very little. Finally, she was commissioned by the Hazelden Foundation, the premiere publisher of books on chemical dependence and recovery, to write about her own recovery.

Beattie has been featured in *Time, People, USA Today, American Health, Glamour,* and in newspapers around the country. A popular speaker on TV, radio, and the lecture circuit, she has appeared on the *Oprah Winfrey Show, Geraldo,* and *Donahue.* She lives in Laguna, California.

JEAN SHINODA BOLEN, M.D.

Dr. Jean Shinoda Bolen is a psychiatrist and Jungian analyst, clinical professor of psychiatry at the University of California Medical Center, and author of *Goddesses in Everywoman, Gods in Everyman, The Tao of Psychology, Ring of Power,* and *Crossing to Avalon.* She is a member of the board of directors of the International Transpersonal Association and a former member of the board of the Ms. Foundation for Women.

Dr. Bolen is in private practice and is an internationally known lecturer and workshop leader. She brings to all aspects of her work an emphasis on the quest for meaning and the need for a spiritual dimension of life, while also taking into account the powerful effects of archetypes within us and family and culture upon us. She is a mystic and activist for whom the inner and outer worlds are equally real.

JOAN BORYSENKO, PH.D.

Dr. Joan Borysenko is the president of Mind/Body Health Sciences, Inc. She is a medical scientist, psychologist, and author whose vision is to reunite medicine, psychology, and spirituality in the service of personal and planetary healing. She has been described as a "rare jewel — respected scientist, gifted therapist, and unabashed mystic." Dr. Borysenko is co-founder and former director of the Mind/Body Clinic at New England Deaconess Hospital and was an instructor in medicine at Harvard Medical School. She holds advanced degrees in cell biology and psychology.

She is the author of many books, including the bestseller *Minding the Body, Mending the Mind; Guilt Is the Teacher, Love Is the Lesson; The Power of the Mind to Heal* (coauthored with her husband, Dr. Miroslav Borysenko), and Joan's latest — *A Pocketful of Miracles*, a book of daily spiritual practice.

NATHANIEL BRANDEN, PH.D.

The name Nathaniel Branden has become synonymous with the psychology of self-esteem, a field he pioneered over thirty years ago. He has done more, perhaps, than any other theorist to awaken America's consciousness to the importance of self-esteem to human well-being. He has been described as the "father of the self-esteem movement."

Dr. Branden is the author of fourteen books, with over three million copies in print. He lectures widely to professional and corporate groups. His books include *The Psychology of Self-Esteem, The Disowned Self, How to Raise Your Self-Esteem,* and *The Six Pillars of Self-Esteem.*

JACK CANFIELD

Jack Canfield is president of the Canfield Training Group in Culver City, California, and a director of the Optimum Performance Training Institute in Pasadena, California. He is a successful businessman and entrepreneur as well as a consultant to numerous Fortune 500 companies, including Campbell's

Soup, GE, NCR, Scott Paper, Clairol, Johnson & Johnson, and Sunkist. His background includes a B.A. from Harvard and a master's degree from the University of Massachusetts.

Jack has published five bestselling books and twelve audio and video training programs, including the #1 *New York Times* bestseller *Chicken Soup for the Soul: 101 Stories to Open the Heart and Rekindle the Spirit*, as well as *A Second Helping of Chicken Soup for the Soul.*

Jack developed the GOALS program for "at-risk" adults. The program is being taught in thirty-eight county welfare programs and several state prisons, including San Quentin.

He has conducted seminars for over 500,000 people in the United States, Mexico, Canada, Europe, Asia, and Australia. Several million more have seen him on television shows such as *Good Morning America*, the *Today* show, *NBC Nightly News*, *20/20*, and the *Oprah Winfrey Show*.

RICHARD CARLSON, PH.D.

Richard Carlson holds a Ph.D. in psychology and is a nationally known stress-management consultant and teacher in the field of personal development and happiness. For two years he wrote a newspaper column called "Prescriptions for Happiness," and he is the author of eight popular books, including *You Can Feel Good Again, You Can Be Happy No Matter What,* and *Shortcut through Therapy*, as well as the newsletter *The Soul Times.*

Dr. Carlson is a frequent lecturer to professional and corporate groups and is on the board of directors of the Street Smart Business School. He is also a popular talk-show guest, having appeared on such shows as *Oprah Winfrey* and *Sally Jessy Raphael*. He is happily married and the father of two children. He lives in Martinez, California.

PHIL COUSINEAU

Phil Cousineau is a freelance writer, editor, poet, filmmaker, and adventure travel guide. He lectures around the world on a wide range of topics, from mythology and film to creativity and mentorship.

His recent books include *UForia, Prayers at 3 A.M.,* and *Soul: Readings from Socrates to Ray Charles.* He is also the author of *The Soul of the World: A Modern Book of Days, Deadlines: A Rhapsody on a Theme of Famous Last Words,* and *The Hero's Journey: Joseph Campbell on His Life and Work.* He is a contributor to five other books. His articles, reviews, and poetry have been published in magazines and newspapers around the country.

Cousineau's screenwriting credits in documentary films include *Ecological Design: Inventing the Future, The Peyote Road, The Red Road to Sobriety, Wiping the Tears of Seven Generations, Eritrea: March to Freedom, The Presence of the Goddess, The Hero's Journey: The World of Joseph Campbell,* and the 1991 Academy Award–nominated *Forever Activists: Stories from the Abraham Lincoln Brigade.*

Cousineau is the winner of the 1991 Fallot Literary Award from the National Association of Independent Publishers. Currently, he is a fellow at the California Institute of Integral Studies and a member of several film societies.

STEPHEN R. COVEY, PH.D.

Dr. Stephen R. Covey is founder and chairman of Covey Leadership Center, a seven-hundred-member international firm. Its mission is to empower people and organizations to significantly increase their performance capability in order to achieve worthwhile purposes through understanding and living Principle-Centered Leadership. He is also founder of the Institute for Principle-Centered Family Living, a nonprofit research and development group dedicated to transforming education and improving the quality of family and community life.

Dr. Covey has taught leadership principles and management skills for more than twenty-five years to leaders in business, government, and education. His consulting portfolio includes more than half the Fortune 500 companies as well as thousands of mid-sized and smaller organizations. Recent awards include the first Thomas Moore College Medallion for continued service to humanity (1990), the Utah Symphony's Fiftieth Anniversary Award for outstanding national and international contributions (1990), the Wilbur M. McFeely Award from the International Management Council for significant contributions to management and education (1991), and the International Entrepreneur of the Year Award from Brigham Young University's Marriott School of Management (1994).

Dr. Covey is the author of several books and numerous articles on leadership, personal and organizational effectiveness, and family and interpersonal relationships. His book *The Seven Habits of Highly Effective People* is a #1 *New York Times* national bestseller, with more than 6 million copies sold. The book is being published in more than 24 languages. Other books include *Principle-Centered Leadership* and his latest bestselling book, *First Things First*. His leadership advisory magazine, *Executive Excellence,* is in its ninth year of publication.

WAYNE DYER, PH.D.

Dr. Wayne Dyer is one of the most widely read authors in the field of self-development. His books include the bestsellers *Your Erroneous Zones, Pulling Your Own Strings,* and *The Sky's the Limit.* He has also written *What Do You Really Want for Your Children, No More Holiday Blues* (a novel), *Gifts from Eykis, You'll See It When You Believe It, Real Magic, Everyday Wisdom, Your Sacred Self,* and *Staying on the Path.*

Dr. Dyer holds a doctorate in counseling psychology. He has taught at many levels of education, from high school to the teaching hospital of the Cornell University Medical College, and has co-authored three textbooks and numerous professional journal articles.

In addition to being an author and teacher, Dr. Dyer is a social commentator who has appeared on thousands of television and radio programs. He lives in Florida and is the proud father of eight "magnificent" children.

BETTY EADIE

Betty Eadie, the seventh of ten children, is the daughter of a Sioux Native American mother. She was raised in rural Nebraska and on the Rosebud Indian Reservation in South Dakota. She is the mother of eight children and the grandmother of eight.

At the age of thirty-one, Ms. Eadie was recovering in the hospital after surgery. She was expected to recover fully, but sudden complications arose. Her near-death experience is considered one of the most amazing ever told. She writes about this experience in *Embraced by the Light*, which has sold over 4.5 million copies and was on the *New York Times* bestseller list for over a year.

Ms. Eadie has given hundreds of talks about her experiences and has made numerous television appearances in the United States and abroad. She lives with her husband, Joe, in the Northwest.

MATTHEW FOX, PH.D.

Matthew Fox is a theologian, educator, and founding director of the Institute in Culture and Creation Spirituality in Oakland, California. In the master's program at the institute, physicists, Native American spiritual leaders, theologians, social activists, Biblical scholars, feminists, psychologists, Sufi dancer leaders, and many artists work together to unleash the New Cosmology.

Silenced by the Vatican in 1989, Dr. Fox was formally dismissed by the Dominican order in the spring of 1993, after a five-year struggle over his views. He is the author or editor of many books, including *Original Blessing, Creation Spirituality, Western Spirituality,* and, most recently, *The Reinvention of Work.* He holds his Ph.D. in the history and theology of spirituality from the Institut catholique in Paris.

ROBERT FULGHUM

Seven years after the publication of his first book, philosopher and essayist Robert Fulghum has more than 14 million copies of his books in print, published in 27 languages and 93 countries. *All I Really Need to Know I Learned in Kindergarten, It Was on Fire When I Lay Down on It, Uh-Oh,* and *Maybe (Maybe Not)* have set records at the top of the *New York Times* bestseller list.

His book and speaking engagements during the fall and winter of 1993 achieved additional success through an unprecedented 40-city tour that raised over $650,000 for charities — benefiting social service organizations such as Habitat for Humanity, Amnesty International, Literacy Volunteers, and the Salvation Army.

In November 1994, he began a nationally syndicated newspaper column through Creators Syndicate. Fulghum has four children, is very happily married to Lynn Edwards, a family physician, and lives on a houseboat in Seattle.

JOHN GRAY, PH.D.

John Gray, Ph.D., is the author of numerous works, including *What Your Mother Couldn't Tell You and Your Father Didn't Know,* as well as the phenomenal bestseller *Men Are from Mars,*

Women Are from Venus, which has sold over 2 million copies in the United States and is available in 26 languages around the world.

An internationally regarded expert in the fields of communication, relationships, and personal growth, Dr. Gray's unique focus is assisting men and women in understanding, respecting, and appreciating their differences. For over twenty years, he has conducted public and private seminars for more than 100,000 participants. In his highly acclaimed books and his popular weekend seminar, "Men, Women, and Relationships," he entertains and inspires his audiences with practical insights and easy-to-use techniques that they can apply to immediately enrich their relationships.

John also knows the serenity of solitude, having lived as a monk for nine years. He spent years studying with Maharishi Mahesh Yogi and received both his B.A. and M.A. in creative intelligence from Maharishi European Research University. He returned to the United States in 1982 and received his Ph.D. in psychology and human sexuality from Columbia Pacific University.

John Gray is a popular speaker on the national lecture circuit and has often appeared on television and radio programs to discuss his work. John has been interviewed on the *Oprah Winfrey Show, Donahue, Good Morning America, Eye to Eye with Connie Chung,* CNBC, and CNN, as well as countless local television and radio programs across the country.

GERALD G. JAMPOLSKY, M.D.

Gerald G. Jampolsky, M.D., is a graduate of Stanford Medical School and a former faculty member of the University of California School of Medicine in San Francisco. He is an internationally recognized authority in the fields of psychiatry, health, business, and education. In 1975, he and some friends established the Center for Attitudinal Healing in Tiburon, California, where children and adults with life-threatening illness may find peace of mind that is transforming for them and their families. In 1982, he founded the "Children as Teachers of Peace" project, which has now been expanded by others internationally. In 1987, he helped cofound the AIDS Hotline for Kids based at the Center.

Jerry has published extensively and is the author of *Love Is Letting Go of Fear, Teach Only Love, Goodbye to Guilt, Out of Darkness into the Light,* and *Love Is the Answer.* His newest book is *One Person Can Make a Difference.*

JON KABAT-ZINN, PH.D.

Dr. Jon Kabat-Zinn is founder and director of the Stress Reduction Clinic at the University of Massachusetts Medical Center; associate professor of medicine, the Division of Preventive and Behavioral Medicine; and executive director of the newly established UMMC Center for Mindfulness in Medicine, Health Care, and Society. He is the author of *Full Catastrophe Living: Using the Wisdom of Your Body and Mind to Face Stress, Pain, and Illness* and *Wherever You Go, There You Are: Mindfulness Meditation in Everyday Life.* With his wife, Myla Kabat-Zinn, he is currently at work on a book on mindful parenting.

Dr. Kabat-Zinn's major research interests are in mind/body interactions for healing and in the clinical applications of mindfulness meditation training for people with chronic pain and stress-related disorders. Dr. Kabat-Zinn is also involved with imaginative personal and organizational solutions to social stress and work stress (the Tao of Work). His work in the stress reduction clinic was featured in Bill Moyers's PBS special

"Healing and the Mind" and in the book of the same title. In 1994, he received the Interface Foundation Career Achievement Award and the New York Open Center's Tenth Year Anniversary Achievement in Medicine and Health Award. Since 1993, he has been a fellow of the Fetzer Institute.

ELISABETH KÜBLER-ROSS, M.D.

Dr. Elisabeth Kübler-Ross was born in Zurich, Switzerland. After receiving her M.D. from the University of Zurich in 1957, she came to New York, where she was a research fellow at Manhattan State Hospital. Further studies led to a degree in psychiatry and her lifelong interest in death and dying.

Dr. Kübler-Ross is considered the world's foremost expert on the subjects of death, dying, and the afterlife. Her books include the classic *On Death and Dying, Living with Death and Dying, AIDS, Questions and Answers on Death and Dying, On Children and Death,* and *Working It Through. Remember the Secret* is her first book for children. She now lives in Arizona.

RABBI HAROLD KUSHNER, PH.D.

Harold Kushner is rabbi laureate of Temple Israel in Natick, Massachusetts, after serving that congregation for twenty-four years. He is best known for *When Bad Things Happen to Good People,* an international bestseller first published in 1981. The book has been translated into 12 languages and was recently selected by members of the Book-of-the-Month Club as one of the ten most influential books of recent years. He has also written *When All You've Ever Wanted Isn't Enough,* which was awarded the Christopher Medal for its contribution to the exaltation of the human spirit, *When Children Ask about God,* and *Who Needs God?* His newest book is *To Life!*

Rabbi Kushner was born in Brooklyn and graduated from Columbia University. He was ordained by the Jewish Theological Seminary in 1960 and was awarded a doctoral degree in Bible by the seminary in 1972. He has five honorary doctorates, has studied at Hebrew University in Jerusalem and Harvard Divinity School, and has taught at Clark University in Worcester, Massachusetts, and the rabbinical school of the Jewish Theological Seminary.

LINDA LEONARD, PH.D.

Dr. Linda Schieise Leonard is a philosopher and a Jungian analyst trained at the C. G. Jung Institute in Zurich, Switzerland. She is the author of the bestselling books *The Wounded Woman*, *On the Way to the Wedding*, *Witness to the Fire*, and *Meeting the Madwoman*. Her books have been published in 12 languages. She has been the recipient of an American Council of Learned Societies postdoctoral fellowship, and in 1994 she was chosen Distinguished Visiting Scholar at the College of Notre Dame in Belmont, California. She has taught at the University of Colorado, Denver, and at San Diego State University.

Currently she is a consultant on creative issues and gives lectures and workshops worldwide. She is a founding member of the Inter-Regional Society of Jungian Analysts and a member of the C. G. Jung Institute of San Francisco.

Her new book, *Creation's Heartbeat: Following the Reindeer Spirit*, will be published by Bantam Books in the fall of 1995. She spent time recently in the Siberian wilderness living with a nomadic group of "reindeer people," the Even tribe, and also traveled to Lapland to study the same people's relation to reindeer and the myths and legends of the native peoples of the Far North.

Stephen Levine

Stephen Levine edited the *San Francisco Oracle* in the late 1960s. After intense practice of mindfulness meditation under the tutelage of an American Buddhist monk, he edited the *Mindfulness Series* for Unity Press. He has written several books, including *Grist for the Mill* (with Ram Dass), *Who Dies?*, *Meetings at the Edge,* and *Healing into Life and Death.*

For the past twenty years, Stephen and his wife, Ondrea, have worked with the terminally ill and those in crisis. Together they share a soul in the deep woods of Northern New Mexico. They write and teach and heal in tandem exploration. Their newest book — *Embracing the Beloved: Relationship as a Path of Awakening* — offers details of much of their ongoing process.

Thomas Moore, Ph.D.

Dr. Thomas Moore is a psychotherapist, a writer, and a prominent lecturer in North America and Europe. He has published many articles and books in the areas of archetypal and Jungian psychology, mythology, imagination, and the arts. His Ph.D. is in the field of religious studies, and he holds master's degrees in both theology and musicology. As a young man, he lived for twelve years as a monk in a Catholic religious order.

Dr. Moore's books include *The Planets Within, Rituals of Imagination, Dark Eros, Care of the Soul: A Guide for Cultivating Depth and Sacredness in Everyday Life, Soul Mates, A Blue Fire* (an anthology of the writings of James Hillman), and his most recent, *Meditations.* He lives with his wife and two children in western Massachusetts. His current projects include further writing on the soulful practice of religion and spirituality.

JACOB NEEDLEMAN, PH.D.

Jacob Needleman is professor of philosophy at San Francisco State University and former director of the Center for the Study of New Religions at Graduate Theological Union. He was educated in philosophy at Harvard, Yale, and the University of Freiberg, Germany. He has also served as research associate at the Rockefeller Institute for Medical Research and was a research fellow at Union Theological Seminary.

Dr. Needleman is the author of *The New Religions, A Sense of the Cosmos, Lost Christianity, The Heart of Philosophy, The Way of the Physician,* and *Sorcerers,* a novel. His most recent book is *Money and the Meaning of Life.* He was general editor of the Penguin Metaphysical Library.

In addition to teaching and writing Dr. Needleman serves as a consultant in the fields of psychology, education, medical ethics, philanthropy, and business, and is increasingly well known as an organizer and moderator of conferences in these fields. He has also been featured on Bill Moyers's acclaimed PBS series *A World of Ideas.*

RAM DASS

Ram Dass was born in 1931 as Richard Alpert. He studied psychology, specializing in human motivation and personality development. Ram Dass received an M.A. from Wesleyan and a Ph.D. from Stanford University. He served on the psychology faculties at Stanford, the University of California, and Harvard University.

In 1974, Ram Dass created the Hanuman Foundation in order to promulgate spiritual awareness and well-being for people living in western cultures. The foundation developed the Living–Dying Project, designed to provide conscious care and support for the terminally ill and dying. It also developed the Prison-Ashram Project, designed to help prison inmates grow spiritually during their incarceration. Both projects now successfully carry on their work as independent nonprofit organizations. Since 1974, the Hanuman Foundation has served as the organizing vehicle for Ram Dass's lectures and workshops, as well as for the publication of his writings, tapes, and electronic media productions. In the past ten years alone, Ram Dass has lectured worldwide in over 230 cities, including the U.S., Canada, eastern and western Europe, and Asia.

Ram Dass has authored a number of spiritual and self-help books, including the classic *Be Here Now, The Only Dance There Is, Grist for the Mill* (with Stephen Levine), *Journey of Awakening: A Meditator's Guidebook, Miracle of Love: Stories of Neem Karoli Baba, How Can I Help?* (with Paul Gorman), and *Compassion in Action* (with Mirabai Bush).

In 1978, Ram Dass cofounded the Seva Foundation — an international service organization working on public health and social justice issues in communities throughout the world. His lectures and workshops have been a primary fundraising and public relations source for Seva's activities.

Ram Dass continues to lecture and teach throughout the world on such topics as utilizing service to others as a spiritual path, aging and its awakening potential, the relationship of business and social responsibility, personal relationships, spiritual awakening and its techniques, and social activism. When not traveling, Ram Dass lives in San Anselmo, California.

ANNE WILSON SCHAEF, PH.D.

Dr. Anne Wilson Schaef is an internationally known writer, lecturer, organizational consultant, philosopher, and workshop leader. She has a Ph.D. in clinical psychology from the Union Institute and did her graduate work at Washington University in St. Louis, Columbia University, Union Theological Seminary, and Teachers' College in Columbia, Missouri, with an internship at Bellevue Hospital in New York City. For over a decade she has conducted yearlong training groups in Living in Process Facilitation in the United States and Europe, and is starting groups in New Zealand and Australia. She has worked in the field of addiction for many years and describes herself as a "recovering" psychotherapist. Her books include *Women's Reality, Co-Dependence: Misunderstood, Mistreated, When Society Becomes an Addict, The Addictive Organization* (with Diane Fassel), *Escape from Intimacy, Meditations for Women Who Do Too Much,* and *Laugh, I Thought I'd Die . . . If I Didn't.* Her most recent book, *Beyond Therapy, Beyond Science,* deals with shifting scientific paradigms and new forms of working with people that are congruent with a new paradigm.

BENJAMIN SHIELD, PH.D.

Dr. Benjamin Shield is a therapist, educator, and lecturer practicing in Santa Monica, California. He holds degrees in biochemistry and biology from the University of California, with advanced studies at the Boston University School of Medicine. His doctorate is in the field of health sciences.

Benjamin's work focuses on the integration of body, mind, and soul while helping individuals reduce levels of pain and achieve an exceptional degree of emotional and physical choice. He believes that healing and spirituality share a common denominator and are accessible to each of us.

Benjamin is a founding board member of the International Association of Yoga Therapists and the American CranioSacral Therapy Association. He is also on the board of directors of the Institute for Psycho-Structural Balancing and is former president of the Founders Board of the Upledger Foundation Brain and Spinal Cord Dysfunction Center. Benjamin has been a frequent guest on local and national television and radio talk shows.

Benjamin has authored numerous articles on psychology, healing, and spirituality. His books and tapes include *Healers on Healing, For the Love of God,* and *Sixty Minutes to Great Relationships.* Most recently, he was a featured guest on the BBC/Canadian TV series *Medicine or Magic?* and was a contributor to the book *Alternative Medicine.*

BERNIE SIEGEL, M.D.

Dr. Bernie Siegel, more than fifteen years ago, began talking about patient empowerment and the choice to live fully and die in peace. As a physician who has cared for and counseled thousands with life-threatening illnesses, Dr. Siegel, who prefers to be called Bernie, embraces a philosophy of living — and dying — that stands at the forefront of medical ethics.

In 1978, Bernie started Exceptional Cancer Patients, a specific form of individual and group therapy utilizing patients' dreams, drawings, and images. ECaP is based on "carefrontation," a loving, safe, therapeutic confrontation that facilitates personal change and healing. This experience led to his desire to make everyone aware of his or her own healing potential.

Like his two previous bestsellers — *Love, Medicine and Miracles* and *Peace, Love and Healing* — the third of Bernie's ever-popular inspirational books, *How to Live between Office Visits: A Guide to Life, Love, and Health,* breaks new ground in the art of healing.

The Siegel family lives in the New Haven area. Bernie and his wife, Bobbie Siegel, have coauthored many articles and five children. The family has innumerable interests and pets. Their home resembles a cross between a family art gallery, a zoo, a museum, and an automobile repair shop.

BRIAN WEISS, M.D.

Dr. Brian Weiss graduated magna cum laude from Columbia University and received his medical degree at the Yale University School of Medicine. After serving his internship at New York University's Bellevue Medical Center, he went on to serve as chief resident in the Department of Psychiatry at the Yale University School of Medicine. He was an associate professor at the University of Miami School of Medicine.

Dr. Weiss also served as chairman of the Department of Psychology at Mt. Sinai Medical Center in Miami, where he now has a full-time private practice. He specialized in many aspects of study and treatment in the psychological field, including depression and anxiety, sleep disorders, substance abuse disorders, Alzheimer's disease, and brain chemistry.

Dr. Weiss is the author of two bestselling books about regression (past life) therapy: *Many Lives, Many Masters* and *Through Time into Healing*.

MARIANNE WILLIAMSON

Marianne Williamson is an internationally acclaimed lecturer and author. Her first book, *A Return to Love,* topped the *New York Times* bestseller list for 35 weeks and was the fifth largest-selling book in America in 1992. Her second book, *A Woman's Worth,* topped the *New York Times* bestseller list for 19 weeks.

Ms. Williamson is a native of Houston, Texas. She has been lecturing professionally on spirituality and metaphysics since 1983. She has done extensive charitable organizing throughout the country in service to people with life-challenging illnesses.

She is the founder of the Centers for Living located in New York and Los Angeles.

Ms. Williamson's newest book is *Illuminata: Thoughts, Prayers, Rites of Passage*. She makes her home in the Santa Barbara area of California.

MARION WOODMAN

Marion Woodman is well known as an international lecturer and workshop leader. Her first career was as a teacher of English and creative theater. Her love of literature and the arts took her into the study of dreams and the creative process that is constantly at work in the unconscious. After her graduation from the C. G. Jung Institute in Zurich, Switzerland, she returned to Canada and focused her practice on addiction and the power of metaphor in understanding addictive behavior.

Gradually, she began to see the loss of the feminine at the core of addictive behavior, both in individuals and in Western culture. She has pioneered bodywork in relation to dreams as a bridge that can connect inner and outer worlds, thus releasing both a new feminine and new masculine consciousness. The marriage of these new energies gives birth to the authentic personality. She is the author of several books and tapes, among them *The Owl Was a Baker's Daughter*, *Addiction to Perfection*, *The Pregnant Virgin*, *The Ravaged Bridegroom*, and *Leaving My Father's House*. A volume of her essays, *Conscious Femininity*, has also recently been published.

The authors are grateful for permission to include the following previously copyrighted material:

OTHER SOURCES

Fr. Alfred D'Souza, quoted in *Seven Choices: Taking the Steps to New Life after Losing Someone You Love,* by Elizabeth Harper Neeld. New York: Delacorte, 1992, 213.

Robert Frost, from "The Gift Outright" (1942).

Edna St. Vincent Millay, from "Renascence" (1917).

Rainer Maria Rilke, from a letter to Franz Xaver Kappus, July 16, 1903, in *Letters to a Young Poet,* by Rainer Maria Rilke, translated by Joan M. Burnham. San Rafael, Calif.: New World, 1992, 35.

Albert Schweitzer, from "Waking the Sleeping Soul," quoted in *The Search for Meaning: Americans Talk about What They Believe and Why,* by Phillip L. Berman. New York: Ballantine, 1993, vi.

Ki no Tsurayuki (c. A.D. 859–945), quoted in *A Treasury of the World's Greatest Letters,* edited by M. Lincoln Schuster. New York: Simon & Schuster, 1940, xlviii.

HANDBOOK
for the
HEART

ORIGINAL WRITINGS
on LOVE

Foreword by
JOHN GRAY

This book is dedicated to you, the reader.
May your life be filled with love.

CONTENTS

Acknowledgments

We offer our gratitude to the following people for their loving assistance in the creation of this book:

Jennifer Josephy and Little, Brown and Company, for their shared belief in our vision.

Patti Breitman, Sheree Bykofsky, and Linda Michaels, for their professionalism and enthusiasm.

Stephen Lamont for his excellent copyediting.

Gay Edelman, Barry Fox, Dr. Pamela DuMond-Shield, Tom Bedell, Mark Lipsman, Steve Hasenberg, and Valerie Harms, for their imagination and dedication.

We especially wish to offer our appreciation and respect to all the participants who shared their wisdom and so freely gave of their heart. They remind us that the best way to teach is to show by example. Our heartfelt thanks to all who were involved with this project.

Foreword

BY *John Gray, Ph.D.*

L OVE HAS BECOME the Holy Grail of our time. People want more of it, suffer from lack of it, and search for it all their lives. This book, *Handbook for the Heart,* dwells on this quest for love and provides the skills we need on our path. In these pages the leading practitioners on matters of the heart examine the many facets of the diamond of love, enabling us to fulfill our deepest longings.

For many of us the difficulty in our relationships is because we have had to adjust to a cultural transition from an old form of coupling to a new way. In the past, people sought marriage partners primarily to create a family and to ensure security. Men worked outside the home; women raised the children. Both parents expected the children to help with the work and take care of them when they were old. Now, however, men and women are more self-sufficient and less dependent on each other for security and survival. Men can raise children, and women hold jobs. As a result, men and women increasingly seek out each other to fulfill long-denied emotional needs.

Therefore, the basis for marriage has changed. We marry not for survival but for the satisfactions of intimacy. Ironically, the reason for so many divorces today is that people want more love, not less. Many feel that their desires for love must be met in order to stay with their partners.

We yearn to feel loved, admired, and appreciated, not just leaned on for financial security. Once people are able to support their families, they can then focus on the quality of their shared connection. New meaning and purpose in life emerges in establishing heartfelt bonds. *Handbook for the Heart* helps you remove the blocks to achieving deep loving relationships.

To attain such love, we must be sensitive to the love we need and know how to get it, as well as how to give the love our partners need. Thus, we must have better forms of communication than those used by our parents. We have to be able to articulate those needs as both we and our partners change over the course of time. It used to be that men and women lived in different worlds, without even attempting to share their innermost thoughts and feelings. My mother, for example, never expected my dad to be a great conversationalist.

Today, men and women have to learn how to negotiate with respect. In today's world, men are no longer responsible for simply one area, e.g., the budget, and women another, e.g., the social schedule. As women are earning more of the income needed to raise a family, they want to have more of a say in how the money is spent. And men want to participate in the planning of their leisure time. The ascendance of love in our relationships also creates a greater capacity for romance and the nurturing of children.

Again, in the past the concept of love was different: a sense of caring grew out of loyalty and shared history. Romance was not important or expected to endure. It was considered loving to sacrifice yourself for your partner. Today, people are no longer willing to stay together in a life of sacrifice. If we sacrifice who we are in a relationship, we lose touch with ourselves and our feelings. To us, loving means passion, partnership, romance, and good communication. Feelings have become enormously significant. Love, intimacy, and closeness are more important than ever before.

To fill my own life with love, I prioritize and carry out the most important acts that create love. In my marriage I've learned it's usually the little things that make a difference. My wife and I have loving rituals, things we do that the other appreciates. For example, when I'm driving my car with my wife, I always slow down at yellow lights and stop. She's grateful because she knows that when I'm driving alone, I often run yellow lights. I'll even say to her, "I did that for you, honey." She usually replies with a chuckle and says, "Thank you very much." Another example is that, even after ten years of marriage, I still bring home fresh-cut flowers. It's the little things that keep romance alive.

With my children, I make sure that I create plenty of uninterrupted time with them when we're doing fun things. I've taught my children that if they need my full attention when I'm busy, they can always pull on my pant leg and I will stop what I'm doing to listen to them. Also, when I travel, I remember to bring them back something from my trip — a tiny token, anything, to make them feel special.

The little things that say "I care" are the most effective in filling a life with love.

One way I make sure to get my own emotional needs met is to take time for activities that I enjoy. Even when my wife thinks we need quality time together, if I'm not in the right mood, I take time to be alone—although I assure her that later we can have our time together, too. When we give to ourselves first, we have more to give to our relationships and family.

So many people, under the illusion of being nice, sacrifice too much of who they are and thus lose their ability to truly love and get the love they need. People suffer from not realizing how vital love is to them. Love is an essential vitamin, especially in a society that emphasizes efficiency, productivity, and virtual reality. Many times the absence of love causes our frustrations, anxieties, illnesses, and fatigue. People don't realize what they are missing.

Handbook for the Heart offers a refuge from the busyness of life and illuminates the joys to be gained from love. To read this book, to hear the words of people who have made it their life's work to define what love is, to articulate how we can most successfully express, give, and receive love, is of immense value—and an extraordinary gift. *Handbook for the Heart* will affect your life in innumerable positive ways, as it has mine.

Introduction

*"It is only with the heart that one can see rightly; what
is essential is invisible to the eye."*

— SAINT-EXUPÉRY (1900−44)

The Little Prince

I F YOU WERE GIVEN one wish for our world, what
would it be? Ours would be, quite simply, that each and
every one of us could feel at peace. And we believe that
the gift of peace begins with hearts filled with love.

Who among us does not desire more love in our lives?
And who among us hasn't sighed, and pushed ahead with
the busyness of our day and our lives, letting the opportunities of love slip away? A hug from a child is shortened to
take a phone call, a friend is seldom contacted because of
distance, a compliment from a mate goes unacknowledged
for a question about a bill, a favorite charity is pushed to
the back of our minds for "later." It seems the truly important, heart-connecting moments are so often neglected.
And our lives, all of our lives, are made smaller.

We know we want and need love, to both give and receive in full measure. But how do we slow down and allow
more love into our lives, when inner and outer pressures
detract us from our heart's deepest desire? There are many

extraordinary individuals who have dedicated their lives to answering just that question. With the knowledge that such role models exist, we asked them directly for specific and practical advice and guidelines on filling our lives with love. "How," we asked them, "do you do it?"

So, the idea for this book was born. We created a "wish list" of possible participants, individuals who have been teaching us—and much of the world—about love for many years. People who have earned the reputation as experts on love. Sometimes we had doubts. Would these wonderful teachers be willing to share their knowledge in an original, single compilation? In the end, though, we let our willingness to take the chance and our need to know rule, and we went forward. We invited each teacher to discuss his or her own way of filling life with love. Almost without exception, the individuals we approached agreed to share their wisdom and insights into why we need to fill our lives with love and, most important, how we can do it.

We were rewarded beyond our greatest imagination. The depth of sincerity of each of the participants is overwhelming. We saw, up close, how each contributor makes an honest and true effort to "walk her walk," to "practice what he preaches." Never before have we met and worked with individuals so completely and sincerely dedicated to a loving existence. The peaceful spiritual leader Mahatma Gandhi once said, "My life is my message." We believe that the same thing is true for each of the participants in this book. Each of them, in a unique and personal way, tells us with certainty how the heart is the fundamental source of our connection with all of life.

Love—giving and receiving from the heart—involves compassion, stillness, gratitude, peace, intimacy and relationship with others, and service. From the perspective of the authors of this collection, love is the only true measure of our success in life. Nothing else ultimately matters. As Mother Teresa is quoted in one of the articles, "We cannot do great things. We can only do small things with great love."

Creating this small thing, this original anthology, is for us an act of great love — for ourselves, for each other, for our families, and for you, our readers. We'd like to thank all the contributors for the richness they have contributed to our own lives and to the lives of so many millions. This project, these writings — these people — have changed and enriched our own lives in profound and remarkable ways. We wish this, most of all, for you — that you, too, will find new ways to bring love into your life and that you find the peace a love-filled heart brings.

From the heart,

BENJAMIN SHIELD, PH.D.
RICHARD CARLSON, PH.D.

1.
The Power of the Heart

"That best portion of a good man's life,
His little, nameless, unremembered acts
Of kindness and of love."

—WILLIAM WORDSWORTH (1770–1850)

THE POWER OF
LOVING-KINDNESS

BY *Sharon Salzberg*

"There is a saying in the Buddhist tradition: 'You can explore the universe looking for somebody who is more deserving of your love and affection than you are yourself, and you will not find that person anywhere.'"

THE POWER OF love or loving-kindness has been denigrated in our culture. There's a sense that a loving person is abused, allows tyranny to reign without protest, and isn't strong. It's almost a sense that love is a weakness. Sometimes there is the idea that the loving heart makes people kind of smirky and sentimental—that because of love, they can't look at suffering clearly or at difficult things within themselves or in the world. I think we have to do a radical re-visioning and come to understand the power of the loving heart. Not only is it innate, but it cannot be destroyed, no matter what our life experience has been, no matter how many scars we bear, how much suffering we have gone through, or how unloved we have felt. We have the capacity to love and to receive love in return.

Living in fear is like being frozen. It's said that the Buddha taught love — particularly *metta*, loving-kindness — as the antidote to fear. There is a beautiful line in a poem by Mary Oliver: "When the thumb of fear lifts, we are so alive." We're oppressed by our fears, our judgments, our guilt — guilt being considered in the Buddhist psychology a quality of self-hatred — and when that oppression lifts, we are so alive. That's the force of love.

Sometimes, if we're fortunate, we experience this love with another person. We might have one being in our life who is a model of unconditional love, so that we don't fear rejection if we're truly honest with this person or if we don't present ourselves in a certain way. We have enormous respect for this person, who means safety and maybe clarity — not mushiness or a phony veneer or an inability to look at difficult and painful things. This person may perceive the difficulty and pain in us, but there is the feeling that he or she views them alongside us, rather than from across some enormous gulf of separation. That is really the essence of a loving heart — the understanding of our nonseparateness.

There is a saying in the Buddhist tradition: "You can explore the universe looking for somebody who is more deserving of your love and affection than you are yourself, and you will not find that person anywhere." We ourselves are as deserving of our love and affection as anyone else. A spiritual practice based on self-hatred can never sustain itself. We have to begin with loving ourselves, being able to embrace all parts of ourselves as well as all parts of the world, in order to understand our capacity to love.

The Buddha said, "If you truly loved yourself, you would never harm another." Harming another is like harming ourselves. Buddhist psychology distinguishes between the force of guilt and the force of remorse—remorse being a full consciousness and sensitivity that we've hurt somebody. Feeling that pain, we let go and then have the energy to move on. Guilt is something else entirely—a continual rehashing of some event, mental flagellation, with tremendous self-hatred. It leaves us strained and exhausted, without the energy to go on and be different.

If self-judgment, criticism, and self-hatred were liberating, we would all have been freed long ago. I don't have anything against those mind states personally—except that they simply don't work. Don't get me wrong; I don't have a philosophical stance that we have to love ourselves, but the fact is, love works and hatred doesn't. Self-hatred may not arise from anything in particular—it may just be a sense of personal humiliation about the fact that we grow older, get sick or disabled, feel that we failed, get angry, or get jealous. We can easily hate, judge, and condemn, but unfortunately, it doesn't end the problems—in some strange way, it intensifies them.

The Buddha said, "Develop a mind so filled with love, it resembles space." We use the words *mind* and *heart* synonymously; the meaning is to develop a heart so filled with love that it resembles space, which can't be marred, can't be ruined—just as if someone were standing in a room throwing paint around in the air. There's nowhere in space for the paint to land. We can develop a mind or heart so filled with love that it's like space—boundless, open, vast, free. Any amount of paint, any irritant, any inner or outer trouble, won't land.

Recently I was in Israel teaching a forgiveness meditation. During the session, someone said he had survived a terrorist attack — he still had some bullets in his body and was in constant pain. He said he didn't think it was possible to forgive, but he did know it was essential to learn to stop hating.

It's clear that if we don't stop hating, nobody will. It has to start with us because not only are we ourselves suffering horribly from the limitation and burning of all that anger, but the world is never going to change unless one person somewhere starts to stop hating.

We develop a loving heart by some form of meditation practice, a process distinct from reading about something or admiring it in a distant way. By meditating for even five minutes a day on a pragmatic level, so that it's not theoretical or even devotional, we can see for ourselves, "What happens when I say this phrase or do this reflection on everybody wanting to be happy? What happens when I sit down for five minutes and wish myself love and safety and peace? What happens when I think of this person I care about so much and am grateful to, or when I think of somebody I really don't like and reflect on the fact that he or she also wants to be happy?" It's an experiment.

Sometimes people feel odd — when they undertake a practice of a loving heart — they think it's artificial and it seems mechanical, but in fact, it's not. I often use the example of planting seeds through harnessing the force of our intention, like planting our garden of love. It will definitely blossom, but we have to take those first steps, to risk or be willing to explore what kind of development can occur in the loving heart.

One technique I like is developing *metta* toward a neutral person. It's interesting because sometimes we have difficulty finding a neutral person. As soon as we think of someone, we have an instant judgment about liking or disliking this person. That's an important revelation. It lets us see that we have an enormous number of neutral people in our lives on whom we've imposed judgments. This can come as a shock to us. It's interesting to consider someone about whom we have no story — just a generic living being, wanting to be happy, like all of us — and offering the same care and cherishing we've just offered ourselves and perhaps someone we love deeply. A sense of separation falls away. Some people, in intensive *metta* during a retreat, contemplate a neutral person and actually have the feelings of falling in love! Not romantically, but in terms of a loving friendship.

One of the tremendous understandings of spiritual practice is the power of the mind. Although we all live in the same world, our individual reality is a function not only of external events but of how they're held in our hearts — the degree of space in our hearts, the vastness or constriction, the contraction or openness of the mind receiving the external events. The spiritual perspective is not that we're sitting in traffic and are really angry and are trying to pretend we're not. Instead, it's an openness to what we're actually feeling; to understanding suffering; to having a great deal of love, kindness, and compassion for ourselves — not being stuck in that first reaction of anger. It's having options, choices — which is what an open heart means, as opposed to a narrow one — and realizing we can look at matters a different way.

In *Lovingkindness,* I tell a story about my friend Sylvia Boorstein being on a plane that developed a problem with its hydraulic system. It had to return to the airport, and every five minutes the pilot would announce the countdown over the PA system, "Thirty-five minutes left to land . . . thirty minutes left to land." The whole time, Sylvia was consciously doing a loving-kindness practice for the people in her immediate family, enveloping them with care and concern and acknowledging her connection to all of them. When the pilot got on the PA system and said, "We have five minutes before we land," Sylvia realized that in five minutes she might be dead. She resumed her loving-kindness practice and found there was no way in the world she could limit herself to opening her heart to just her immediate family. The only thing she could do at that moment, when she might have only five minutes to live, was to open her heart to all beings everywhere. This was without any contrivance or force or pretentiousness.

Metta is not a fabricated decision like "Now I am a very spiritual person and therefore I will love all beings"; nor does it mean that if we're really seething with rage or filled with fear, we're somehow going to overlay a nice little veneer and pretend and be smiling all the time. It's not that at all. *Metta* is the moment Sylvia had when the sense of "us and them" crumbled. It was born of the understanding that she might soon be dead — so why bother upholding all those boundaries and barriers? With the collapse of those boundaries, the effortless, natural love for all beings wells up. That's the moment we look for. That's the moment when we are so alive.

Our practice shows us our own strength. Very early on, one of my teachers said something wonderful to me: "The Buddha's enlightenment solved the Buddha's problems; now you solve yours." Our practice shows us that "I do have the wisdom, I do have the strength, I do have the loving capacity, in real-time, real-life situations, to look at things in a different way." That's what our practice gives us.

HEART SOUNDS

BY *Deepak Chopra, M.D.*

*"The way to fill your life with love is very simple: if
you want more love, give more love."*

FILLING OUR LIVES with love is so important because love is the only true reality. Ultimately, whatever we're doing in life, we do because we are
seeking love. Love is God. It is the experience of the
sacred. Everything we do, we do for love. Someone once
said, "The Nobel laureates are looking for love. The
award is but a consolation prize." Since there is nothing
else that really matters, it behooves us all to make love the
true priority in our lives. We need to recognize the importance of love and we need to do so not just with lip service
but by integrating love into our very being.

Love is the ultimate experience because all forms of
love are expressions of God. People often think about
love as an emotion or a sentiment. But love is so much
more! Deep emotions and sentiments can be extremely

nurturing, yes. But love is truly the ultimate reality. It is the experience of unity consciousness — meaning that the observer and the observed are experienced as one, the seer and the scenery are experienced as one, the lover and the beloved are experienced as one. Love is the experiential knowledge that we are all the same being: we are all one. We only appear in different disguises; our essential nature is shared. And it is the awareness of our essential nature that allows us to give and receive love freely.

When you have this experiential knowledge of unity consciousness, this profound understanding that we are all one, you become unable to hurt others or to be hurt. Instead, there is only love, ecstasy, and joy. Saint Augustine said, "I'm in love with loving." When you ask, "What is the purpose of love?" the answer is "There is no purpose." Love is its own reward. And the more love you give, the more love you receive. In fact, when the love is unconditional and from the heart, the return is directly proportional to the giving. You receive as much as you give. And so the way to fill your life with love is very simple: if you want more love, give more love.

You see, the universe operates through dynamic exchange; giving and receiving are merely different aspects of the energy flow in the universe. As we decide to give what we also seek — love — we keep the flow of love circulating in our lives and in the world. In offering love to others, we ensure that there is always plenty for ourselves. As long as we are giving love, there is no need to worry about getting enough. It will come. It comes the moment that we offer love to another, because receiving is the same as giving. They are simply two different aspects of the flow of energy in the universe.

There are specific ways you can participate in the energy flow. Humans have three profound needs: appreciation, attention, and affection. Attending to these needs brings more love into your life on a day-to-day, moment-to-moment basis.

Appreciation means telling others that you care for and treasure them. It's important to express this appreciation as often as you can. I try my best to find something special to honor and admire in every human being I encounter. I think it's only right to tell people what I see. My action satisfies my need to appreciate as well as their need to be appreciated.

Attention is the ability to listen with the totality of your being. It means taking the time to be truly present to others instead of being distracted by your own thoughts or letting your mind wander. In my own life, I try my best to be fully present, whether I'm with a waitress, someone who asks a question at one of my lectures, a family member, someone I work with, a friend, or someone on the other end of the phone. The other person deserves my undivided attention. And when I offer it, both of us are served.

Affection is touching somebody in a loving manner. It means showing someone, in an open, loving way, that I care for him or her. Showing affection, with gentle gestures and touches, is a wonderful way to fill your life with love. A simple handclasp, a light stroking, a big bear hug keep the energy of love flowing in both people's lives.

Messages about loving come to us from our hearts as well as from our bodies. I recognize that both my heart and my body are very intelligent sources that allow me to make karmically correct choices, choices that are governed by love rather than by rationality. I have learned not to trust my intellect over my heart. In a business situation, for example, my intellect or rational mind may tell me that something is not a good idea. It might say, "Don't do it," but my heart might say, "You should do it." In these cases I always follow my heart. I believe that the best decisions — karmically correct decisions — are always made from a place of love.

My best advice is this. With every encounter, with every single human being you meet, ask yourself one simple question: "What can I give this person?" Don't be concerned with what you can get back, but focus entirely on what you can do for him or her. And what you do can be quite simple. When I go to someone's home, for example, I often bring a small gift or pick a flower. What you give doesn't have to be something material. There is always something you can offer, and the giving is always very powerful. You can say something nice, or even silently wish the person happiness or some other type of goodwill. Even the thought of blessing someone, sending loving thoughts, or giving a simple silent prayer has the power to affect others.

If you start bringing love into your life, consciously and deliberately filling your life with love, you begin to see miracles all around you. Your life becomes an expression of love, and you see things you never thought possible happening in both your inner and your outer life. If you strive to give love, all else begins to come to you.

By participating in the flow of love in the universe, we can affect the whole world. We are the world! The outer world is but an expression of our inner world. Whatever is happening in our inner world is reflected "out there." The so-called criminals of society, deluded dreamers, the misfits, are nothing other than projections of our collective shadow-self. Once we confront this truth, we realize that there is no sense in trying to go out and change the world. If we would just change ourselves, the world would transform and take care of itself.

It is easy, so easy, to get distracted and say, "Oh, my God, look at all the bad that's happening in the world." But we can't give in to that notion; we have to keep our focus on the love. There does seem to be a newfound acceptance in the idea of a critical mass, a definite change in the collective psyche of the world, as more and more people make love a priority. Real change is happening. By giving love, always love, we can continue to influence what happens in the rest of the world. If enough of us embrace love, the world will eventually be saturated with love. The love in the world begins with the love within ourselves.

The Heart Is
Always Open

BY *Stephen and Ondrea Levine*

"People say life is so short. That isn't true at all. Life is so long that we don't have a moment to waste without forgiveness and loving-kindness. Life is so long that without spiritual practice, very few people are alive enough to die on their deathbeds. Most people have died years and years before."

JUST AS THE sun is always shining, the heart is always open. We don't need to do anything to be more loving except let go of what blocks the natural luminescence of the heart. Being more loving is a process of watching the fears and desires that make us unloving. To be truly loving means living in the present — not in the past or in the future — and trying to meet even the closed heart with kindness.

Of course, there are distractions — there's a lot of noise out there in a world of gluttony and ambition. But nothing outside can pull us from our center. Desire pulls from within. We're simply fishing — for delights, for safety, for pride. We can't blame the fish for our interest and excitement in catching them! I think it was Hari Dass who said that one of his most profound recognitions was the element of suffering that is in pleasure. We hold on to pleasure, desiring to prolong its impermanence, and the rope that burns as it's dragged beyond our grasp. If we work on our own desire system — if we remove our hooks from the water — then fish become a beautiful thing. Instead of carp for our plates, they become something we can sit and watch, like koi, those large Japanese goldfish. Just as our perception of the fish swimming in the water is altered, our relationship to the objects of our desires changes radically. Desire then isn't what draws us out of ourselves; it becomes what re-minds us as it arises. It becomes something that opens our heart, because nothing opens the heart like watching what closes it, distracts it, dilutes it, or confuses it.

Our conditioning came about from continuous building, and we free ourselves the same way: a moment of mercy here, a millisecond of forgiveness there. These flashes may seem like so little, but people come to us all the time and say, "You know, if I'm going to be truthful, I'd have to say my heart's open maybe two minutes a week." They're really concerned, and we laugh — we almost swoon. We tell them, "In this world, on this plane of suffering, it's a miracle that the heart is open at all." But that it doesn't happen all at once is good, because none of us, almost none of us, is prepared for the enormity of our great heart — we'd pass out.

People do all this arduous spiritual work to understand the great heart of the divine. When we get there, we discover that nothing has any meaning in itself; all meaning is added by the mind. The only rational act of a lifetime is love. When we get to the great truth, nothing makes any sense but love. The rest of it was just the confusion we created to avoid suffering. Love gives us an opportunity to let go into the enormity, the very source of satisfaction, which is our true nature and which we merely glimpse each time we fulfill a desire. In that millisecond when desire is absent, we experience what we call satisfaction. This is not because the desire was fulfilled, but because the nature of satisfaction is a parting of the clouds, a moment when desire is absent from the mind and when love expresses itself effortlessly, naturally, radiantly.

People say to us, "If I could just find the right mate, I'd be happy the rest of my life." That's being drawn out by desires, by the fishhook in the water. A relationship does not in itself make us happy. Nothing makes us happy except the work we do inside, because we're only truly happy when our heart is open. But relationships are a forum for that inner work. Nothing teaches us how unloving we are like relationships do. They put us in a position where we're confronted daily with our holding, our fears, our expectations, our anger, our distrust. In the world — even in the meditation hall or the monastery — we can participate on our own terms. We can meditate when we want, pray when we want. If an untoward thought or feeling arises, no one knows it but us. We can keep up the pretense of being a person who loves God. But in a relationship we can't do that. All pretenses eventually burst into flames and destroy the structural integrity of the relationship.

The difficulties in relationships are one of their most precious gifts — provided we have a partner with whom we can let go and not be abused for letting go. As we become more spiritual, one of the difficulties is that we may have a tendency to stay in a bad relationship because we think that it's good for our personal development. That's a tricky one. The idea that we can't be a good person unless we can be abused does not help the world. Letting ourselves be abused is not an act of compassion; it may actually be an act of self-righteousness. The difficulty with relationships is either that fear keeps us from committing or that we commit blindly and are caught by our own desires and expectations. If our partners are what we love most in the world, we and our partners are in big trouble. If our partners are the *people* we love most in the world, and if God or the truth — whatever we choose to call it — is what we love most, then the relationship with those people is our most profound desire.

People say life is so short. That isn't true at all. Life is so long that we don't have a moment to waste without forgiveness and loving-kindness. Life is so long that without spiritual practice, very few people are alive enough to die on their deathbeds. Most people have died years and years before. We've sold off a spiritual arm, a spiritual leg. We've denied so many parts of our true nature, so many parts of our heart — it's phenomenal how much we have died. Death isn't the problem; the problem is how dead we lived — how little the priority of the heart has motivated us; how much, day to day, we have tripped and fallen headlong into another unconscious moment, seeing someone else as the object of the mind instead of as the subject of the heart.

Relationships give us continual opportunities to be aware. People hold pieces of silk over their heads and jump out of airplanes, calling it skydiving, or jump off bridges while attached to bungee cords. When asked, "Why do you do these dangerous sports?" they say, "Because it makes me feel so alive." When we're trying to survive, all our awareness is brought to that situation. Where our awareness is, there's our aliveness. Usually our awareness is diffuse, like the sun on a winter day. But, as with the sun on a winter day, we can focus awareness through a magnifying glass and put a blazing pinpoint of light where we want it.

A relationship does the same thing. Relationships are the ultimate danger sport because, moment to moment, we don't know whether we'll survive — whether our self-image will emerge intact. Ideally, it won't! The more intact our self-image, the more isolated we are from the enormity of the truth. The more we let go of our fears, the more we can let go of our expectations and be concerned about whether the other person is feeling loved instead of whether we are feeling loved. As Saint Francis said, "It's time to love instead of looking to be loved." If we love, we'll be more loved than we ever imagined. Nothing is more sublime than an open heart.

VALUING LOVE

BY *Nathaniel Branden, Ph.D.*

"How do I bring love into my life? My answer is that I focus day after day principally on what I care most about in this world—on what I most respect and admire. That is what I give my time and attention to."

I DO NOT KNOW if there has ever been a time in history when the word *love* has been used so promiscuously as it is at present.

We are told constantly that we must "love" everyone. Leaders of movements declare that they "love" followers they have never met. Enthusiasts of personal-growth workshops and encounter-group weekends emerge from such experiences announcing that they "love" all people everywhere.

Just as a currency, in the process of becoming more and more inflated, has less and less purchasing power, so words, through an analogous process of inflation, through being used less and less discriminately, are progressively emptied of meaning.

It is possible to feel benevolence and goodwill toward human beings one does not know or does not know very well. It is not possible to feel love. Aristotle made this observation twenty-five hundred years ago, and we still need to remember it. In forgetting it, all we accomplish is the destruction of the concept of love.

Love by its very nature entails a process of selection, of discrimination. Love is our response to what represents our highest values. Love is a response to distinctive characteristics possessed by some beings but not by all. Otherwise, what would be the tribute of love?

If love between adults does not imply admiration, if it does not imply an appreciation of traits and qualities that the recipient of love possesses, what meaning or significance would love have and why would anyone consider it desirable?

In his book *The Art of Loving*, Erich Fromm wrote: "In essence, all human beings are identical. We are all part of One; we are One. This being so, it should not make any difference whom we love."

Really? If we were to ask our lovers why they care for us, consider what our reaction would be if told, "Why shouldn't I love you? All human beings are identical. Therefore, it doesn't make any difference whom I love. So it might as well be you." Not very inspiring, is it?

So I find the advocacy of "universal love" puzzling — if one takes words literally. Not everyone condemns sexual promiscuity, but I have never heard of anyone who hails it as an outstanding virtue. But *spiritual* promiscuity? Is *that* an outstanding virtue? Why? Is the spirit so much less important than the body?

In commenting on this paradox, Ayn Rand wrote in *Atlas Shrugged:* "A morality that professes the belief that the values of the spirit are more precious than matter, a morality that teaches you to scorn a whore who gives her body indiscriminately to all men — the same morality demands that you surrender your soul in promiscuous love for all comers."

My own impression is that people who talk of "loving" everyone are, in fact, expressing a wish or a plea that everyone love them. But to take love — above all, love between adults — *seriously*, to treat the concept with respect and distinguish it from generalized benevolence or goodwill, is to appreciate that it is a unique experience possible between some people but not between all.

Consider the case of romantic love. When two adults with significant spiritual and psychological affinities encounter each other, and if they have evolved to a decent level of maturity — if they are beyond the level of merely struggling to make their relationship "work" — then romantic love can become a pathway, not only to sexual and emotional happiness but also to higher reaches of human growth. It can become a context for a continuing encounter with the self, through the process of interaction with another self. Two consciousnesses, each dedicated to personal evolution, can provide an extraordinary stimulus and challenge to each other.

But such a possibility presupposes self-esteem. The first love affair we must consummate successfully is with ourselves; only then are we ready for a relationship with another. A person who feels unworthy and unlovable is not ready for romantic love.

Of course, there are other kinds of love besides romantic love. What I feel for my grandchildren is a different kind of love. What it has in common with romantic love, however, is that I see in my grandchildren values and traits that touch my heart. But it would be a corruption of language to say that I "love" my grandchildren the same as I "love" children whom I do not even know. Whatever my feelings for other children, the experience is entirely different.

Apart from what I feel for my wife, Devers — who is the highest value in my life — writing is my paramount passion. What this means, practically, is that a good deal of my time and energy is devoted to writing. This has to do with *living* one's values, not simply professing them.

You ask, "How do I bring love into my life?" My answer is that I focus day after day principally on what I care most about in this world — on what I most respect and admire. That is what I give my time and attention to.

Since my highest priorities are my marriage and my work, I give the greatest part of my time and energy to them. With regard to my wife, I frequently communicate to her my awareness of all the traits and characteristics in her that I so much love, respect, appreciate, and admire.

We all want to be seen, understood, appreciated. I call this the need for the experience of psychological visibility. I strive to make my wife feel visible to me.

I also spend a great deal of time thinking about the things I love. I am keenly aware of how much there is in my life to appreciate and enjoy. I dwell on that every day. I do not take anything good in my life for granted.

I am always aware of our mortality. I know that if I love someone, the time to express it is today. If I value something, the time to honor it is today.

The Best-Kept Secret

by *Barry Neil Kaufman*

"If perceptions lead to behaviors, can our thoughts bring love into our lives? Absolutely. I know for a fact that we can make the choice to love, that we can make that choice come alive, and that it's sustainable, renewable, and ever-deepening."

I FINALLY HAPPENED UPON a simple definition of love that has allowed me to activate it in my life in ways that astound me. My definition is threefold: love is accepting and nonjudgmental; love is wanting the best for another person; and love is doing something useful to help another person realize his or her potential.

An initial awareness that has been a guiding point and beacon in my life, and one that may actually be the best-kept secret on this planet, is simply this: love is a choice. I never realized this as I was growing up. Instead, it almost seemed to me that love fell out of the sky and hit you on the head or was otherwise magically manifested. And I believe that this idea is not an uncommon one. In our culture, love is viewed as a passive experience, something that just "happens to you." We see love more as a reaction than an action, and we have systematically learned to become wallflowers in the dance of love. Even the way we speak of it — "I fell in love" — makes it sound as if it were some sort of colossal accident, like falling down the stairs. Then later we'll say, "I fell out of love," again as if it weren't within our control. Many people never understand that love really comes from an opening-of-the-heart decision that we can make at any time in our lives.

Yes, love is a choice; it doesn't just happen. But to love, you must first find the happiness within yourself, because when you are unhappy, you are not loving. Once you learn to be happy, you can learn to open your heart to loving. You must also create a place where you refrain from judging those around you, a place of learning, a place where you are present for others at any given moment. Then, when you bring happiness alive in your own life as well as in the lives of others, you are able to love and be loved in return.

I have an unflinchingly optimistic bias. I believe that everyone is lovable — we have only to learn how to see the lovability in others. I also believe that everyone, with absolutely no exceptions, can give love and that one single loving person changes the world.

But how we experience the world and love depends entirely on how we decide to see the world — that is, what we "make up" about the world. I call this "the big make-believe." My wife, Samahria, and I found this truth in our lives when we had a very special child, a child who was autistic and retarded — conditions that all the experts said were incurable and irreversible. They looked at our little boy and said, "Bad, terrible, awful." But we looked at the same child and said, "Wonderful, special, opportunity."

In truth, he wasn't bad, terrible, or awful; nor was he wonderful or an opportunity — these were just things that people "made up" about him. But the important thing is that these beliefs, these perceptions, these labels, led to behaviors. "Bad, terrible, awful" led to distress, despair, and inaction. "Wonderful, special, opportunity" led to optimism, hopefulness, and an incredible amount of creativity and action.

If perceptions lead to behaviors, can our thoughts bring love into our lives? Absolutely. I know for a fact that we can make the choice to love, that we can make that choice come alive, and that it's sustainable, renewable, and ever-deepening. I decided long ago that I wanted to bring love alive, not simply as a mysterious experience beyond my control but as a living principle. And one of the most profound and loving experiences of my life occurred while I was doing just that.

Samahria and I have adopted several children from backgrounds of severe abuse and violence. As we were driving to the airport to pick up one of the children for the first time, I was thinking that the only thing I knew about this little guy was that he was five years old, that when he was two and a half his mom had died, and that his father had tried to kill him by slitting his throat. He had then been put in the back wards of an orphanage. When we were called and asked, "Would you take this little boy, because nobody else will?" we immediately replied, "Absolutely!" because we wanted to open our hearts and our family to him. As we were driving to the airport, I realized that I didn't know this little person but was going to open my arms to him. He would be my son, and I would make a commitment to be his poppy for as long as he wanted me. When we arrived at the airport waiting room and the crowd began to surge through the door, I saw a man I recognized from the orphanage. He was holding the hand of this very frail little five-year-old boy. I dropped down on one knee so I wouldn't seem too large and intimidating and opened my arms to him. I must have been about two hundred feet away, but at some point he saw me, recognized who I was, and started to run toward me. And as I watched my little Robby run toward me, it was as if each step were being taken in slow motion. When he took the first step I thought, "I love you and you are my son." And when he took another step I thought, "And now I love you more and you are my son," and when he took another I thought, "And now I love you even more." By the time he jumped into my arms, I realized that I had accessed the deepest vein of love that I had ever experienced and that I was as passionate about and committed to this little stranger as I was to my other children.

In the definition of love that I gave earlier, I suggested first truly accepting a person and not judging; second, looking into a person's eyes and deeply wanting the best for him or her; and third, taking some sort of positive action to help that person realize his or her potential. I'd like to add the idea of becoming an indiscriminate lover. This kind of indiscriminate loving has nothing to do with sexuality or promiscuity — it's about developing the ability to love anyone and everyone without requiring anything in return. Most of the time we are stingy with our love, thinking, "Well, I'll only love these five people." We do this because we see love as a limited resource. But the most powerful way to develop love is to be indiscriminate, in the sense of not having any requirements for loving. Instead, we immediately open our hearts to the bus driver, the waitress, the flight attendant, and the mail carrier because we want to. And the more we "practice" love this way, the more our lives are filled with love. You can observe the same principle in action when you keep lifting a barbell. Eventually your body responds by increasing the power and size of your biceps. It's a basic tenet of life that the parts of you on which you focus the most attention become the parts that are the most developed. Unfortunately, in our culture we tend to focus an awesome amount of attention on anger, fear, anxiety, judgment, and so on. Just imagine what would happen if we decided to focus on love instead!

One of my kids once said to me, "But, Poppy, if you love everybody, we're not too special to you. You love every stranger on the street, but what about us?" I shared with him that although I might feel I could love a hundred people, a thousand people, or as many people as I could reach out to, each one of those experiences would be special and personal. I didn't mean that when I turned to my son and held out my hand, my love for him would be diminished. It would actually be enhanced, because the more a person focuses on loving, the stronger the ability to love becomes. So I could say that in choosing to love indiscriminately, I make myself a stronger lover and make my ability to love even more powerful.

The focus on love is very important. Some people say, "I want a big car," "I want a better love relationship," or "I want my children to listen to me." Invariably I ask them, "Why do you want those things?" They reply, "Because they'll make me feel good." This mythology implies that when we get what we want, we feel good. But what really happens is that when we get what we think we want, we experience only a temporary feeling of pleasure, inner ease, or peace of mind. The ultimate "feel good" is truly found by filling ourselves with love.

I have discovered that there are certain shortcuts to love and to the happiness that you must have in order to love. First of all, you must learn to be present in each unfolding moment. Instead of living in the past or worrying about the future, make every attempt to concentrate on "right now," because happiness and love are both in the present moment.

Second, make love and happiness priorities in your life. The pursuit of love and happiness often seems to be more tangential than focused. We put a vast amount of time, energy, and money into educating ourselves and pursuing careers, into shopping for furniture, clothes, and vehicles. But we don't expend nearly as much effort to establish a basis for love, happiness, and peace of mind. The decision to put real, focused energy into making love and happiness active states of mind can truly transform your life.

Third, be aware of when you are judging others. Try to let go of those judgments, because they are walls between people. Judgments create hostility, while letting go of them allows you to embrace and love others. If you lead with love, others respond with love.

Next is gratitude — a wonderful precursor to happiness and love. We are often like harried consumers who rush into the store to buy dozens of doughnuts but, once they get home, moan and groan about the holes in the doughnuts. We forget to see the abundance of doughnuts — we see only what's lacking. As you go through your daily activities, allow yourself to look for substance and abundance, rather than focusing on the holes. This attitude goes a long way toward opening your heart, your mind, and your spirit to happy, loving feelings.

And finally, strive for authenticity in both thought and action. One of the great causes of alienation from both ourselves and others is that we avoid presenting who we really are. We often do so for the best of reasons — we don't want to reveal who we are because we're afraid of rejection. But the result is an incredible amount of internal dissonance between the masks and roles we create and our real feelings. By peeling away the masks, dropping the roles, and sharing our true feelings, we can make real connections with our inner selves and with others. That's bridge-building material, bonding material. That's an act of love.

I have an expression that I share with people: we have learned to become beggars of love. Not eaters of love, but beggars. We hold out our cups, asking people to love us — "Will you please love me?" — because we believe that we will feel better if people love us. Unfortunately, the effort is in vain, for we can only really experience love when we fill ourselves with love and when we are willing to pour that love into other people's cups. In order to love others, we must first give ourselves the experience of love inside. At the Option Institute we teach that the one who loves most, wins. That's the heart and soul of the experience of love.

Years ago, when I put myself on the road of the perpetual seeker of love and happiness, I was always searching but didn't have a lot of time. Once I decided that I wanted to change my philosophy from "I seek" to "I find," I realized that in order to "find" I would have to make it a central pursuit in my life. And when I made the pursuit of love and happiness central, I did "find." When I gave this quest the space, the commitment, and the perseverance and reverence, I was able to transform my dream into reality. And by making this an active, central pursuit in your life, you can also bring love and happiness alive for yourself, so that you do not spend your life searching—but finding.

2.

Heart and Soul

"If you have a particular faith or religion, that is good. But you can survive without it if you have a love, compassion, and tolerance. The clear proof of a person's love of God is if that person genuinely shows love to fellow human beings."

— THE DALAI LAMA

TO LOVE AND BE LOVED

BY *Rabbi Harold Kushner*

"None of us has the power to make someone else love us. But we all have the power to give away love, to love other people. And if we do so, we change the kind of person we are, and we change the kind of world we live in."

I WAS IN Oklahoma City a few weeks after the terrible bombing in which so many died, meeting with families who had lost relatives. I asked them, "Of everything that has happened in the last ten weeks, what has helped you most to bear your burden?" And they kept giving me the same answer: the outpouring of support and sympathy from friends and strangers, the validation that they were people worth caring about, that they were right in feeling their pain and grief. The understanding from others made their losses easier to endure.

My wife and I had the same experience in our personal life. Our son died at an early age. When we found out how desperately ill he was, I first had to understand that this wasn't something God was doing to us. We came to understand that God was not punishing us, God was grieving with us. Knowing God was on our side liberated a lot of love and helped us handle the problems better. In the same way, when people reached out to us, it gave us the same message and the same reassurance. People coming forward, just to say that they wanted to help, that they wished there was more they could do, made a difference.

People need to feel understood and supported. Many members of my congregation come to me for counsel. I've learned that they are looking not for advice — often they already know the answer — but for understanding. And I give them my concern, my sense that they are worth caring about and that their problems are worth taking seriously. Receiving this message is immensely therapeutic for them.

I often see how this need simply to be loved with understanding manifests itself in married couples. The wife starts to tell the husband her problems. After a minute he interrupts and tells her what to do about them, because he's geared up to be a problem solver. But she's very unhappy, because she doesn't want his advice. She wants fifteen minutes of his undivided attention. She wants validation that her problems are as important to him as they are to her. And if he would just hold still and listen for those fifteen minutes, she would get the message that he cares about her.

People can do this for one another, can love one another with understanding. All around me I see many people whose lives are not as fulfilling as they might be, simply because these people are too involved with themselves. I think our society puts too much emphasis on finding someone who will love you; our culture focuses too much on being loved and not enough on being a loving person.

It's much easier to be a loving person, to give away love. This ability is something you can have control over. None of us has the power to make someone else love us. But we all have the power to give away love, to love other people. And if we do so, we change the kind of person we are, and we change the kind of world we live in.

This attitude is what works for me in my own marriage. The essence of marital love, I have learned, is not romance, but forgiveness — accepting a person's imperfections and understanding that each of us has his or her quirks that would drive our mates crazy but for the love between us. When I'm in a bad mood, I can only hope that my wife is prepared to write it off as just a bad mood, not the essential me.

Some years ago I read a wonderful newspaper column. A woman sees two children in a playground get into a fight. One of them says, "I hate you. I never want to play with you again." For two or three minutes they play separately, and then they come back and start playing with each other again. The observer says to a woman sitting next to her, "How do children do that? Be so angry one moment and together the next?" And the neighbor says, "Oh, it's easy. They choose happiness over righteousness."

That is the advice I give a lot of married couples. Choose happiness over righteousness. Even if you're right, don't demand recognition of the fact. Sacrifice the victory for the sake of a happy marriage. In a happy marriage there are no winners and losers, only two people who agree to put up with each other — exasperating as that may be.

The rewards are certainly worth it. There is a satisfaction you can find only in a marriage, as you make yourself part of a larger entity. We see this in the biblical injunction that "therefore shall a man leave his father and mother and cleave unto his wife and they shall become one." You achieve a sense of wholeness, not just when you find someone with whom to sleep and live but when you can really join with another person and feel his or her joy, feel his or her pain. There's a sense of expansion of your own self. The emptiness in your life is filled in a way that you can't get from any other human experience.

If you work it right, possessing a sense that there is something greater than you the individual, whether it be spirituality or a child, also creates a sense of happiness and love. I think we all need some sort of force to pull us out of our narcissism and our overconcern for ourselves. Having a child can do this. I've seen how a child changes people, just knowing that this other life is dependent on them. A sense of religious commitment can do this, too. It opens the heart, bringing a sense that you owe something to a cause greater than your own well-being or your own satisfactions. I think human beings are created to be this way, and when we act selfishly and narcissistically, we're acting against our essential nature. People are not meant to be selfish.

People are meant to be loving, and they are meant to be intermittently happy. I suspect that people who are happy all the time probably don't realize what's going on around them. There is so much pain in the world, only by shutting our eyes to it could we always be happy. But we do have the power to always be loving, always be caring. And from time to time, we have a moment of happiness that justifies everything that leads up to it.

This runs counter to a lot of the messages all around us: that if we just get a certain something—a better car, a better neighborhood, a better pair of sneakers—then we'll be happy. Of course, this frame of mind doesn't work. It only makes us more insecure. Advertisers need to make us feel anxious so that we'll buy whatever they're selling to make us feel better. And insecurity makes it hard for us to feel worthy of love, to believe that others will accept us if they really know us, and ultimately to be accepting of other people.

Someone once wrote: "Happiness is always a by-product. You don't make yourself happy by chasing happiness. You make yourself happy by being a good person." The happiest people I know are people who don't even think about being happy. They just think about being good neighbors, good people. And then happiness sort of sneaks in the back window while they're busy doing good.

This attitude works in relationships as well. I always worry about a relationship in which one or both parties are constantly taking the temperature of the relationship and measuring whether they're happy. I suspect that such an appraisal leads to asking questions like, "Would I be happier if I were in a relationship with somebody else?" Instead of asking themselves, "Am I happy?" I think they should ask themselves, "Is there something I can do to make this a better relationship? What else can I give to it?" If they do that enough, they'll turn around one day and realize happiness has snuck up on them.

Being loving toward others, and creating a relationship in which they love us, is a reciprocal process. We begin by being loving toward ourselves, seeing ourselves as capable of loving, capable of giving things away. It's a very stunted person who can't give him- or herself away emotionally because of being afraid there won't be much left if he or she does. Loving ourselves doesn't mean narcissism and self-worship. It means accepting the imperfections in ourselves and realizing that nobody expects us to be perfect. Self-love means seeing that not every mistake is a permanent stain on our self-esteem and our sense of worthiness. That's how you love yourself. I worry about people whose major goal in life is getting enough love, because I think they end up being takers rather than givers.

It helps to have some moral code in achieving these things. We act against our essential nature when we are dishonest or devious or selfish. And acting against our essential nature impinges on our ability to give and receive love and on our ability to experience happiness. For example, adultery corrodes a marriage because it introduces an element of dishonesty.

I have trouble understanding people who do things that, in the long run, are only going to hurt them. This self-damage could be in the way they eat and drink or behave with their families. Probably what is happening is that they're not confident that they'll get enough love, so they go out and steal it, just as people who feel they don't have enough money rob people. People who are worried that they're not going to get enough love try to get love by unethical means. This isn't just limited to marital infidelity. For example, a woman trying to get love by illicit means might pretend to be someone she isn't. She wears a mask when she's suppressing her own individuality, her own needs and wants. She's hoping to be loved by people who wouldn't love her if they knew what she was really like.

I don't think people who do this realize how inherently contradictory it is. How can it be real, nourishing love when it's gained dishonestly? When they are hiding their true nature? It is always a futile pursuit, it always catches up with them. And ironically, they stay hungry.

I think in the long run we love people who, by accepting us, enable us to be better than we otherwise would be. We love someone who reflects to us an image of ourselves that makes us feel good about ourselves. We love someone who frees up the creative and emotional energies that otherwise would remain dormant. We love someone, too, who helps us to be a loving person.

Some religions, like some people, have the kind of message that liberates our own ability to love. If the message of the religion is "God loves you despite your shortcomings," your heart is opened to giving and receiving love. But if the message we hear is "You have sinned, you have fallen short, you're no good, God is disappointed in you," we're going to tighten up. It turns us into emotional misers, unable to give away love. But if the message is "God knows exactly who you are, and loves you anyway," we are permitted to love and to forgive — ourselves and the other imperfect people in our lives.

There are a lot of religious spokespeople who don't agree with me, but I believe that God really did make us in his own image — a model of love and forgiveness that we can emulate. This is very important. This is how I try to live my life.

I recognize that I need love in the same way that I need food and sleep and exercise. I understand that my soul would shrivel up from malnutrition if I didn't love, didn't give love and receive love. One of the things that works for me, helps me fill my heart with love, is the series of Jewish prayers that focus on being grateful for all the things around us that we might otherwise take for granted. The first words of prayer when Jews wake up in the morning are to thank God that they're still alive and awake, that their bodies work, their arms, their legs, their eyes, their minds work, that they have clothes to wear and food to eat and things to look forward to. When your heart is filled with gratitude, when you can just go out and feel how lucky you are that the world is there for you, and how lucky you are that there are people out there trying to enrich your world, it's a lot easier to be loving—to yourself and to others.

HEARTWORK

BY *Marianne Williamson*

"That's what we're talking about here: whether the spirit of love is in charge of our thought forms. And if it is, we're more charitable; we give people a break. We bless instead of condemn. We support instead of deride. We forgive instead of attack. We love instead of fear."

PEOPLE DON'T NEED to be reminded of love's importance. What people are looking for are the what and how of love. The culture in which we have grown up is dominated by a severely loveless mentality, and fully recognizing this is crucial to our healing as a nation. Without that conscious recognition, we fail to understand what difficult work it is internally, as well as externally, to avoid complicity with loveless cultural stimuli and to resist effectively their persuasiveness.

The great teachings of the ages apply as much to the experience of this culture at this time as they do to any culture at any other time. The heart lives in an eternal realm.

The only way we can reach that realm is to bypass the cacophony of the world, to reach deep into our own hearts for the silence that waits for each of us.

If we wake up in the morning and head directly into the turmoil of the world — reading the headlines, watching or listening to the news as the status quo defines it — then the mind has no opportunity to escape the world's hysteria. But if we meditate and pray before we see the headlines, or at least before we head off into our worldly activities, then our hope and faith remain firm.

I think we're on the earth to bring healing to the world, but we can hardly do so when we ourselves are too wounded. We are all heir to the fear that runs rampant in this culture. When we do not turn toward God, we become expressions of the hysteria. Behavior modification or mere suppression of the panic is not enough to transmute our minds or the conditions around us. Only love can do that.

The world's greatest need, I believe, is for serious spiritual practice. Pascal wrote: "All of humanity's problems stem from man's inability to sit quietly in a room alone."

In the *Course of Miracles*, it says that five minutes spent with the Holy Spirit in the morning is enough to guarantee that He will be in charge of our thought forms throughout the day. That's what we're talking about here: whether the spirit of love is in charge of our thought forms. And if it is, we're more charitable; we give people a break. We bless instead of condemn. We support instead of deride. We forgive instead of attack. We love instead of fear.

We are all heir to the darkness of this world, and we are all heir to the gifts of God. To choose His gifts over the false gifts of the world is a moment-by-moment choice, a moment-by-moment decision. But we live in a world where the stimulus of fear is so loud, so insidious, and so constantly bombarding us that the work of resistance is serious work indeed.

It's a kind of muscle training. If you want a new body, you have to work for it; if you want a new mind, you have to work for it also. Spiritual practice takes a very deep effort, to soften our own hearts, to quiet our own fears, to renew our own souls. It all begins within us, and the work can be grueling.

My most difficult spiritual challenge of the past few years has been my relationship with my daughter. I never knew how hard parenting would be. I don't mean physically, but emotionally. Whatever intimacy issues that I have are magnified in my relationship with her.

I have had to work to become someone who can read to her for an hour without jumping up to answer the phone. I have had to work to get myself to take her to school and pick her up, myself, consistently, rather than always choosing to put work first. These might sound like small things, but to me they were big things. Work, particularly its adrenaline-driven dimensions, has become an American addiction — and it's a killer. It doesn't let you rest. A driven woman is not much of a mother, so I have worked very hard to reclaim my quiet. Things are better now, but I realize the level of sustained effort it takes to be the mother I want to be. I know in my heart that I can write books or give lectures to lots of people, and that's great, but being a good parent is much more important than any other job.

As Gandhi said, "We must *be* the change."

THE WELLSPRING OF
THE HEART

BY *Jack Kornfield*

"The questions asked at the end of his or her life are very simple ones: 'Did I love well? Did I love the people around me, my community, the earth, in a deep way?'"

IF YOU WANT to love, take the time to listen to your heart. In most ancient and wise cultures, it is a regular practice for people to talk to their heart. There are rituals, stories, and meditative skills in every spiritual tradition that awaken the voice of the heart. To live wisely, this practice is essential, because our heart is the source of our connection to and intimacy with all of life. And life *is* love. This mysterious quality of love is all around us, as real as gravity.

Yet how often we forget about love! Love begins by recognizing what most deeply fulfills us is not what we have or what we do, but the state of our heart. The Indian mystic poet Kabir wrote: "Are you looking for Me? I am in the next seat. My shoulder is against yours." Here he speaks of our longing for the Beloved.

Our heart is very near, yet in modern life a remarkable swoon comes over us in the complexity and busyness of our time, and we forget what matters most. We think we have time, but no one knows for sure how much time he or she really has. In his teachings to Carlos Castaneda, Don Juan uses death as an advisor to remind us of these values:

> Death is our eternal companion. It is always to our left at an arm's length. It has always been watching us, and it always will until the day it taps us. The thing to do when you're impatient with your life, turn to your left and ask advice from your death. An immense amount of pettiness is dropped if your death makes a gesture to you, or if you catch a glimpse of it, or if you just catch the feeling that your companion is there watching you.

If you have the privilege of being at the bedside of someone having a conscious death, the questions asked at the end of his or her life are very simple ones: "Did I love well? Did I love the people around me, my community, the earth, in a deep way?" And perhaps, "Did I live fully? Did I offer myself to life?"

In the heart of each of us, there is a voice of knowing, a song that can remind us of what we most value and long for, what we have known since we were a child. There is a tribe in East Africa that recognizes this song even before birth. In this tribe the birth date of a child is not considered the day of his or her physical birth or even the day of conception, as in other village cultures. For this tribe the birth date is the first time the child is a thought in his or her mother's mind. Aware of her intention to conceive a child with a particular man, the mother goes off to sit alone under a great tree. There she sits and listens deeply, until she can hear the song of the child she hopes will be born. Once she has heard this song, she returns to her village and teaches it to the father, so they can sing it together as they make love, inviting the child to join them. After the child is conceived, she sings the song to the baby in her womb. She then teaches it to the old women and midwives of the village, so that throughout the labor and at the miraculous moment of birth itself, the child is greeted with its song. After the birth all the villagers learn the song of their new member and sing it to the child when he or she falls or hurts him- or herself. It is sung in times of triumph or in rituals and initiations. When the child grows up, this song becomes a part of his or her marriage ceremony; and at the end of life, his or her loved ones gather around the deathbed and sing the song for the last time.

Hearing such a story brings a yearning for such listening, for our own lives and song to be held and guided from such a place of respect. But we have been distracted and drawn into the marketplace. Our lives are complex, and our times are materialistic, ambitious, outer-directed. So often we have forgotten how to listen. It is difficult to be in touch with our heart in the midst of a busy life.

Anne Wilson Schaef, who writes about the addicted society, tells us that

the best adjusted person in modern society is the person who is not dead and not alive, just numb, a zombie. When you're dead, you're not able to contribute work to the society, and when you're fully alive you must constantly say no to many of the processes of society—the racism, the polluted environment, the nuclear threat, the arms race, drinking unsafe water, and eating carcinogenic foods. Thus, it is in the interest of modern consumer society to promote those things that take the edge off and keep us busy with our fixes, or keep us slightly numbed out and zombie-like. In this way, our modern consumer society functions as an addict.

No wonder we have difficulty staying in touch with our heart! When we do speak with our heart, we must ask the most honest questions we can. How do we feel about the way we are living? Is it conducive to ease, creativity, wholeness, respect? Or have the responsibilities of our adult life made a prison for our body and spirit?

For many of us, our loss of innocence and connection began years ago in childhood, when they became buried to allow us to survive our schools, families, religion, and culture. And so part of the art of living from the heart is reclaiming this childlike capacity to listen to our heart. The famous American painter James McNeill Whistler attended West Point Military Academy in the 1850s. In his engineering class, the instructor asked all students to draw a model of a bridge. Whistler drew a beautiful stone arched bridge, complete with two young boys fishing from it. The lieutenant, very angry, said, "This is a military exercise. Get those children off the bridge." So Whistler redrew it and put the boys fishing from the bank of the river. The lieutenant got even angrier and said, "I told you to get them completely out of the picture." So in the last version, Whistler drew the stone bridge and the river, and added two little tombstones on the riverside with children's names on them! This is a symbol of the way that many of us have lost our heart and, ultimately, lost connection with ourselves. In fact, it took Whistler many years of painting to reawaken the spirit of the child in himself. Like Whistler, most of us must find our own way to reclaim our buried tears and grief and, passing through them, rediscover a renewed source of playfulness and joy.

The great traditions of meditation and prayer, of contemplative life, offer ways that help us to listen deeply, to restore this lost connection. One of the qualities they foster that allows us to stay in touch with our heart is stillness. We need to step out of "doing" time, to "being." We need a Sabbath, a regular holy day, a regular time to stop and reconnect with the spirit that moves through all things. Even doing too many good deeds can be a problem for us. As Thomas Merton said, "To allow oneself to be carried away by a multitude of conflicting concerns, to surrender to too many demands, to commit oneself to too many good projects, to want to help everyone and everything, is itself to succumb to the violence of our time."

So what we seek in living from the heart is a rhythm in life that includes time for renewal in nature: time to walk for no purpose at all; time to sit still; time to listen to the sounds of life around us; time to listen to our bodies; time to listen to our hearts. Meditation can teach us this art with the simple grace of following our breath in and out until we feel the life rhythm that always moves in our bodies. Then we can listen to the stories the mind is telling, to the longings of the heart, and to the things we most deeply value. Meditation cultivates a quality of sacred attention. It is a prayer that doesn't ask for what we want, but opens us to hear, "Not my will but Thine": a prayer that listens with the whole being.

This kind of respect of self, in stillness, in nature, in prayer, can naturally extend to touch the hearts of others. When we listen to another, we can meet him or her with an agenda or with openness. We can try to get our point across, defend ourselves, accomplish just what we want, or protect ourselves. All this comes from what in the spiritual world is called "the body of fear." Or we can listen with sacred attention, with respect, in order to learn what is true in the heart of this other being.

This love, this connection of the heart, this intimacy, is not far away. As Mother Teresa says, "In this world, we cannot do great things. We can only do small things with great love." It's not very complicated to do these small things. When we become still, the path is obvious. It is made of the moments and the days of being there for ourselves and our children, listening to our colleagues, and honoring the environment. When we are present with our heart, we offer a respect to ourselves and to others in any situation.

Even in our modern technological world, a renewal of this respect is possible. For example, a series of medical facilities based on a patient-centered model called Plaintree Hospitals are opening up. Classical music plays softly in the background. Patients wear their own robes and pajamas, sleep on flowered sheets, and are encouraged to sleep as late as they like in the morning. Friends and family are welcome to visit at any time convenient for the patient. They are encouraged to help and cook and care for the patient. The idea makes so much sense. And this is true of ways of the heart as well. What we most care for, what we most need to do, is right there — when we take the time to listen.

Sometimes, however, we become afraid. We don't recognize that the heart has the capacity to be open in the midst of all things. I have a friend, a businessman, who began to meditate. He began to have so much chest pain that he thought he was having a heart attack. We worked together and he breathed gently into the pain, putting his hand on his heart. When he let himself feel the busyness that had run his life for such a long time, tears welled up for the things he'd left undone in his family and his community. The pains of his heart subsided. And he realized that he could live in a very different way.

Often when we first try to listen to the heart, there is sorrow. The unfinished business we've run from, the grief not felt, the losses that are part of our measure of sorrow, the tears of the world, make themselves known. We can open to them, too, and listen in a sacred or respectful way; we can allow the greatness of our heart to unfold. A woman I know tells the story of how each morning on her way to work she passed a homeless man; for months she dropped coins into his cup and gradually developed a nodding relationship with him. Then one day she realized that she had never looked him in the eye. She felt that if she ever truly did so, he'd end up in her living room the next week. She realized that she had closed down.

Like this woman, we are all afraid that we cannot hold the sorrow and beauty of the world. And it is true that the heart has its seasons, just as a flower opens to the sunlight and closes to the night. We need to be respectful of those rhythms. But we can't close down for long. It is our true nature to have an open heart, as much as it is the true nature of a flower to open in the sunlight. Sometimes this is called our Buddha nature, or our divine nature. But whatever we call it, know that each heart has an enormous capacity to hold the world. We are intimately connected with all things, and whether we let ourselves know it or not, our heart feels all that is true in life. Mahatma Gandhi used to say it this way: "I believe in the essential unity of all that lives. Therefore, I believe that if one person gains spiritually, the whole world gains, and that if one person falls, the whole world falls to that extent."

This is not just a philosophy. My wife and I were traveling in India some years ago; we were visiting a mountaintop temple of a great sage, a woman named Vimala Thakar. My wife began to have very painful visions of the death of her brother, which I thought were just part of her meditation process. But quite sadly, one week later we received a telegram that read "Your brother has died, a suicide." The way he had died was exactly what my wife had seen in her vision — and we learned from the telegram that her vision had come on the very night of her brother's death. Here we were, halfway around the earth, and yet my wife knew very well what had happened to her brother and how it had happened. We have all heard such stories. This is because in reality we *are* all connected.

So the work of our heart, the work of taking time, to listen, to live our values, to love well, is also our gift to the whole of the world. Through our inner courage, we awaken to the greatest capacity of human life, the one true human freedom: to love in the midst of all things. Viktor Frankl, the famous psychiatrist who lived through the Holocaust, wrote:

> We who lived in the concentration camps can remember those who walked through the huts comforting others, giving away their last piece of bread. They may have been few in number, but they offer sufficient proof that everything can be taken from a human being but one thing — the last of our freedoms — to choose our spirit in any given set of circumstances.

The power of the heart is enormous and transformative. Each of us has our own gifts that come from the flowering of our heart. It may be to plant a garden; run an ethical business; be a teacher or a healer, an artist or a parent. For some the journey to the heart's generosity is long and hard; but even those who are abused as children can grow out of those difficult circumstances to be beautiful adults in our community. I have seen it in my work again and again. Always those wounded adults remember one person — a teacher, a grandparent, a friend — who saw them or touched them or loved them, even in the midst of grave abuse and torment. And it is on this love that they base their healing.

The strength of the heart is its ability to nurture all that is beautiful in human life. It requires from us a great mercy and forgiveness — not judgment but the tenderness that weeps at the sorrow of another as if it were our own and that is willing to offer quick forgiveness. By forgiveness, I do not mean condoning what causes suffering to us or to others. Forgiveness, in the end, is simply the statement that we shall not put another human being out of our heart. That we are willing to let go of the pain of the past so that we can start again on the basis of love. There is a story of two ex–prisoners of war who met many years later. One asked the other, "Have you forgiven your captors yet?" And the second man said, "No, never!" And the first one said, "Well, then, they still have you in prison, don't they?"

So the work of the heart is simply the work of mercy for ourselves and for others. It is as natural to us as our own breath. It is who we are. As Thomas Merton wrote:

> Then it was as if I suddenly saw the secret beauty of their hearts, the depths of their hearts where neither sin nor knowledge can reach the core of their reality, the

person that each one is in God's eyes. If only they could see themselves as they really are. If only we could see each other that way, there would be no more need for war or hatred, no more need for cruelty or greed. I suppose the big problem would be that we would fall down and worship each other.

This is the work of the heart. It comes from the intention to listen, to take time to feel your breath, to sense your heart beating in your body, to look at the movement of the clouds and the change of the season. Ask your heart, "If my life were only a little bit longer, what is most important, what do I value, how do I want to live?" As we practice listening to the heart and bringing it forth in our actions, in our tongue, we discover that love itself changes our universe. It is contagious — we catch it from one another. And the power of loving-kindness, the power of those living from the heart, makes the power of armies and technology seem like child's play. For it is the heart force that brings all life, that creates all life, that moves through us. It is never too late to touch this fountain. So take time to listen, to allow that wellspring to be known in your own life.

THE BASICS OF LOVE

BY *Betty Eadie*

"The more you notice the love, the miracles, and the beauty around you, the more love comes into your life. The more you love, the greater your ability to love. And the process perpetuates itself. As you love the world and the people in it, you find this love manifests itself and returns to you."

FILLING YOUR LIFE with love—both giving and receiving—is one of the most difficult aspects of life to master. At least it was for me, for mine was not always a lovable world. Nor are all people loving or easy to love. To make matters worse, many of us have been raised in families that have taught us the opposite— to be nonloving.

I had to learn not only how to give love but also how to receive it. It is often easier to act in a loving manner than to acknowledge the love of others or to trust in the love of others.

I learned to fill my life with love by first learning to love myself. I found that when I wasn't acting in loving ways to others, it was invariably because something unacceptable was going on inside me. At those times, it seemed that most of the people in my life were bothering and annoying me. Fortunately, I discovered that this bother was stemming from something missing within me, from a lack of self-esteem — self-love — and it usually had nothing to do with "them." I knew that to fully love others, first I had to feel love for myself.

It's easy to find fault in others, but much more difficult to look at ourselves and our own faults with honesty. We're often in denial about our own faults; we don't like to see them too clearly. After taking a look at my own flaws — some of which I could change, others of which I simply had to accept — I was gradually able to recognize my faults as parts of me that needed ongoing work. Rather than insisting that I was perfect and that everyone else was to blame, I was able to begin loving and accepting myself as never before. And, having learned to accept and love myself, I was able to extend love and acceptance to others. I was free to start loving the less than perfect parts of other people as well.

Of course, my near-death experience affected my outlook on life, filling me with a desire to become a more loving individual. (I would like to think that I would have become more loving anyway. Time and age have a way of encouraging this!) At this point in my life I don't focus on the many reasons why I wanted to become more loving. Instead, I try to focus and act on the many possibilities for being a loving person that arise each day. Often a simple desire to change is all you really need to begin.

One of the ways I practice love is to think about how I would feel in a given circumstance if the roles were reversed. How would I want someone to respond to me? I then try to act accordingly. And you know, it really works. When we make a genuine attempt to treat others as we would like to be treated, we become much kinder, more compassionate, and more tolerant. No one wants to be hurt or to be treated unkindly or disrespectfully. And although many of us were taught to treat others as we would like to be treated, we usually insist that others extend this courtesy to *us* before we do so. We have to reverse this process. If we were the ones to offer love and kindness, even if we didn't always get something in return, we would live in a much more loving world.

It's important to love and appreciate the little things in life, all the beauty that God has created. I know it sounds terribly simplistic, but as I go about my day, I try to appreciate *everything* I see: a bird, a tree, a flower, something unusual happening. My goal is to love what I see and to thank God for showing it to me. When I do, it's as though the universe opens up and envelops me in love. As I receive this love, I can't help become increasingly open and available for more. A wonderful expanding cycle begins to take place. The more you notice the love, the miracles, and the beauty around you, the more love comes into your life. The more you love, the greater your ability to love. And the process perpetuates itself. As you love the world and the people in it, you find this love manifests itself and returns to you.

As you focus on being a more loving person — without worrying about what you are getting in return — you find that plenty of love *does* flow into your life. You don't have to do anything, it just happens. People who are loving and giving attract kindred souls into their lives, for it is easy to love those who are themselves loving. You attract loving people and acts of kindness into your life as you yourself become more loving. It's a giant circle of love that begins with you.

When you act in a loving fashion, an important ripple effect takes place. And even in those rare instances when your love for someone is not returned, it's a good idea simply to keep loving. This doesn't mean that you should allow yourself to be taken advantage of, but rather that you become a model of love and loving behavior. You may be able to help lead that person to another level, where he or she might be kinder somewhere down the road.

We often think the big things are what really matter, but that's not always true. Never underestimate the importance of loving acts. One tiny kind deed can make a world of difference — and you may never even know it. You can probably remember, somewhere back in your life, something that someone said or did that made a big difference to you. This person may have said one simple little thing that stuck with you forever. I remember being in a hospital when I was a little girl, probably when I was around twelve years old. A nurse came into the room and when I opened my eyes, she said to another nurse, "Such love and kindness come out of this little girl's eyes." That comment has stuck with me to this day. It has helped me to think of myself as a kind, loving person. I look upon the nurse's comment as an affirmation of love. To this day, I like to share my love through my eyes. (Eyes are, of course, "the window to the soul.") I'm sure that this wonderful nurse would never remember saying her kind words, nor could she imagine the impact her kindness has had on my life. In a sense, then, she has indirectly helped everyone that I have helped.

The wisest words about love come from the Bible: Do unto others as you would have them do unto you. I have found this to be good advice — always stop and think before you respond or act out of unkindness or harshness. Imagine how you would feel, and how you would like to be treated, if you were in that person's shoes. The true blessing of offering love comes when you don't need to do something for someone, but you do it anyway — for no other reason than your desire to be loving. In these instances, you, as well as the person you are loving, are truly blessed.

LOVE ENOUGH FOR ALL

BY *Stephen R. Covey, Ph.D.*

*"Individuals can affect the world by becoming a model
or an example in their small circle of influence. Just as a
rock thrown into a pond causes ripples to gradually keep
going out until eventually they are very small, so our
acts influence the ecology of the entire human race."*

I LOOK UPON LOVE as the supreme activity of life. Developing love in yourself has to take priority. You need to draw upon the divine energy from God so that you have the power to manifest or express this kind of love. Then the word *love* is no longer a noun. This word *love* becomes a verb. It's something that you do, a sacrifice you make.

A couple came to me to talk about the unhappiness in their marriage. The husband said, "What do you suggest I do, because the feeling isn't in our marriage anymore?" I said, "Well then, *just love her.*" He said, "Well, Stephen, the problem is that the feeling isn't there. It really isn't, not on my part, not on her part; but we are still concerned because we have children." I said, "Where did you get this concept that love is a feeling? Love is a verb; love is something you do. Look at any mother who goes to the Valley of the Shadow of Death to bring a child into the world. The love she has for that child didn't come from the child, it came from her, because she sacrificed for the child. Love — the feeling — is the result, the fruit, of love. The concept of love as a feeling comes from Hollywood. It's selfish and immature, not holy and divine."

This was an exciting new thought for the husband. If love is truly a verb, if forgiveness is a verb, if kindness is a verb, then you can do something about it. But if love is just a feeling, you feel almost helpless because you think you have no control over your feelings. Ultimately, your feelings are a function of your actions. Since you have control over your actions, you therefore have control over your feelings. As you gradually discover this, you gain the maturity to love — whether you are loved in return or not.

The key to love means having a source of unconditional love that you can draw upon endlessly. To me, the way God loves his children is a kind of "fatherly" love that is a rich, unconditional love. "Brotherly" love, which is more conditional, is great; but when push comes to shove in life, brotherly love tends to break down into personal differences. It is during these times that people need to embrace the divine fatherly love.

When you love God first, you love your spouse more. When you love God first, you love your children more. You should always love God first, not people first. Then you have the power to love people with rich and unconditional fatherly love. You may even have to be strong and strict with people sometimes, but that's what a father does with a son or daughter. You transcend the personal when you love God; yet in doing so, you feed the heart and soul of both you and the other person.

To tap into this source of boundless love takes spiritual effort; but when it comes, it is like being nourished by a spring. If I neglect that spring, that source of nourishment, for only a few days or sometimes for even a few hours — if the stresses of life are great enough — then my ability to love unconditionally is no longer there.

I find that just as you have a one-on-one relationship with God, you must have a one-on-one relationship with all the key people in your life and teach them to have a similar relationship with the key people in their lives, so that the water of this love "goes to the end of the row," as the farmer might say. It's important to have private visits with every key person in your life on a regular basis. I try to do so with my married children at least monthly, the un-married ones at least weekly, and with my wife and children at home daily.

I believe the true test of any family is how the parents treat the child who challenges them the most. If you can show unconditional love toward that one child, then all the other children know that the love expressed toward them is also unconditional. But if you cannot show that uncon-ditional love to the one who tries your patience, who may even repel you emotionally, the moment you don't affirm their value, all the other children question the love that you give to them. They wonder, Well, if I hit your nerve, will I also be withdrawn from this affection?

I remember one time when I was with my little boy and I was being unkind and critical of someone. My surprised son turned to me and asked, "Dad, do you love me?" He meant, "Do I have to worry that if I do something wrong, your love will be withdrawn just as it was toward that person?" Assuring him that I loved him unconditionally, I owned up to my mistake and said that only God is perfect and that I, too, needed to work on my own mind and heart.

A powerful source of the ability to love intrinsically is to give service anonymously, when no one knows the source, not even the recipient. If the recipient does know, there should be no effort to get any mileage or recognition out of it. You should not even tell your own heart that you know. A powerful affirmation comes inside your soul when you give anonymous service in this way. When your service is seen, you can transfer all the credit and the glory to God, who gave you the gift and the resources to do it.

When acting unconditionally, you learn not to take either credit or criticism personally. You have to be impervious to how people treat you, to maintain your own sense of personal worth and security. Your behavior has to come from your integrity and a deeply imbedded set of principles and values that ultimately are centered upon God.

Love in the workplace is the cement that enables all the connections to flow smoothly. Without it, the workplace is a machine without lubricant. Love in the workplace manifests itself in many ways: empathy, respect, courtesies, kindness, keeping promises to other people, never talking behind another's back in a negative way. If you have concerns or criticisms, go directly to the person and share them with an "I" message rather than a "you" message. When you have concerns, you say, "My perception is" or "My feeling is," which is a softer form of giving feedback. It's important to care enough to give feedback to everyone — customers, suppliers, and all your associates inside the company.

The word *love* may be too saccharine for some people in the business context; if so, *caring* will suffice. Sincerity, sacrifice, service, respect, dignity, fairness, and patience are manifestations of love and caring. It doesn't matter what words are used, because the focus is on building good relationships. Relationships in selling, relationships in consulting — they're all about love.

Love makes the world go around, no question about it. The absence of it makes people defensive so that they are not vulnerable. Most people don't know how to tap into the unconditional supply of love, so if they see only conditional sources being taken away, they become cynical and develop different reactions, which psychologists call projection, rationalization, intellectualization, denial, and so forth. When people put on the armor of God that Saint Paul talked about, they have spirit and the word with them and have no need to defend themselves with sarcasm or cynicism.

Self-control and self-esteem are necessary to forget yourself. Then you become capable of really living outside yourself with love. Otherwise, you become narcissistic and see the world through your own very narrow frame. You live love on your terms but don't include a frame of reference for other people. You begin to make deposits into their emotional bank account, but these deposits may not truly reflect the unique realities or needs of those people at all. What you perceive as deposits may actually be very low-level deposits or even possible withdrawals.

We also affect the world by being prayerful. Prayer taps into the energy of God, bringing the heavenly forces on the other side to bear on this side. When someone prays in faith for someone, although he or she may not be connected in time or space (perhaps that person is on a different continent, or perhaps that person is in prison), I don't know how it happens, but the energy of God touches that person in the form of protection or perhaps a sense of peace and comfort. Fundamentally, I believe the kindest thing we can ever do for other people is to give them love and prayer. They may not ever know we are doing it.

Individuals can affect the world by becoming a model or an example in their small circle of influence. Just as a rock thrown into a pond causes ripples to gradually keep going out until eventually they are very small, so our acts influence the ecology of the entire human race. The poet Robert Browning once said, "One man's death diminishes me no matter where it is." We are all part of one another and so, interwoven; it's a kind of divine architectural ecology that encompasses us all and cannot be violated.

3.

Giving and Receiving

"Love cures people — both the ones who give it and the ones who receive it."

— DR. KARL MENNINGER (1893 – 1990)

THE BIRTHRIGHT OF
OUR HEART

BY *Benjamin Shield, Ph.D.*

"This is the essence that gives breath to our bodies and to our souls. This is the breath of God. It infuses each of us with life and purpose. It endows us with the grace to give and receive the way our bodies breathe out and breathe in."

LOVE IS THERE — always. Yet it is often difficult to fully embrace this wellspring of love that resides within ourselves and is available to us each and every moment. It is not something that we must create, it *is* us. Love is our essence — the fundamental energy that nourishes us. It is our birthright.

From our creation we are sent on a journey to reclaim our birthright. When we encounter obstacles along the way, we continue the journey — not by overpowering something *outside* ourselves, but by letting go of something *inside* ourselves. We do this by keeping our hearts open, risking vulnerability, letting go of past hurtful experiences that block our ability to love, and allowing others to love us.

We could say that love is like the sun. Clouds may pass over it and temporarily block its warmth. But the sun, like our essence, continues to shine. Our lives may move between joy and disappointment, but the love within us never diminishes. We can ignore, hinder, and even deny this love — but we cannot destroy it. We can forget love, but love does not forget us.

Love creates the strong foundation for our lives. And it is often the simplest of loving moments that continue to strengthen this foundation. I am often reminded of a story that I heard some time ago. A radio commentator was talking about her vacation at a beautiful seaside town in Mexico. One afternoon she saw an elderly couple strolling hand in hand along the beach. They were clearly in love, and there was something about them that made the commentator feel that they had been married forever.

Later that day she saw this same couple at dinner. Her curiosity got the better of her, and she apologetically introduced herself and asked the secret of their wonderful relationship. The answer surprised her.

The woman was genuinely amused. "Our secret is that my husband has always been a bit hard of hearing! You see, we were married during the Depression. Both of us worked two, sometimes three, jobs just to make ends meet. One day I came home so exhausted, I said to my husband, 'I'm so tired, my *teeth* hurt!' Well, he took me by the hand, sat me down, took off my shoes, and lovingly rubbed my *feet!*"

She continued, "I think you understand the mix-up! But from that day on, this became our little ritual. At the end of each day, my husband has always lovingly rubbed my feet. With this simple act, he shows me daily how much he loves me and, in turn, I remember how much I love him. And no matter what else is going on in our lives, or in the world, we always remember how easy it is to love each other."

There are many times that I find myself afraid to take the risk of loving, to become vulnerable and tenderly open-hearted with another human being. The wounds from hurtful experiences have created fears and obstacles that hinder my ability to love. Learning to identify and remove those fears is one of life's most challenging processes. When I feel overwhelmed and afraid to love, I try to remind myself that love, not fear, is the template upon which our world is built.

Much of my inner work involves releasing the fears — past, present, and future — that interfere with my access to love and love's access to me. This is a lifelong process of facing myself consciously, discovering that my fears are just masks for old pain and not premonitions about the future. In this process of letting go, I try to focus on those things in my life that nourish the experience of love. I try to focus on those things that help me to let my ego boundaries melt, to lose my self-importance, and to release my daily worries.

We do not have to sequester ourselves in a monastery to do this. The unique, daily moments that each of us have in our lives can continually reconnect us with love. Watching my dog, Annie, play with her friends, I feel the unabashed joy she experiences. Listening to music such as Beethoven's "Moonlight Sonata" wash over me and infuse me with its beauty softens the harsh edges of the day. Simple acts, such as taking a walk in the woods, holding a door open for a stranger, or just remembering to breathe deeply and consciously are all things that help me to give up some of my limitations, to let myself expand, become more spacious, and to move myself gently toward that center of my being, into the heart of love.

This ongoing process of connecting with my center enables me to merge more fully with others. When this occurs, my perspective widens, my senses sharpen, and I become more permeable to the love within me and to the love given by those around me.

Love is more than thought and feeling. Love is behavior. It means spending time with our children as they struggle bravely to read. It means being with friends as we allow them the space and opportunity to share their lives, their dreams, and sometimes their tears. It means really trying to see things through another's eyes. We become renewed by giving our love away—in our relationships, our work, our communities, and most important, to ourselves.

Equally important is the action of letting love *in*. We do harm to ourselves and to those around us when we withhold the events of our day, when we brush off a compliment, or when we refuse to let our mates hold and comfort us. We not only starve our own heart, but at the same time deprive our partners' heart of the joy of giving.

Sometimes love is not found in the "doing." It is often discovered in the quiet moments, in the nurturing of ourselves or others, in the space we create in our lives for love to enter.

The folly of chasing after love is reflected in the story of the Zen student searching for enlightenment. He was so overzealous that he spent morning, noon, and night meditating and praying, and seldom stopped to eat or sleep. His Zen teacher worried as he watched his student become weaker and more exhausted each day. Eventually, he sat down with him and expressed his concern.

"Why do you not eat and get the rest that your body and spirit deserve?" he asked.

"Because I seek enlightenment and there is not a moment to waste."

The teacher placed his hand on the student's shoulder and replied, "What makes you rush ahead after enlightenment? Perhaps all your hurrying carries you *away* from what you seek. Maybe enlightenment is actually behind you, and all you need to do is stand still and let it catch up with you!"

This story reminds me that we can choose to judge ourselves, or to love ourselves. When we are in judgment, we become carried away by the failures and heartbreaks of the past or transported forward into the idealistic fantasies of the future. We hurry backward and forward, desperately seeking the love that already rests patiently inside our own hearts, waiting to be discovered. In the moments that we consciously transcend judgment, self-criticism, and self-doubt, we create the environment for compassion and love for ourselves as well as others.

The effects of experiencing genuine compassion reach far beyond our own lives. It can transform our world in ways we could never imagine. Rollo May once described compassion as being in a music shop, and plucking a single string of one violin. Then, the same string on all the other violins in the shop begins to resonate.

It is the willingness to receive and *be* received that is the most fulfilling and enduring of our shared moments. Through our willingness to participate in and to witness each other's growth, we become guardians of each other's souls, guides for each other's journeys. Then we can lead each other into the light as well as into the dark places—the abyss of old hurts, childhood wounds, and long-held fears, which must be illuminated and understood if we are to grow.

The poet Rainer Maria Rilke wrote: "For one human being to love another; that is perhaps the most difficult of all our tasks, the ultimate, the last test and proof, the work for which all other work is but preparation." I often find that the degree to which I am able to accomplish this labor of love is proportional to the degree of importance that I give to it; that the expression of love is the highest priority and good that we can accomplish while we are here on earth.

Love is there—always. It lives as we live. This is the essence that gives breath to our bodies and to our souls. This is the breath of God. It infuses each of us with life and purpose. It endows us with the grace to give and receive the way our bodies breathe out and breathe in. In the end, the measure of our lives will be the sum total of the love that we have shared; of those selfless, loving moments that coalesce to define a life whose marrow and being is the expression of our birthright.

THE SMOKE AROUND THE HEART

BY *Joan Borysenko, Ph.D.*

"People want to be of service but worry about being selfish. Yet if you're not of service to yourself, you are being selfish, because you'll never be able in a loving way to connect with a larger network, let alone with one other person."

IT'S AN INVIOLABLE LAW. And that's the nicest part about it: What you give, you also receive.

I recently attended the wedding shower of a friend. In her midforties, she was marrying for the first time. In the perennial optimism of marriage, it was hoped to be the only time. There were about a dozen women there, and in what I thought was a sweet as well as useful idea, we were all asked to comment on what the most critical aspect of a loving relationship is.

It was as fascinating to hear what others said — each in her turn serious, funny, or outright ribald — as it was to wonder what would come to me when my turn came.

What I tried to say is this: *One of the most important aspects of a loving relationship is gratitude to the other for the gifts he or she bestows.* And this is a gratitude that must be acknowledged and must be spoken. It's vitally important to be constantly thanking other people for the loving things they do.

This act falls under the general category of what I call Not Taking Anything for Granted: not taking life for granted, not taking other people for granted, but recognizing that every time someone presents you with an act of kindness, he or she has given you a gift. It's a simple process of acknowledgment: Ah, this is a gift; it didn't have to be. And then thanking the person for it.

You need to stay alert to the fact that love itself is a gift. To receive it, you have to do something, like say, "Thanks." It's such a simple thing, like the old Shaker song, "Simple Gifts." Just because they're simple doesn't mean they're not valuable.

Another part of the giving and receiving of love is the importance of honesty and communication. Because often what passes for love is not love at all. An analogy is that what often passes for patience is not really patience at all but impatience, strained to its absolute limit. Frequently, what is considered loving is accepting from another things that are less than what you would wish them to be, yet not saying anything about it. Then you store up these moments, resentments build, and eventually stacks blow. This unspoken debris blocks the paths for both giving and receiving.

To keep the channels open and clear requires a willingness to talk about the things that are difficult. And that is hard for many people. It's hard to say something when you think someone else is not going to like hearing it. How could that be thought of as loving? But it is loving. And the more you can whittle down the time between the realization that something needs to be said and actually saying it, the better off you are. Honest communication is a skill, and it correlates with your ability to be able to truly give and receive love.

This notion is sometimes obscured in spirituality. When people think of spirituality, love, the sense of interconnectedness and loving-kindness, the ability to give and receive love, it gets a little fuzzy and sounds so wonderful. "I love you and you love me and, gee, isn't it all great?"

There are wonderful spiritual principles at work in this world, but it's too easy to forget the very basic psychological processes that are also a vital part of it. God, remember, lives in the details.

The details for everyone — but in some ways, I believe, particularly for women — are to learn to be self-aware, honest, and able to handle their emotional lives in a way that's going to be best for them. Then it will also work for others. Women tend to be very nurturing, very compassionate, very good at giving love. They are a little bit less good at receiving it in return. If they bury their own needs, they don't receive what they need and eventually start to build resentment about giving to others. Then they're in the bind that has many names, one of them being codependency.

The net result: They've given away themselves, and now there's nothing left. In their compassion and desire to help everybody, they lose themselves or fall into a rut of manipulation. But in the end, they find there's nothing left to give, no peace of mind, and all this goodwill has become pitched into a well of anger.

I'm often asked in workshops, "How is it that I can aim

for living a life of compassion and forgiveness, but wind up bitter, burned out, and codependent?"

Often we teach a kind of meditation in workshops that the Tibetan Buddhist tradition calls *Tonglen*, meaning the meditation of giving and receiving. It's a very graphic visualization exercise. You do it first for yourself, because Buddhists understand that unless you give something to yourself first, you won't have anything to give anybody else anyway. You have to take care of yourself first.

Then you do it for loved ones. Then you do it for people you might be in conflict with. And, gradually, you do it further and further out. If you were practicing the true Tibetan Buddhist method, you would do it for all the beings on all seven levels of creation.

First you visualize your own pain as smoke around your heart. You inhale that smoke into the light within your own heart and then when that smoke dissipates, you exhale your heart-light back to yourself. And you do that for others—breathing in their pain and breathing back your happiness, the wholeness of your own true nature. What tends to happen when people do this is, first, relief—because people inherently know that if they don't take care of themselves, there is no way to take care of anybody else.

But what's so wonderful about the Tibetan image is that when you compassionately take on the pain of someone else, you don't store it. It burns up, dissipates in your own heart, and leaves you with extra energy in the form of light; it illuminates you, even as you breathe it back at them.

The meditation exercise points up this basic psychological principle—that you need to make sure that you take care of yourself first. When you don't, the bind you get into is taking on others' pain and problems and then looking for your payback. So you walk around like an emotional beggar with your heart hanging out. And the recipients of your beneficence are disempowered and probably resentful.

Untangling this process is a serious problem, discovering the difference between truly giving and receiving love, and storing others' psychic pain or trying to fix their life. You can disempower them and injure yourself, because you've given without leaving enough for yourself.

There's a wonderful poem by Mary Oliver, "The Journey," which ends with the line that the only person you can save is yourself. Nothing could be truer. People want to be of service but worry about being selfish. Yet if you're not of service to yourself, you are being selfish, because you'll never be able in a loving way to connect with a larger network, let alone with one other person.

I wish there were a term other than *codependency*, because people tend to associate that word only with addiction. I think that codependency involves a much larger principle. You can tell that there's something wrong with the personal equation in a relationship if you don't feel enough love coming back to you. Again, it's a very simple thing, a "what's wrong with this picture?" scenario. But you need to look at the picture in two ways — directly at yourself and also at the situation.

It's like the notion of surrender in the Serenity Prayer, in which you ask for the serenity to accept the things you cannot change, the courage to change the things you can, and the wisdom to know the difference. If you look at your life and say, "Something's wrong; I'm pissed off all the

٭e, and I'm not getting the love that I need," it would be ridiculous to add, "Well, gee, if everything was spiritually right, I could just surrender to this situation and keep loving everybody and feel fine."

It may be exactly the wrong tack to surrender to the situation. You may need to tell your friend to find somebody else to hang out with, you may need to get out of your marriage, or you may need to use tough love with your children. You can't tiptoe past the basic feedback of the psychological world in which we live, hoping to ascend to the larger, richer spiritual realm. Saying "If I just gave and received love properly, everything would fall into line" is a little too easy, I'm afraid. It's the old spiritual bypass routine.

It's not easy to learn to ask for what you need. It's not easy to ask a child, a friend, or a spouse for what you need. Nor is it easy for people to ask the Great Spirit, to ask the great mystery, for what they need, either. But it must be learned. I don't know an easy way of learning to do it, but we learn by doing. Just ask. The Great Spirit isn't a mind reader, and neither is your spouse.

I've always been in favor of recognizing the need for mucking around in the mines — learning the basic principles we need to deal with. Even the dark side has its lessons. Anger is a great teacher in learning to give and receive love, because it's pure feedback. It's a clanging gong that announces, "Something is radically wrong." The message may be painful, but it's also simple and clear.

The joyous message is also simple and clear. Being grateful, encouraging other people, saying "What you did made my life better" encourages others to do more of that, to be more loving — until, we hope, you're surrounded by encouraging people, who make you feel good simply being in their presence.

It's an inviolable law. And that's the nicest part about it: What you give, you also receive. The expression of gratitude is itself a simple gift. But the effect is huge: it creates more love in the world.

GOD IS LOVE

BY *Hugh and Gayle Prather*

"Indeed love heals, but being loved does not. Being loved merely holds the door open for healing, for happiness, for fulfillment, for 'getting our needs met.' But to walk through that door, we must love."

OURS IS THE first generation to blame our parents. Now we lead the way again in becoming the first generation to blame our children. To sum it all up, one final self-help book must be written: *I'm a Victim — You're Not.*

So when our attention turns to love, we quite consistently believe that the only love worth having is love that is directed at us. In all our relationships — social, romantic, political, parental — we are interested in only those who can commit to *us*, amuse *us*, meet *our* needs. We have turned the prayer of Saint Francis on its head. The doctrine of our times now reads "May I not so much seek to console, as to be consoled. To understand, as to be understood. To love, as to be loved. For it is in getting that I receive."

Even a casual look around at the devastated families, abandoned children, and betrayed friendships should make it plain that this approach does not work. How much more evidence do we need that some truths never change? Perhaps in the realm of the eternal, giving and receiving are simultaneous. But in the temporal world, giving comes first. This basic truth is at the heart of every major religion and mystical teaching that has come to earth over the last several thousand years. You experience love by loving. It is that simple.

It would be impossible for the two of us to talk about love in anything other than devotional terms. Trying to do otherwise would force us to leave out most of what we have learned in the past eighteen years of counseling families and especially what we have learned in the thirty-one years of our marriage, the most important lesson being the extraordinary potential of love to transform those who exercise it.

Let us give an example. After almost fifteen years of a marriage in which Gayle committed to Hugh, but Hugh played out his family's old pattern of disloyalty, Hugh finally started coming to his senses. He realized that he had in Gayle someone who truly loved him. In fact, Gayle was perhaps the only person in Hugh's life who had ever loved him unconditionally. And yet, despite having had someone stand by him for fifteen years, someone who saw the goodness in him more clearly than he saw it in himself, Hugh had remained basically untouched by this love.

How could that be? Doesn't love heal?

Indeed love heals, but being loved does not. Being loved merely holds the door open for healing, for happiness, for fulfillment, for "getting our needs met." But to walk through that door, we must love. If being loved healed, all creatures great and small would now be perfect, for God has loved them all and always will.

During the many years that Gayle was committed to Hugh, she grew spiritually, she was basically happy, and most of the damage she still carried from childhood was released. Hugh, who did little more during this time than devote himself to his own pleasure, did not grow spiritually, was not freed from the effects of his childhood, and was not only unhappy but was periodically suicidal. It was not until Hugh committed to Gayle and, yes — as co-dependent as it sounds — put Gayle's happiness first that Hugh was finally healed of his destructive pattern.

Please remember that this occurred many years after the honeymoon period. Gayle no longer had youth. She never had money. She was merely a person. But a funny thing happens when we love a person — any person. We are acting a little like God. And when we act a little like God, we feel a little like God.

At that fifteen-year juncture in our marriage, we made a joint decision never to leave each other, never even to threaten to leave — no matter how angry we became. And we set aside time each day to work on various aspects of our relationship. We made these work sessions sacred and tried never to skip or interrupt one. We don't think it's a coincidence that within weeks of making this commitment, we both began to feel God's presence and that a few months later our first child was born.

Everyone is well acquainted with the fear of "loving too much." For example, people fear that having a life partner demands endless sacrifice: no more free evenings and weekends. No more leaving and returning as they wish.

No more spending money on themselves alone. No more time to pursue their long-term goals. In short, no more *them*. Yet once they have abandoned their dreams and succumbed to having a permanent partner, they discover that their fears are just beginning. For now comes parenthood. A mistake in their child's nutrition could lead to a fatal illness. A mistake in discipline could create a sociopath. A mistake in education could wipe out entire career opportunities. As their children mature, people worry that if they don't push them out of the nest quickly enough, sons will be emasculated and daughters will become "caregivers."

Most little children not only love their parents but know with all their being that their parents love them. In working with families in which there is abuse, time and again we have been awed by how powerful is children's perception of the spiritual bond between themselves and their parents. Even when they are being horrendously mistreated, these little ones refuse to believe that their parents do not love them. We have observed that the amount and duration of abuse necessary to convince these kids otherwise amazes and inspires us all over again.

Judging by how many adults seek to go back and reconnect with parents who abandoned them, searching sometimes for years to locate them, we suspect that the spiritual knowledge of the connection between two people is never completely lost to anyone. It's interesting how often the adults who undertake this search are happy with how their adopted or foster parents have treated them. Being raised lovingly appears to make people *more* likely to seek out other love connections. These adult children often do not have even childhood memories of the lost parent, but they will say, as one man was recently quoted in our local paper,

"I will always think of my adoptive mother who raised me as my real mom, but I still want to find my natural mother." The untouchable connection between spirit and spirit, between soul and soul, between God and the children of God, is a gentle memory that lies quietly in every heart. When we choose to do so, we can awaken it and know love.

Although the following attitude is no longer prevalent in most hospitals, in the 1970s when we started our support group for parents who were grieving the loss of a child, hospital personnel often discouraged parents from "getting too attached" to a baby who was dying, explaining that there was really nothing that could be done for their baby and that if they allowed themselves to become deeply bonded to the child, the loss when the child died would only be that much more painful.

However, some parents chose not to take this advice, instead devoting themselves in every possible way to loving their infant daughter or son. They would touch them, feed them if allowed to, pray for them, or just stay in the hospital and watch over them. In our grief-support group we noticed a marked difference between those parents who had held back on their love and those who hadn't. Contrary to what was predicted, the feeling of loss was much greater for the moms or dads who had distanced themselves, and their grief was particularly resistant to healing. But the parents who had loved without caution healed quickly and usually turned immediately to helping other parents. They were also much more likely to feel the comforting presence of their child in their daily life. They either knew or came to know that it was something much more than the child's body that they loved.

Does any of this mean that because we love someone,

we now must give up all the things we like to do? Does it mean we must let our spouse, our child, our parent, or our boss become a tyrant, the cruel princess or prince of our kingdom? Does it mean that every whim and proclivity of our partner or our kids somehow carries more wisdom or spiritual correctness than our own thoughts and desires? Obviously not. But it does mean that there will be many times when it will *appear* that we must sacrifice our plans for the welfare of someone else.

The mistake we are now making is in thinking we know what love *looks* like. Love isn't getting on our hands and knees, wiping up the footprints of a saint. It isn't necessarily more loving to say yes than to say no, to be submissive than to be firm, to disregard our own needs than to meet them. In fact, loving is not a behavior at all; it is a quality of the heart and mind. But the fear we now have about that quality is crippling our chances for personal happiness and growth. It is, in fact, keeping us from experiencing God.

Eventually, we see that where we expected sacrifice, our love laid a gift; where we expected boredom, our love laid a new interest; where we expected a dead-end day, our love transformed it into fulfillment. In making these seemingly endless sacrifices, we received a reality far more lasting than had we gone about our usual loveless life in our usual loveless way.

God is the river of light in which we all bathe. This brilliance flows through the core of every living thing. Nothing within the warring, separated images of the world reflects the unity of God, and yet the unseen waters of love surround us in all circumstances — no matter how petty or shameful or tragic they may be.

The uncomplicated reason that the experience of God must follow our decision to make another person's happiness as important as our own is that God *is* oneness. God is what creates and sustains and joins the spirit. God is our shared heart and mind. Although within the world God goes unrecognized, those who see their oneness with just one other living thing cannot fail to see God.

LOVING INSIDE OUT

BY *Patricia Love, Ed.D.*

*"I believe that we invite people into our lives, especially
our partners, to be our teachers. The irony of this is that,
having invited them to be our teachers, we then go kicking and screaming into the classroom!"*

FILLING MY LIFE with love starts with controlling
my mind. Over the years, I have learned that I possess not only an active mind but a slippery one. If
I'm not attentive, my mind can drift to wherever there is
energy, sometimes toward the negative areas. For years I
drove myself with negative energy, constantly criticizing
myself for what I was doing wrong. It has been a continual process of discovering that I have a choice about how
I see myself and my life, how I feel about things. The more
positive choices I make, the more love flows freely into
my life.

Now I understand that self-love is about honoring ourselves, literally actualizing the love in our life in ways that

are unique and real to us. I have learned that I must love myself first. This has become a conscious task and, at times, a very difficult one. One day at a time, I still have to focus my deliberate intention to offset my history, to remind myself that I am lovable and loved.

The outcome of nurturing this internal fullness is love; I get full, then the people who are close to me get full. I am present for them, raw and fresh. Living this way has freed me to be a conduit, a channel for love to flow through to others and then back to me. Anyone can do this with her or his life. Just trust the process, stay with it, and understand that it doesn't always work in an orderly fashion.

I believe that we invite people into our lives, especially our partners, to be our teachers. The irony of this is that, having invited them to be our teachers, we then go kicking and screaming into the classroom! But if we can trust our choice, and trust the progress of our education, we can learn much as we follow the path that our partners lay out for us. Our partners are in a unique position to give us an invitation into ourselves, lead us into our blind spots.

One way that our partners offer us teachings is through sexual intimacy. This is a unique contribution our partners make and can continue to make through all our years together. Yet sometimes we forget that after the initial physical passion fades, there is something deeper to create, to allow to unfold. So often we lose out on this wonderful teaching place of trust and love and mutually discovered wisdom because we get lost in how to communicate our needs and desires. Without a way to understand each other, we get bogged down in lost expectations and misunderstandings. We need to listen to our partners, truly listen, to allow the intimacy to grow. If we can find a way to do this, we will know a deep peacefulness that comes from the growth of love and trust and shared history. The commitment, the loyalty, the love we share can create a unique well of love to draw upon for all the areas of life.

The lessons our partners teach also come from areas of apparent conflict. One of the things I find in my own practice is that the partners often have their own answers, for the relationship, for themselves, and for each other. They just need a midwife to birth the solutions, a safe environment in which to listen for the lessons. Ironically, if we can let ourselves listen, truly listen to what our mates are telling us, move beyond the style or the tone or the particular words, we may hear that they are speaking some piece of our own truth. Listening for this message is a difficult, humbling task, but if we can let down our walls enough to let it happen, we achieve new and ever-deepening intimacy.

Communication is essential in creating intimacy. We need to open ourselves to the real messages our partners are sending us, not only about ourselves but about the partners' own needs and desires. When we can receive the true messages and respond unselfishly sometimes, focusing on our mates' needs, we find deep and lasting partner-love. When this happens around sexual needs and practices, greater fulfillment results. But it needs to happen outside the bedroom as well. The partners need to connect regularly throughout each day, freely and fully sharing thoughts, feelings, dreams, and desires. We may still need to discuss who should pay what bill when, but we shouldn't forget to give a little hug and little kiss as we're passing by! In the same way that we listen more freely, less critically, we need to speak more carefully, choose our words more wisely. So often I have seen how couples get caught up in the feeling of the moment, forgetting to measure their words. The sparks fly, and the message gets lost. Learning to communicate carefully is work — hard work. It may be the hardest work we ever do. But all relationships involve work. There are no perfect partners, no perfect relationships. There are relationships, though, in which the partners' needs are met, in which the bond is nourished and therefore endures and provides the teaching that keeps us ever-growing.

Another feature of a deep and meaningful relationship is a willingness of the partners to let the other take center stage sometimes. To be mindful not only of our own needs but of our partners', to be willing to put the other first sometimes, is an essential part of creating a loving, enduring bond. Sincere and loving sacrifice is a beautiful, necessary gift: we may, for example, decide to make love even when we don't feel like it, just because our partners need us. By the same token, our mates may sometimes decide to respect our requirement for solitude, even when they want closeness just then.

Of course, even though we admit our partners into our lives as teachers, we don't follow blindly. Doing so would be as destructive as ignoring their role in our own development as people. We must learn to trust our own inner wisdom. For years I denied my intuition, my gut feelings, and my mental acuity. It was a terrible, painful deprivation that I've worked to overcome. We all need to trust our own minds, our own feelings, our own emotions, our senses, and our bodies. When we do so, there is a wonderful blending of the inner and the outer. We can become receptive to our partners, and the lessons they have for us.

Some people find themselves continually rejecting the lessons their partners and the people close to them offer. They feel that others are letting them down. Sometimes our loved ones do fail us, but just as often the gap may actually be caused by our own lack of self-trust. If we keep saying, "I trust these people and they keep disappointing me," then it may be that we are actually disappointing ourselves. If we are out of harmony with ourselves, not listening to our own inner whisperings about what is safe and true, the proper messages can't get through. And we feel let down.

When we deny ourselves the benefits of our own inner wisdom, we deny ourselves self-love and self-care, and we're less effective and fulfilled in our own lives — for what we are blind to in ourselves, we are blind to in others. But when we tune in to our own deepest messages, we can create a space of love around us and can live in a context of love that nurtures not only ourselves but the world.

THE MIRROR OF LOVE

BY *Harville Hendrix, Ph.D.*

"One of my favorite sayings is that love does not create marriage — intentional, conscious marriage creates love. The same is true in all relationships. Love is born in the midst of conflict. And this is how we have been able to keep the dream of love and romance alive."

MY WIFE, HELEN, and I have known each other for eighteen years and have been married for thirteen. Recently, we were asked to present a keynote address on the subject of "keeping the dream alive." We were asked to talk about our relationship and the techniques we have devised to keep our love growing and thriving. At first, Helen and I were intimidated — we certainly didn't want to present ourselves as models, but we also didn't want to present ourselves as too flawed. Finally, we decided we'd just tell the truth — that our current relationship is the result of thirteen years of struggle, years that have been every bit as challenging for us as for anybody else.

One of the major difficulties that we encountered over the years was an inability to make romantic moments last. It seemed that every time we created a romantic moment, whether it was reading poetry to each other, going to a movie, or having dinner at a fine restaurant, we just couldn't seem to hold it. It would last for that evening, maybe — but we would definitely blow it within a few days, if not that very night. Then we'd be back into tension with each other. So, at a certain point, we both just stopped trying to be romantic. Why work at what wasn't working?

Once we realized what was happening, we began to look at our relationship with a critical eye. We found that our romantic moments were sabotaged when we became analytical of a trait or behavior in the other person. For instance, we would have different points of view about a movie and we'd show little appreciation for the other's ideas. We would criticize each other. And then we made an interesting discovery: we each possessed the very same traits that we criticized in the other. And not wanting to accept a particular disliked trait in ourselves, we would assign it to the other. We came to understand that rejection of a trait or behavior in the other was actually a form of self-rejection. We concluded that unconscious self-hatred was the source of our conflict and probably fueled the power struggles of many (if not all) couples.

Not only does this unconscious self-hatred get in the way of expressing love, it also interferes with receiving love. You cannot feel worthy of accepting love if you unconsciously hate yourself or even hate some parts of yourself. We finally realized that in order to increase our self-love, we had to learn to love in the other person the trait we most disliked in ourselves. And we had to stop criticizing each other, because the more we criticized a disliked trait in the other, the more we increased our unconscious self-hatred. We theorized that the deeper recesses of the brain aren't able to distinguish between the inside and the outside, and so they receive the acceptance and love that we give to each other as if it were self-love. It also translates our criticisms of each other into self-rejection. Putting it all together, we came to the conclusion that self-love is the paradoxical achievement of loving another, *especially* that part of the other which we reject in ourselves.

To this end, we created a system for developing what we call a conscious marriage. In such a relationship, conflict that usually tears apart couples is reframed as an unconscious attempt to resolve issues and connect at a deeper level. Criticism, the coercive language of conflict, creates defense and distance rather than contact. What people need to do as couples is to cooperate with their unconscious, which is trying to maintain the couple's essential connection and restore their original wholeness. To do so, we developed a special form of communication that we believe is essential to any relationship, especially a loving one. This process is called intentional dialogue and was inspired by the Jewish philosopher and theologian Martin Buber.

The process includes three steps. The first step involves what we call direct mirroring. It is designed to help the listener hear the other person without any interpretation or emotional reaction: the listener merely reflects back the speaker's words. All emotional interpretations of what the words mean are dropped. The listener merely paraphrases back to the speaker what the speaker just said, *without judgment.*

Step two is what I call validation. Once the listener has heard the other person without adding any interpretation, he or she then must try to see the issue from the other's point of view. An example could sound something like, "What you are saying to me makes sense, *because* . . ." Then the listener completes the sentence, filling in the blanks after *because*. Another example: "Given the fact that I was late, it makes sense to me that you would think I didn't care or that I didn't take my obligation seriously." This statement forces the listener to see that the logic in the other person's mind is equal in value and truth to the logic and truth in his or her own mind. It's a very self-transcendent act and a great equalizer!

The third part of the dialogue process is empathic relating, or truly understanding the partner's feelings. When you are able to mirror the feelings of the other person, validate the other, and see through his or her eyes, then you have become empathic. An instance of empathic relating: "Given the sense of what you are experiencing, I can imagine that you must feel hurt or excited or angry." Amazingly, if you keep practicing empathic behavior, you find that you eventually begin to experience the actual feelings and inner world of the other person. Through empathy, you share the center and experience of your essential connectedness while retaining your unique individuality. We call it freeing the partner from the prison of our conceptions.

Helen and I, with the help of Buber, see this process as discovering the "thou-ness" of the other person without surrendering the "I-ness" of yourself. I am not really capable of loving you until I surrender my position that my way is the right way, until I can see the logic of the way your mind works, and until I can experience your feelings as yours, separate from mine. It's when I can truly see and experience your "thou-ness" that I can begin to love. Up to that point, what I may profess to love is actually what I imagine you to be. I am only really loving my own representation and therefore am really only loving myself. True love is when I can experience and honor your otherness, apart from my needs and expectations. And I can maintain that love, even though my experience of you may not always be either satisfying to me or a way to serve my needs.

We have also been able to use this process when dealing with our children. Just recently, I was frustrated with Hunter, who is ten, and began to express my feelings in a strong way. Instead of reacting by defending himself, he began to mirror my thoughts and feelings, which rapidly brought the tension to an end. Another time, during a car trip, I was expressing some anger to my wife about something she had done. My daughter Leah then leaned over the front seat and whispered into Helen's ear, "Mirror him, Mom." That effectively ended the scene! But the best part of all this is that the level of emotional connection between Helen and me is now being experienced by our children.

Helen and I also use intentional dialogue with our adult children. Whenever they are upset with us, we invite them into dialogue. The conversation sometimes is very long, but it always ends with connection rather than conflict, distance, and alienation. The dialogue process creates such a level of connectedness that the energy just flows.

You can also use this process for responding to positive experiences, not just conflictual ones, and it enhances the communication and deepens the connection between you and the other person. Mirroring the positive reinforces the experience — in turn reinforcing the behavior that brought about the good experience in the first place.

In my work and in my life I have seen how feelings of being unloved have more to do with a person's own unconscious self-hatred and self-rejection than with a true absence of love. These unconscious feelings can make it impossible for someone to take in any information that counters them — namely, that the person is loved. So the question is, How can you get in touch with your unconscious self-hatred and begin to modulate it?

You can do this by becoming aware of what you really don't like in your partner or your children or in humankind in general. What is it that really bugs you? I find that I get annoyed when my wife, Helen, overindulges in sweets or spends what I think is too much time on the telephone. But then I also sometimes overindulge or withdraw from people by spending too much time on the computer. Once you can truthfully figure out what bothers you in other people, you probably have accessed your own self-hatred, which has then been projected on someone else.

How do you transcend this projection? I have found that I can learn from looking at the function of a behavior in Helen's life (let's say, talking on the telephone) and seeing what it means for my life. Then I try to figure out if there's some part of my own behavior that is like hers (being on the computer too long). If I reframe Helen's behavior as functional for her, serving her in an important way, and value it — even support it and love it — I can then begin to experience what I call parallel self-love. While I am loving her, I am also loving myself. I have bypassed the unconscious self-hatred. Every time I look at another person without judgment but with understanding and empathy, I am doing the same thing for myself. The result is that I experience the love I give.

As we have increased our own self-love through loving each other, we have found that we don't need to set up romantic events and times to express our love. We have created a safe place and, as a result, feel romantic all the time. If we get too busy, then we can just go back to the intentional dialogue system and give ourselves some time to reconnect. And there doesn't have to be a conflict for us to communicate in this way. It is my belief that it's in the safe space of seeing the other as a "thou" that love is born and sustained. One of my favorite sayings is that love does not create marriage — intentional, conscious marriage creates love. The same is true in all relationships. Love is born in the midst of conflict. And this is how we have been able to keep the dream of love and romance alive.

4.

Love Is a Verb

"The love we give away is the only love we keep."

— ELBERT HUBBARD (1859–1915)

LISTENING

FOR LOVE

BY *James and Salle Merrill Redfield*

"When our intention is geared toward love, when we trust that the deeper, mystical part of us is always lying beneath these negative feelings waiting for a chance to surface, the letting go becomes easier. It's almost as though we're getting out of our own way so that we can come back to this mystical state of love, this most natural state of being."

B RINGING LOVE INTO your life is the way to lead the most fulfilling life. Love is the force, the energy that animates creativity and peace in each one of us. And on the collective level, when we center ourselves and bring love into our being, we engage in the historical process, in purposeful evolution.

History is all about trying to pull more and more love into the physical dimension. Throughout the whole story of human civilization, we see watershed moments in which more love, understanding, and connectedness — and, consequently, more peace—have been brought into our world. This happens as each person brings more and more love into his or her everyday consciousness, not just when he or she thinks about it or when someone brings up the subject, but as an ongoing state of being. As more people act lovingly, they bring even more love into the world. Loving, we believe, is the very purpose of human existence.

Our opportunities for healing the world have grown even greater. Technology has created a smaller world, a smaller community for humanity. We're all so much closer together than ever before. It's more difficult to deny the pain that exists elsewhere. The pain in the war-torn parts of the world is really our own pain, a pain that we all share. Our own individual actions are extremely important because we are all part of this larger matrix, a global web. Our own acts of love build energy that we can all draw upon. Even a little bit of love on our part can create an important foundation for future generations to build upon.

In our own personal lives, we bring in love in two ways: by actively seeking it and by clearing the way for it to come. This is an everyday process. When the two of us wake up in the morning we try to express how much love we are feeling. If we're slamming doors and "kicking the dog," it means there is some frustration and irritation in ourselves that needs to be cleared. At that point, when we're honest and address our feelings, it simply becomes a matter of "letting go," which clears the way and allows the love to return.

How do we "let go" and clear the way? By being completely honest, fully acknowledging our feelings, no matter what they are, no matter how nonloving they might be.

It is only when we are fully conscious of our feelings that we can process them and let them go. When we recognize negative feelings — instead of denying them — they can pass through us, thereby clearing the way for love to re-enter our lives. The two of us transcend our own negativity by making sure we're not identifying with it. We all have nonloving as well as loving feelings within us, but the nonloving part of ourselves is not the "true self." The true, or higher, part of the self is always seeking the state that mystics talk about, the state in which we are filled with a universal love and a peaceful euphoria.

The key to this state of mind lies in letting go and accepting whatever is happening in our lives at the moment. This acceptance doesn't mean we can't or shouldn't strive to be in a different place or to improve our life. Everyone's life is always flowing, and we all need to participate in the forward movement. But, at the same time, we need to accept whatever is in the moment.

Most of our frustration, anger, and nonlove in life is the result of wanting life to be different. We need to recognize and accept these feelings — and then let them go. (It's simple — but not easy!) If we identify with our negative, nonloving feelings, if we dwell on them and hold on to them, if we believe that they are all we have, it's extremely difficult to release them. But when our intention is geared toward love, when we trust that the deeper, mystical part of us is always lying beneath these negative feelings waiting for a chance to surface, the letting go becomes easier. It's almost as though we're getting out of our own way so that we can come back to this mystical state of love, this most natural state of being. Life is a continual process of first noticing and accepting what interferes with our loving feelings, then allowing the negative to leave so that the love can return. This is a day-to-day, moment-to-moment experience. As we trust in the process, we open ourselves to greater and greater amounts of love.

We can help others in this process, as they can help us, and so, actively bring love into our lives. Listening—really listening—is a critical part of filling our lives, and the world, with love. It's important to listen at a deep level to those around us and to enter into a dialogue with them, validating what they are saying. The more we listen in this fashion, the greater the love, respect, and compassion we feel for one another. Sometimes we are in such a hurry that we forget where the other person is coming from—are they hurt, confused, angry, or in need of love? Slowing down and listening lets us hear the truth in the moment. And it's the key to better understanding others and ourselves.

Try this powerful exercise: find someone whom you can really listen to, and who will listen to you, and ask him or her to simply sit quietly with you and repeat back what you say. This simple act of hearing your own words mirrored back, perhaps as much as anything else, allows you to feel truly heard and understood. (You will probably then want to let the other person have a turn, with you reflecting back his or her words.)

Developing listening skills is especially helpful in dealing with another person's anger. If we're angry at each other but take the time to slow down and really pay attention to what is happening within the person with whom we are in conflict, almost without exception we can say to ourselves, "I've felt that way, too." That realization enables us to bring forth our compassion and understanding in almost any situation. We can say to ourselves, "She's not a terrible, mean person, as it might seem on the surface, but rather a person in pain who needs love." Staying in this loving, listening frame of mind—and staying out of the negative—gives us the clarity to solve problems rather than latch onto them and make them worse. On a personal level, this type of listening keeps the two of us very bonded and connected. It's difficult at times, particularly if we're disagreeing, but that is when we need it most.

Similarly, an interaction may be driven by what is going on inside ourselves. We may see this in the rise of judgmental, nonloving thoughts. When we can let go of these negative thoughts and feelings, we can stop blaming the other person and re-ignite our own loving feelings that, in turn, allow us to truly love this person. Then we have the power to change the situation, because we have changed ourselves. If we wait for the other person to change first, we're missing the opportunity to grow and to expand our own love. (And we're setting ourselves up for disappointment! Each of us is on his or her own journey, responsible for his or her own course corrections; we can only change ourselves, not others.) Love, remember, comes from inside of us. It's not something we wait to get. The amount of love that we have inside ourselves defines the amount we can give to others. So, in a sense, the most important inner work is simply learning to love ourselves fully. This allows us to do our part in filling the world with love.

Even horrible situations can be seen as opportunities to learn more about our own nonloving ways. When we take a look at the hatred around the world, we can see that we all have prejudices, anger, and mistrust we need to let go. We can all make a difference on the global level by working on ourselves as individuals. The anger in ourselves can be replaced with love. As we awaken to ever-present love, we can begin to visualize this love expanding into other parts of the world.

A natural extension of filling our lives with love is not trying to control where life is going. And then, something synchronistic occurs — someone calls, we get an inspired idea to pursue that day, we cross paths with someone we haven't seen in years. Once we let go, our higher selves take over and life takes its own course. Days become more productive, creative, enjoyable, and filled with wonderful, mysterious events.

As the process continues, we get in touch with whatever our greatest contribution might be. This is different for everybody. Some of us might lead prayer vigils for the war-torn parts of the world. Others might raise our children, transform our given occupation, or simply smile at our customers. No one's contribution is more important than anyone else's. We're all simply doing what we're led to do by our higher selves. And we make our best contribution to the ongoing spiritual evolution of the world.

The love we all want is available. It starts within us, but it's everywhere else, too. "Seek and you will find." Don't be willing to accept an ordinary life and don't be willing to accept the models of our previous generations. We have the potential to transcend and break through previous forms of negativity by redefining reality and what we believe possible. If we look for love, we will surely find it. At first it can take some "faking it till you make it," meaning that filling our lives with love begins with the intention to do so as well as knowing that it is possible. And as we hold on to this vision, and work with it, the experiences we are looking for begin to enter our lives. Have patience, let go — and love will happen.

LOVE WINS

BY *Samahria Lyte Kaufman*

"Living love passionately — and the key word is pas-sionately — creates joy all around us. The passion ig-nites the love into flames that are seen and felt by anyone with whom we're engaged."

WE LOVE ONLY to the extent that we ourselves are happy. Before we can truly love an-other, we have to learn to love and accept ourselves. For me this process was difficult, as I did not love myself at all.

I took the first step when I began to cease judging those negative characteristics I perceived in myself. I began to learn to accept who and how I was, without needing to change all these things. Once I accepted an aspect of my-self, then changing it was much easier. I realized I was at every moment doing the best I could.

I decided that the power for creating my own happi-ness — my own unhappiness as well — was in my hands and no one else's. This power was not dependent upon what others said or the situations that arose in my life. I was not a victim, but in fact a creator.

I made happiness and love my first priority — even before I got what I wanted in any given situation or knew whether life was going to work out the way I thought best. Like the carrot in front of the horse, I held this priority before my eyes, and this focus helped me change myself. With each change I made, I became happier; and the happier I became, the more loving I was.

An example of how powerful these changes can be involves the story of my son, Raun. At eighteen months old, Raun was diagnosed as autistic. The slide into autism took about six months, during which time he went from a child who looked at everyone, laughing and enjoying his interactions with people, to a child who was completely disconnected from people.

We sought out everybody we could to research what treatments were being done with autistic children. The main form of therapy back then was — and is still today — behavior modification. We saw that these children's behaviors were being judged as bad and inappropriate. We didn't feel that way about Raun. Our conclusion was that he was acting in this manner because he needed to; he must be taking care of himself in some way.

With that in mind, I began to work with him myself, twelve hours a day, seven days a week, for three and a half years. At that time he was diagnosed as autistic but also as having an I.Q. below 30, and he was totally mute and unresponsive. Just a few months ago, at age twenty-two, Raun graduated from Brown University with a degree in biomedical ethics.

Every time I think about this transformation, I realize it was a miracle made possible because of love. Had I not worked on my own heart so dramatically to learn how to be happy and love myself, I would not have been able to love and, most important, to accept him exactly as he was.

I have a daily practice that helps me create a more loving way of dealing with the world. When I begin to feel even the slightest bit uncomfortable or challenged, I do one of two things. I first question myself to determine what is happening and how I am feeling about it. Then I ask if there is anything that I think I'm going to get from this discomfort. This self-questioning helps me to uncover previously held beliefs that might be counterproductive or even hurtful to who I am now. Once I discover these beliefs that are causing the pain or unhappiness, I can choose to keep or discard them. If I discard these old beliefs, I find my life becomes much more effective. Second, I can realize that what I want is to feel good and loving at that moment—and this becomes my first priority. Then I make that realization into a decision to feel loving.

I feel that when we love in the fullest way possible, without worrying whether our love is reciprocated equally, we are immensely rewarded. Thus, the one who loves the most, wins. It serves me well, because then I don't feel sorry for myself if I love someone more than he or she loves me.

I try to assume the best about people, which doesn't mean being naive. It means knowing that each person has a reason for whatever he or she is doing. We can give other people the benefit of the doubt and stay open to listening and trying to understand them.

It's important to express and demonstrate love—not

only in words but in actions, giving what's important and meaningful to the other person. Often people don't make their love tangible; they don't do the things that matter to the other person, so the other person doesn't *perceive* that he or she is loved.

If someone does something we don't like, we can see it as an opportunity to grow stronger and more loving. When I am dealing with someone who is angry or attacking, rather than seeing myself as put down or hurt by that person, I just say to myself, "This is an incredible opportunity for me; this is happening right now to benefit me." I can ask myself, "What am I going to do with it?" I can get angry right back, I can feel hurt, I can feel diminished in some way, or I can love more and try to express what I think and feel from a perspective of personal strength and power. So we actually use occasions where others are unhappy with us to empower ourselves to feel stronger and more loving. This has been so enlivening for me.

Love is a decision that we can make anytime under any condition, but first we have to know that it is a decision. Everyone wants to love more and be loved more — everyone. Just remember that opening up our awareness, even in a situation that doesn't feel so loving, can soften everything.

Everything I do is based on creating a happy, loving attitude toward myself and others. This is my main aim and focus. When we make our attitude the most important thing, we can inspire others and show by example what it's like to bring forth and share an attitude of love. When people really experience that attitude from another person, they want it for themselves. Living love passionately — and the key word is *passionately* — creates joy all around us. The passion ignites the love into flames that are seen and felt by anyone with whom we're engaged.

When we are more loving, we are more likely to create miracles in our lives. Part of this process is learning to stay present within each moment. Living in the present is very freeing and brings me immediate comfort. Another important ingredient is gratitude. Being grateful is a powerful tool in feeling love toward everything or everyone in our lives. The energy of love we emanate changes everything around us for the better. Person by person, moment to moment, as we love, we change the world.

A Loving Prescription

BY *Andrew Weil, M.D.*

"I doubt that there is much I could do to promote a more loving way of dealing with the world if I weren't connected to that same loving force in myself. Thus, as with so many areas of my life, the work begins within."

I LIVE IN AN especially magical and remote area of the Tucson Valley, bordering a national park. It's a wild and spectacular place of natural beauty. I garden on my land and work to maintain it as a beautiful place around me. This activity helps me stay centered. And this beautiful place is where I meet my patients. Patients come to my home, and I see them in a room that I live in.

It's far from town, so the trip is difficult for some. Patients arrive with much anticipation and expectation. But I don't really receive them as a doctor. I relate to my patients on a very personal level. I don't use any of the formalities that people usually associate with doctors.

Possibly I belabor the old "physician, heal thyself" line, but I doubt that there is much I could do to promote a more loving way of dealing with the world if I weren't connected to that same loving force in myself. Thus, as with so many areas of my life, the work begins within.

My mornings begin in meditation. It's something I do when I first arise, to help keep me centered for the day and able to deal with whatever comes along. It's not hard for me to remember the time before I used to meditate, a time when my moods were far more erratic than they are now.

Part of my meditation is the Buddhist heart meditation. The heart meditation is to imagine filling your heart with love, and then expanding that love out in ever-widening circles. First, open your heart to your immediate vicinity and to the people in your community. Then send love out to the state, to the country, and eventually to the entire world. It is a visual and mental meditation. When I do this practice, I go right through the evolutionary chain. First I cultivate plants and project a lot of love onto them. Then I relate to my pets. I feel great love for my dogs and parrot and send love to them. Next I relate to my children and stepchildren, and on it goes.

I know that my experience of the world is very much determined by my perceptions of it. My consciousness influences and also limits what I see. So by connecting to the source in myself that is loving, I am able to see the love around me. Then the resonance with others can begin.

I think that's what falling in love is all about — you're really projecting what you feel inside you onto another person or onto something out there. I think if people can recognize that this falling-in-love impulse comes from an inner source, then there's always a way of connecting with it — certainly not only in the romantic sense.

The true definition of healing is "to make whole." Too seldom are physicians trained to realize that the remedy can come not necessarily in the form of a pill but in an intangible ingredient we can only wish could be encapsulated.

Love is the one source of sustaining comfort in life, and it is of such force that it has miraculous powers of healing in the physical, mental, and spiritual realms. We must try to cultivate that force and to experience it as habitually as possible.

There's no doubt in my mind of the relationship between mental and emotional states and the state of our health and resistance to disease. I've seen it. A number of my patients have experienced the complete disappearance of chronic symptoms — including severe back pain and auto-immune diseases like lupus — through fortuitously falling in love. Being in a state of love releases such positive energies to flow freely around the body, it can cure any number of ailments.

Do I prescribe falling in love? In a way, I do — though obviously I can't send my patients to the pharmacy for this particular elixir. I often don't even talk directly to patients about love and loving. Yet it is always behind my ideas and my questions to them.

All physicians want to do well for their patients. Yet there is so little being taught to medical doctors today about emotional states and their influences on health. There's nothing about spiritual experiences and their influences on health. There's little about the art of medicine — including the art of listening, communication, and suggestion in the service of healing. I think doctors are relatively untrained in such areas, and I believe it would be healthier for everyone if this were changed.

I look at my patients not just as physical bodies but as mental and emotional beings as well. I am always thinking of suggestions to give them that might enable them to be in healthier mental states. These might be very specific, simple, sensible ideas, such as recommending that patients spend more time in nature, that they buy flowers and keep them in their environment, that they seek out the company of friends who make them feel good. I might recommend to some that they meditate. My suggestions are very individualized, depending on my sense of each patient, what they're open to, and what they're ready for.

Relationships are the greatest challenge that we face as human beings. If living one's own life is difficult, living with another person is incredibly difficult. Yet this is the way in which we really refine our personalities. We are thrown headfirst into all the areas of our deficiencies, forced to confront the many issues that we still need to learn. Yet it is because of this challenge that relationships become a part of our spiritual work.

Just as love flows from within and expands into widening circles, so relationships move in cyclical forms. There is something cyclical about the nature of love between people that allows people to fall away from love and then return to it. We keep recreating it. My wife and I experience this process when I find myself frequently on the road. During the separations, the homecomings tend to get better. I think this is part of the nature of a loving relationship. A relationship is constantly changing. And particularly over time, an underlying theme emerges: coming back together again and reexperiencing the other person in a way that is ever more loving throughout the years.

Eventually couples become families, and the challenge is sparked again. When we constantly live around people, and cycle in and out of other people's behavior (some of which can be very annoying at times), sometimes we have to withdraw from family interactions and get ourselves centered again before reentering the fray. For example, my breathing exercises are a useful emergency measure to help center myself. In our home we do some simple ceremonial rituals, and we're fairly physical—we hug a lot. All these family traditions and ceremonies serve to help us grow together.

And so does time alone, which is important and begins this cycle again. It is absolutely essential to carve out time for oneself. Otherwise, the swirling demands of daily life may obscure the crucial lesson: that all these inner reserves of love are easily accessible.

At any given moment, everything we need is there. All the lessons are there. All the love we need is there. We don't have to look outside ourselves; the source is within and always present, always there. If we can be open to that, and experience it, then we are fluent in the language of healing.

DRAWING FROM THE WELL OF SELF-LOVE

BY *Louise L. Hay*

"No matter how much we give love, if we don't give it to ourselves, nobody can love us enough. If we are in relationships with people who don't have self-love, no matter how much we love them, it will never be enough because they are not giving it to themselves on the inside."

LOVE IS A natural thing; it is simply there, if we don't push it away. We are each born with love in us. Unfortunately, as we move through life, most of us accumulate blocks to loving. If we can just get the blocks out of the way, the love naturally fills our being.

If we don't fill our lives with love, we are miserable. Even though it is that simple, it still took me a long time to learn this. I used to be someone filled with resentment and self-pity, and I really didn't know what love was like. I thought it was something that I had to go out and find. It wasn't until I was able to let go of seeking love from the outside that I was able to understand what real love is.

I had to learn how to identify and push away my blocks to loving. Most of the blocks, I realized, had to do with my thinking. I am very aware that we can only think one thought at a time. So I refuse to think the negative thoughts that keep the love out. If I find those other thoughts creeping in, I just say to myself, "Louise, you don't have to think this way. You can think of something wonderful." Sometimes to break a flow of negative thoughts that is threatening, I repeat to myself simple words, such as *love, peace, joy, contentment,* and this act becomes enough to break my cycle of negative thinking. Then, automatically and unconsciously, the other loving thoughts come flowing in.

It's important for me to remember that I can choose to be happy. Most of all, I like to choose grateful thoughts because the more I am grateful for all the good things (I don't mean possessions but the joys of living), the more they come to me.

Many people contact me for help with health issues, even very serious ones. All I do is teach them to love themselves. They learn to look at what has gotten in the way of their love and health. Were they judging themselves as not being good enough? As they examine their beliefs in the light of reason, they often realize how silly those ideas are. I have people look into a mirror, just look into their own eyes, and say, "I love you." For most people, this is very difficult. So I immediately say, "Okay, what is wrong with you?" It always turns out to be some silly thing, like "My hips are too big" or "I am a bad person." "Okay," I ask, "why are you a bad person? What have you done?" Usually it is nothing, absolutely nothing.

So where do these thoughts come from? Mostly, it's old childhood voices that they carry with them. Many people are much better at giving love than at receiving love, because they don't feel worthy of receiving love. It comes down to the old "I am not good enough." That self-perception usually goes back either to some horrendous childhood incident or to just a relentless series of negative comments given to children over long periods of time. Society wants us to follow rules.

Society does not seek creativity; it demands conformity. In order to conform, people have to give up parts of themselves. Parents want little children to conform to their rules; then the children go to school and the school wants them to conform to its rules — and the individual becomes lost along the way. When we can adopt a sane viewpoint and really look at these things with a conscious mind, we find that there is really nothing in the way of love, and a huge weight drops off. I do believe that we have come to this planet to love ourselves in spite of whatever obstacles others or we ourselves have put in our paths.

Another way to bring more love into our lives is to be willing to forgive. That's a hard one. But lack of forgiveness locks up our hearts, keeps us in bitterness, holds us in resentment. It is a perfect breeding ground for self-pity. We can't love when we buy into all that. We have to look at all these negative thought patterns in the clear light, and learn to let them go.

When we let old thought patterns go, when we learn to forgive, we can love ourselves better. And when we love who we are, when we have self-worth and self-esteem, people will recognize that and treat us differently. Opening the channels to this universal energy brings good into our lives, and miracles literally happen. Good is out there, waiting to come into our lives, as long as we open ourselves to it. But if we close the doors with all the bitterness, the resentment, the anger, and the unforgiveness, our lives will be miserable and loveless.

We don't even need to go out and look for the good. We just have to release our own junk, the junk within us. When a person who eats lots of junk food decides to eat healthfully, over a period of time his or her health becomes stronger and stronger. That person hasn't really done anything, is not looking for help; he or she is simply taking care of his or her body. The junk goes out of the body and is eliminated. The same thing happens with our minds; as we eliminate the junk, the truth comes in.

One of the ways I actively bring love into my life is with my pet animals. I don't buy animals, I rescue them. All my animals have a history of abuse. But a year of love does wonders for all of them. What incredible changes are possible! I had one dog who was very difficult. Three times in the first three weeks she lived with me, I said, "I am going to take her back, I can't handle it." But a year later, this dog is my dream pet. People are no more complicated than animals. Get the fear out of the way, get the abuse out of the way, let people know they are loved and wanted and will be taken care of, and their true personalities come out.

However, there is one way in which people are different. For humans, self-love is the most important. No matter how much we give love, if we don't give it to ourselves, nobody can love us enough. If we are in relationships with people who don't have self-love, no matter how much we love them, it will never be enough because they are not giving it to themselves on the inside, and they will not trust ours. They can't let our love in because they haven't created a place to receive what we've offered, a place to receive love.

Once again, it's really as simple as loving ourselves. I am a very simple lady with very, very simple ideas about life. I always focus on looking for what stands in the way of the natural love flow and letting that obstacle go. Then we can start just to appreciate who we are and know that we are unique and special and wonderful and that there's nobody in the whole world like us, never has been and never will be.

Over the years I've developed my love rituals. I wake up in the morning with a little extra time to snuggle in bed. I say, "Oh, isn't this delicious and so comfortable and isn't it wonderful that I have this great bed to sleep in and the dogs that sleep with me!" Then I am practicing being grateful for the day. I always know that it is going to be a wonderful day and that there will be incredible experiences in it. Some of them I can expect, and some of them I cannot. I program my day with gratitude.

The last thing I do at night is also an expression of gratitude. Right before I go to sleep, I reaffirm what a wonderful day it had been. Sometimes the day would have included unpleasant experiences, but to me these are always about growth, so I am grateful for them as well.

Of course, everyone has crises. I have a little routine when a crisis occurs. As quickly as possible I say to myself, "All right now, out of this experience I know only good is coming. This is for my highest good, this is a wonderful experience, all is well, and I am safe." During a crisis I repeat this passage over and over, until my thoughts become clear. It's amazing: after practicing it a few times, the mind clears, and either a solution is found very quickly or something happens to allow the crisis to resolve itself.

Another thing I ask for every day is deeper understanding, so that I am able to see life's issues with more clarity. I think the people who create the most havoc in the world are people who once were abused as children and now have very little understanding of how life works. I am very aware that my thoughts and my words are creating my future. Knowing this, I carefully practice what I think, what I say, and what I do with other people. I know that what I give out will always come back to me. This doesn't mean that I never get angry. Everybody gets angry. But now my anger doesn't last the way it used to. Something that I used to stew about for three weeks now may take three minutes. And, consequently, I find that I have far fewer problems in my life.

I have also learned to give myself more love by working less. I used to work ten-hour days, seven days a week. I don't do that anymore. Mainly, I try my best to stay in my garden. I have a wonderful vegetable garden. I eat out of it as much as possible. I have fruit trees and lots of flowers and a pond with fish in it. I take care of it mostly by myself, because my gardening is my joy. I think I am just a farmer at heart.

Being overwhelmed by the details of our lives, by overwork, can squeeze the love out of our lives. I think it makes us terribly impatient. Recently I took two years off to restore my soul. I spent that time on my knees in my garden. I found I was giving so much to others that no matter how much I gave, it was never enough. I said, "Okay, I am going to decide how much I give." I suffered a lot of guilt. But I realized that I don't have to do it all; there are many wonderful teachers out there. As a teacher, I understand that my students must have many, many teachers, must study and learn from many people.

We each have to find our own way, balancing the details of our lives. But we all need love. My advice is to be loving and be very aware that everything we do and say and think is coming back to us. So if we love ourselves and love life and love everybody around us, we will find that our own lives will fill with an abundance of all that is good.

HEART TUGS

BY *Victoria Moran*

"You don't have to ponder the hows *and* whys *of what makes an act loving, or which situations contain the potential for love. When an opportunity to be loving presents itself, you know it. There is no doubt."*

I T IS CHALLENGING to talk about filling your life with love, for there is no single activity that can be called "showing love." It is easy, for example, to identify the activity of "washing dishes": that's the thing you do with dishes, soap, and water while standing at the kitchen sink. You're aware of what you are doing when you are washing dishes, and you are doing it deliberately.

Since there is no activity called "showing love," your love must be expressed in other ways, often through very mundane activities. You usually do not plan to be loving — you certainly don't make a notation in the daily schedule to be loving at 10:15. And often you're not aware of the fact that you are being loving.

If someone said, "Would you die for your child?" every parent would immediately reply, "Yes! Bring in the gurney, wheel me out of here." But suppose it's 8:00 at night, at the end of a long day. You're exhausted and your daughter asks, "Would you play chess with me?" When you drag your tired body and mind to the table for twenty minutes of chess, you are being loving.

Sometimes, many times, you do things that you really don't want to do at the moment, like playing with a child when you're tired and would prefer to just collapse into bed. You do these things because you are driven to do so by your love for the person, for humanity, for whatever touches your heart. And these acts of love, even if done reluctantly, help you to rise above your own problems and negativity.

I was given a tremendous lift by love some years ago when the woman who had helped to raise me was in the hospital, in a coma. One evening the doctor called and said, "I think we can save her with surgery. Can you come to the hospital now?"

I didn't want to go right then. You see, I had a history of food addiction. I had just begun recovery, and it was very important to me that I stuck to a regular eating schedule. I clung to those three meals a day because I didn't know what else to do. I thought they were my lifeline, but I was now being called on to be a lifeline for another human being. I even asked the doctor if I had to go to the hospital at that moment. He said, "Yes, come right now."

There was no question that I would go, but I worried about getting my next meal on schedule. After I had done what was required at the hospital and signed the papers, the doctor said, "It's going to be four or five hours. Why don't you go down to the cafeteria and get something to eat."

We went to the cafeteria, but it was closed; we had to eat dinner out of the vending machines. Here I was, just two months removed from binge eating, about to eat from the food addicts' slot machine! And yet, it was absolutely all right. I made the best choices possible from the ones available, and I got through that tense time without falling back into addiction. I was able to do so because my love for this woman, my acting out of that love, had lifted me above my own needs.

Just as the act of love can lift you above the problems of everyday life, actions can create love. One day, while waiting to get a massage, I saw two adorable little boys playing in the hallway. They had found a baby starling. The sensible approach would have been to mind my own business and keep my massage appointment, but I felt a tug in my heart. The bird needed care, so I said to the younger of the two boys, "Would you like me to take this bird to a bird doctor who can help it live?" The little five-year-old looked at me with his great big eyes and said, "I would really like that." Then he asked, "Will they bring it back?"

I replied, "We want this bird to be able to fly away and build a nest and have a family." That was harder for the little boy to accept, but he and his brother agreed, so I took the bird to a wildlife center, just across the state line in Kansas. The people there said, "Oh, this is a Missouri bird. We can't take a Missouri bird, that's against the law." They gave me the name of a wildlife center in Missouri to call, but it was after hours. Reluctantly, I took the bird home for the night.

The next morning I called the place in Missouri, but they said, "Starlings aren't protected in this state. If you bring it here, we'll have to euthanatize it." So I kept the young bird in my office at home, feeding it every two hours with soaked dry cat food and chopped blueberries. We have three cats and a bird dog, so we had to make my office into Fort Knox to keep them away from the little guy. We had to feed Chirpy as often as any baby. We couldn't go to the movies; we couldn't even be away from the house for more than two hours at a time. This responsibility was really a nuisance, but I became attached to the little bird. As much as I was thrilled to let Chirpy go and be a bird, I had fallen in love with him. Interacting with another being had created a great deal of love, even though the interaction was tedious and Chirpy had spent only eleven days in my world before being released to his own.

If someone were to ask me how to become a more loving person, I would simply tell him or her to follow the tugs that come from the heart. I think that everyone gets these gentle urges and should listen to them. Even if they sound absolutely insane, they may be worth going with. Recently my daughter and I were driving home from a health food store in a not very savory part of town. I make it a point to drive through any area of town that I jolly well feel like, because avoiding certain places is part of what makes them unsavory. Anyway, as we were approaching a stoplight, I saw a man dragging a woman down the street. At first, I thought that she was ill, that she was having some kind of seizure, and that he was helping her. But the looks on their faces, and the looks from the bystanders, gave a different impression.

I said, "Rachael, is that woman being attacked?" I was driving, so I couldn't quite see. Rachael craned her neck out the window, took a good look, and answered excitedly,

"Yes, yes, she's being attacked!" So I stopped at the red light, said, "Wait here," locked Rachael in the car, and went after the abused woman.

I have fairly extensive self-defense training. I know how to take care of myself if I have to, so I wasn't thinking over the situation. I was responding. I charged up to the man, who by that time had dragged the woman into a small office area. Everyone else was watching him, fearful, as I shouted at the top of my lungs, "Cut it out!"

Now, I'm a small person, in my midforties. I do not present an imposing physical threat. But the incongruity of the situation — this little person challenging a big guy — must have been powerful, because he just stood there, speechless. His mouth was moving, but nothing came out. I took a good look at the woman. Her face was red and swollen: she had obviously been punched. I continued, in a lower voice, "This woman looks as if she's in distress." He kept moving his mouth, but no words came out.

Then, to my surprise, the battered woman leaned over and kissed him on the cheek. This was evidently a he-beats-me-but-I-love-him-anyway situation. I had done my part, so I left. The rest was up to them.

As I returned to my car and drove away, I was filled with doubts. Did I want every thug in the city to have my license plate number? How could I have done this with my child in the car? But later, several people I respect told me that if they had been that woman, they would have wanted someone to step forward to help them.

The point of this story is not that I'm a hero or that I deserve a medal. Clearly, the battered woman didn't even want my help. The point is simply that you don't have to ponder the *hows* and *whys* of what makes an act loving, or which situations contain the potential for love. When an opportunity to be loving presents itself, you know it. There is no doubt. Whether it's returning a purse you find in the street, offering your seat to an elderly person on the bus, smiling at a clerk, or playing another game of chess with your child. Love is like a bell that's always ringing. All you have to do is listen. And the more you listen, the more you see opportunities to show love to others.

When I was at the lowest point of my life, I felt that I had only two things — and they weren't any publications or acclaim. One was taking care of Dede, the woman who had helped bring me up, during her difficult times. The other was the assistance that I had given to other people who suffered from food addictions. If I had died at that rock-bottom moment, I could have taken those two things with me to wherever it is that we go next. They were better than money or anything else. They were love.

Today, I would say that love is my religion. Love is the thing that I want permeating my life. Perhaps that is why Tibet is my favorite place to visit. The Tibetans have infused their everyday lives with spirituality and devotion. In Tibet you see people carrying out the ordinary business of life with their fingers on their prayer beads. They're praying along on their prayer beads as they barter in the marketplace, as they shop, as they carry their children on their backs. They walk while spinning prayer wheels, and their prayers go up to the heavens. Religion, spirituality, and everyday life are all entwined. For Tibetans, life, religion, and spirituality are all one thing, the same thing. Wouldn't it be nice to make life and love one and the same? To use everything as another opportunity to be loving?

It can be done. Life and love can be one. When you're loving people, you bring out the love within them. You may not see it every time, but the love you give gets passed along. It makes a chain that can transform the very nature of the world.

5.

A Gathering
of the Heart

---

*"There is no feeling in a human heart which
exists in that heart alone — which is not, in
some form or degree, in every heart."*

—GEORGE MACDONALD (1824–1905)

A Celebration

of Love

BY *Leo Buscaglia, Ph.D.*

"In life and in love, there is only that moment, the now. The only reality we know is what we experience this very second. Reality is not what has passed or what has yet to come into being. Grabbing hold of this simple idea makes life magical because it brings love alive."

PERHAPS THE BEST WAY for us to fill our lives with love is to consider what love is all about. The act of loving is a continuing process of building upon the love that is already there—inside of us. Love is always present in all men and women. However, at every point in a person's life, love can be in a different stage of development. Love is always in the process of becoming.

Sometimes love may be difficult to recognize because it has a different manner of revealing itself to and through each person. To expect others to love in the same way you do at that moment is unrealistic and even foolish. Only you are you. Only you can respond to love, can give love, and can feel love as you do. The adventure lies in the discovery of love in yourself and in others. The excitement comes from understanding what love *is*, rather than what you insist it must be.

Cultures vary greatly in their attitudes toward displays of emotion. For example, when I visit my relatives in Italy, there is never any doubt about their love so sweetly and warmly expressed. I instantaneously feel their joy and excitement at my presence. I become caught up in their cries of happiness, their exclamations of love, the hugs, and the kisses. I am delighted with their emotional demonstrations, partially because I was raised with such noisy and physical outpourings of love. It's understandable, however, that this type of experience can be overwhelming or even frightening to those who are unaccustomed to such a showering of feeling.

Indeed, many people in our culture are extremely separated, especially physically, from others. In some parts of the world, both men and women kiss, embrace, walk hand in hand or arm in arm. In certain areas in the United States, however, this kind of behavior would be considered quite strange, if not illegal! I consider this attitude to be a shame, as touching can often be a form of communication far more powerful than mere speaking. To put your arm about another person, or on his or her shoulder, is a way of saying, "I feel with you," or "I care." Sadly, I have seen people crying while others can only look on in uneasy embarrassment. Someone may offer a handkerchief, but seldom an embrace. This does not mean that the uncomfortable onlookers are not loving people. They simply have limited means of expressing their love. The trick is to look past the cultural limitations to the true love that lies within and, most important, to encourage that love to bloom.

One of the more difficult concepts to grasp is that love lives in the present moment. Unfortunately, most of us are either stuck in yesterday or anxiously waiting for tomorrow. We have lost sight of the present moment.

Some look back fondly to "the good old days," trying to recreate past happiness and security. Others live strictly for tomorrow, spending their lives collecting achievements and external rewards in preparation for some grand tomorrow. We amass, or try to amass, great fortunes and store them away. We deny ourselves and our families daily to buy large insurance policies or other forms of future "security." Our lives are largely directed toward some nebulous future or perhaps even toward death itself. We are so concerned with tomorrow that we have lost sight of the purpose and potential joy of daily life and of loving today.

But we must remember that life is a process, not the goal. Life is all about striving to get there and enjoying the journey, not simply the arrival.

In life and in love, there is only that moment, the now. The only reality we know is what we experience this very second. Reality is not what has passed or what has yet to come into being. Grabbing hold of this simple idea makes life magical because it brings love alive. This understanding does not mean, however, that we should live for the moment. It does mean that we should strive to live *in* the moment, which is a very different thing.

Of course, the past has value and there are unknown treasures in the future. Only the moment, however, has true value, for it is here and can be lived fully. The rest is merely our imagination. Love knows this, for love does not look back. Instead, love experiences the past and takes the best from it. Nor does love look forward, for it realizes that tomorrow's dream remains awaiting and may never come. No, love is neither past nor present. Thankfully, love is now! And it is only in the *now* that love can be a reality. All else is but memory or hope.

There's an old Buddhist *koan* (a difficult question designed to force a student beyond logic toward illumination) that I shared in my book *LOVE*. This koan tells of a monk running from a hungry bear. He dashes to the edge of a cliff and stops, realizing that he must either jump or be eaten. He leaps off the cliff, but as he falls, he grabs hold of a small clump of wood jutting out from the face of the cliff. The poor monk looks down, only to see a starving tiger circling below, waiting for him to fall. Just at that moment, two hungry gophers on the side of the mountain begin to gnaw at the clump of wood from which he is suspended. The hungry bear is above, the starving tiger below, and the gophers are to his side. Looking beyond the gophers, he spies a wild strawberry bush and a giant, red, ripe, juicy berry within his reach, ready to be eaten. He plucks it, puts it in his mouth and eats it, exclaiming with delight, "How delicious!"

Such stories can teach us so much about where love resides — in the moment. Love revels in and grows in the moment. Love basks in the joy of the moment. As you immerse yourself in every moment, you discover more of what love wants to offer you. As a result, your life begins to fill with more love.

Adding love to life is always good. But as we fill our lives with love, we should consider the *type* of love we look to. The greatest love is what gives all, expecting nothing in return. Love is always willing, even delighted, to receive in return, but it never asks for anything—other than to be allowed to continue being. This is the purest love. It is also the most delightful love, for it can never be painful. You see, if nothing is expected in return, we can never be deceived or disappointed. Love can only be painful when it demands something in return.

The concept of pure love that gives without taking sounds simple, but its practice is not easy. Few of us are strong enough to give without expectations. But *real* love comes without strings attached. And it is only real love that is given without expectations.

If we love fully and deeply, then we have no choice but to believe, trust, accept, and hope that our love will be returned. But there are no guarantees. If we wait to love until certain of receiving equal love in return, we may wait forever. Indeed, if we love with any expectation whatsoever, we eventually are disappointed, for it's quite improbable that anyone is able to meet all of our needs, regardless of the strength of his or her love or devotion.

Buddhism teaches us that we move closer toward enlightenment when we cease desiring. Expecting something from others as our "right" is a prescription for unhappiness. Perhaps we can never totally surrender our wants, but the extent to which we can live without demands or expectations of others is the extent to which we are free from disillusionment and disappointment. Others give us only what they are able to, when they are able to, not necessarily what we desire them to give. When we cease placing conditions on love, we take a giant step toward learning to love.

So how do we surrender our wants and develop pure love? Even the greatest guru cannot give you love. He can only help by guiding you, offering insights, suggestions, and encouragement. That is why I believe that a total immersion in life is the best classroom for learning to love. Where do I start? An excellent way to begin is by taking loving chances. Consciously choose to participate actively in love and, most important, trust that you are capable of changing.

We cannot change until we believe in our abilities, until we trust in ourselves. But trust alone is not enough: We must also work at it. We cannot simply will our lives to be filled with love. No, we must do the willing *and* the filling.

The overweight person who yearns for a beautiful physique cannot lose weight and develop muscles by desire alone. So it is with love. The desire for love is important, but only through action can love manifest itself. *Love* is a verb, an action word. If we want to love, we must *move* toward love by reaching out to others in love.

Since we live in an imperfect world in which our love is not always returned, it helps to reinforce ourselves in order to continue loving. The lover must often say, "I love because I must, because I will. I love for myself, not for others. I love first for the joy it brings to me, and only secondly for the joy it gives to others. If others return my love and reinforce me, that is good. If they do not, that is also good, for I *will* to love." Lovers must remember that we live for the joy of loving. We hope others do the same thing, but we neither expect nor demand that they do. When they do, we are doubly delighted.

Unfortunately, we sometimes stand in the way of our own love. Our lives are intricate tapestries of relationships. In these relationships, our motivations, desires, needs, and dreams are enmeshed, woven tightly together. We can learn much about ourselves by examining the patterns of our relationships. As we study the tapestries of our lives, it becomes clear that some of the threads block the growth of our love.

In order to enrich our lives with the brilliancy of the colors and threads and patterns of love, we *must* be willing and able to give up certain destructive characteristics — such as the need to be constantly in control, to be always right, to be free of conflict and frustration, to change others for our needs, to be loved by everyone, and to possess.

Even the healthiest among us has some problems relating to others. Whenever two or more individuals move toward one another, even willingly and in love, the processes that bring them together and keep them together are monumentally complex. Balance and security are shaken. Brand-new behaviors are required, or the relationships will fail.

As I noted in concluding my book *Loving Each Other,* there are several strategies we can use to deal with these problems:

We can deny that they exist.

We can acknowledge their existence but avoid doing anything about them.

We can harden ourselves against them and live with them.

We can view them as irreversible and terminate the relationship.

Or we can rise to the challenge of becoming more loving. We can understand that the more we learn about problem solving in relationships, the greater is our ability to love one another.

I hope that you accept the last possibility, for it is my wish that you fill your life with love.

The Dance of the Wounded Heart

BY *Gabrielle Roth*

"It may be a natural impulse to love one another, but how can we love someone if our own heart is stuck? How do we let someone in if we won't let ourselves out?"

NOT LONG AGO I was riding in a taxi when the driver gave me a gift. He told me that in his native town in Africa, whenever you board a bus, it is customary to greet everybody onboard. You greet each person! And if you don't, the other passengers will think you mad.

The reasoning behind this act is simple — when you get on, you enter the community of people who are riding the bus. As a recognition of this community, you greet each person; it's unheard of that someone would not.

Yet how different we are in the Western world. Such behavior in a midtown Manhattan bus would be unthinkable. Here the person greeting each passenger would be thought absolutely mad.

We crave recognition, yet we don't give it. We want respect, yet we don't take the opportunity to show respect for one another. We're all on the bus, all part of a community, but most often we act as though we're the only one present.

Why is it so difficult for us to love? Love is the natural impulse of the heart. It's the vibe that connects us — to ourselves, to partners, to the community. Certainly we have all been conditioned to love our neighbors as ourselves. Unfortunately, we do just that.

Most modern Western people don't have much love for themselves. The heart is on hold. Waiting to exhale. Waiting to be moved, to be loved, to be seen for who we are. Passively sitting on a volcano. We need to move.

Movement is my master, my teacher. For the past thirty years, I have been falling in love with the dance. I just keep moving. I move alone, move with partners, move in community. Through movement and over time I have come to trust what the body has to say about the heart. It is often a sad, angry, scared message, shoved behind a mask. What it would really like to say when it gets on the bus is "I'm not okay and I hope you're not, either." But nothing is said at all.

It may be a natural impulse to love one another, but how can we love someone if our own heart is stuck? How do we let someone in if we won't let ourselves out?

So many people in our culture have wounded hearts, cutting off our ability to see one another, hear one another clearly. We don't often ask the questions that should be asked: "What does this person need from me right now? What is my offering? What can I give to this other person? How can I give this other person what he or she needs to grow and change, even if it means growing and changing beyond me?"

We have forgotten how to love. We ask, "What can I get out of this relationship? Why aren't you giving me this? How come I'm not getting that?"

We undervalue ourselves. The bottom line is that we don't think we deserve love. This utter lack of self-esteem is paralyzing. If we don't love ourselves, we can't imagine somebody else loving us and yet we want it so badly but we won't let ourselves have it because we might lose it and we already have. Self-negation: You love me? Not possible. You love me? What do you really want? You love me? What's wrong with you?

Some of us rarely lose touch with ourselves but struggle to connect this very same self to another. Some of us resist the group. Fear puts all systems on hold.

That's why I dance. Movement is my practice. Every day I dance the five rhythms: flowing, staccato, chaos, lyrical, and stillness. I call this movement practice the Wave because the rhythms create a wave of energy, the key to unlocking the chambers in my heart. The moment I begin dancing, I know how I feel. My body can't lie.

The message isn't always comforting. There are ghosts trapped in the body, moments of terror, rage, and grief that wander and wail in our physical landscape. Rousting these shadow emotions is a cathartic exercise, not for the weak of heart.

Luckily, the heart is a muscle with soul. Put the psyche into motion, and it heals itself. As soon as your body gets moving, your heart pumps, passions begin to rise. Molecules begin to shift; you know you are alive.

Sometimes being alive is scary. As energy starts to flow,

it sweeps those ghosts through the dancing body like dark clouds in a ferocious sky. The dancing heart goes through the pain. Suffering is part of us, but so is the instinct to express it artistically. You have style, nerve, spontaneity, to spare. In movement, energy is awakened, flowing in and out with your breath.

Movement is my master; I give myself to it totally, all my secrets, all my sorrows, all my fears. I surrender to the dance and let it break my heart a thousand times a day.

I believe that to release the energy which is love, you have to be able to move through the fear that is bonded to the ego, the fear that holds the whole heart in a rigid space or leaves no space for it at all.

I often picture the ego as an extremely efficient Captain Control. Holding the breath. Keeping it all tight and secure. Nothing spontaneous.

Security is a mirage. Life is insecure by its nature. I prefer to practice being insecure. I prefer to practice letting go. I prefer to practice feeling. Fear is a dance. I dance it, it dances me. Movement catalyzes freedom.

Freedom is being in the moment: no past, no future. This innocence heals the wounded heart. Whatever you are holding in your heart, let it go. Perhaps you need to grieve or rage or laugh till you completely fall apart. Do it. To dance is to love your body.

Loving your body opens your heart. If it's not happening in your body, it's not happening. If it's not happening in your body, love is just an abstraction. Love is energy, and energy is motion.

As I practice moving the five rhythms, each rhythm is a teacher. Each takes me into the depths of myself, purifies me, releases all the parts of me; even the parts I deny dance. The rhythms nourish my soul. Each time I nourish my soul, I loosen the ego's hold.

Body, heart, and mind, unified as one — that is the soul. It's not abstract. It's real energy, a real presence that thrives when people are connected — all systems kick in, the psyche is fluid.

My practice is to keep moving. By being responsible for my own energies, I can be responsive to others. Every day I empty out the past. The movements of the Wave are also like the movements of the snake, because I shed the old Gabrielle so that a new one may be born. I have a lot of past to empty out; some parts of it I will be letting go of forever, some parts won't let go of me. I just keep dancing. I dance to give myself permission to be — to be real, honest, raw, vulnerable, and all the things I have been told not to be.

I dance till I am empty. I dance till I am full. My dance is my prayer. I sweat my prayers.

Beginning with Love

by *John Robbins*

"Give away your love, freely and without expectation. Give it away, and soon your life will be filled with love, and you will have set others on the path of love and peace."

I HAVE BEEN WITH a number of people who were dying and listened to them express regrets over their nearly completed lives. I've heard men say, "I wish I had spent more time with my children, my family, and those that I love," but I've never heard, or even heard of, a single dying person who said, "I wish I'd spent more time with my business or at the office." Being near death offers a person a level of deep sobriety and profound sincerity that most of us do not normally approach. The greatest regrets of almost everyone have to do with not having expressed enough love. The message to us, the living, is clear: love is the single most important aspect of life.

The measure of our lives and the influence that we have on the world and one another is determined by the degree of love and openness in our hearts. If someone is in pain, and if I can allow room in my heart for that pain, then I can be a healing factor in that person's life.

The amount of love and openness in my heart is the basic criterion I use to evaluate myself and my actions. Much of my work, for example, involves social action. I often find myself confronting representatives from the National Cattleman's Association, the National Rifle Association, or other people whose actions seem to me to be very destructive. I find that it's a real test, one of the greatest challenges of social action work, to remain in balance and in a "loving space" with these people, despite the vast differences in our positions and goals. I don't mean this in an egotistic sense of "I'm better than they are and my positions are right, but I'm going to tolerate them." Rather, I'm referring to a genuine sense of acceptance, respect, and love. If we don't keep our hearts open, even to those people whose actions we oppose, we become part of the problem, perpetuating what we are attempting to change: a lack of love.

The importance of infusing every action with love became clear to me many years ago, when I was involved in a peace march in the San Francisco Bay Area. The situation became rather intense when the police were called out and tear gas canisters were fired into the crowd. A man walking beside me actually hit an Oakland police officer over the head with the sign he was carrying, a sign that read PEACE! This action has stuck with me as a metaphor for the contradictory desires with which we often struggle.

The key question is, How can we keep our loving centers in the midst of chaos, confusion, and even insanity? How do we work passionately for peace, for example, without hating our "enemy"? Perhaps part of the solution to these dilemmas comes from recognizing the central importance of love and from acknowledging the fundamental fact that love begins with ourselves. I may not respect or support someone's actions; I may oppose and in some instances even put my life on the line to stop him or her, yet I will not (if I can help it) allow my opposition to anyone's behavior interfere with my relationship to his or her soul.

I always try to remember that there is pain, suffering, and confusion within each of us. I have no doubt that if I knew other people's entire stories, regardless of their positions on certain aspects of life, I would have compassion and understanding for their predicaments and their choices. If I knew what their childhoods were like, the turmoil and difficulties they undoubtedly faced, the pressures that impinge upon their goals and actions, the structures of their psyches and how they feel forced to obey certain impulses, I would most certainly feel compassion and love for them, rather than judging them negatively.

It is particularly hard to bring compassion into our relationships when we feel ourselves to be unlovable. Swimming in a media soup of soap operas, codependent "love" songs, and other forms of popular culture, many of us have learned to moan and complain when we feel that no one loves us. While it's true that feeling unloved is miserable, there is something that we all can do to begin to fill our lives with love. And that something is simply to give our love to others. We can always do that, because love isn't something that we "get" or "find." Rather, it is something that we create within ourselves and give to others.

I never really felt a part of my family while I was growing up. I felt alienated. I didn't know how to love my sisters and my parents. Like most parents, mine wanted me to conform to their expectations, to follow the script that they had in mind for my life. I would have done so in order to please them, but I couldn't, because what they wanted for me was contrary to my inner callings and my destiny. This difference made them unhappy with me and contributed to quite a bit of pain in my family. I often felt like a total failure when I could not please my parents.

However, early on I realized that I could please my cat by petting her. When she purred and loved me back, I realized that my love made a difference to this beautiful animal; and this love meant a lot to me. I discovered that when I found a place to pour out my love, I felt better. I was happiest when I was loving her, petting her, talking to her, and looking after her needs.

As an adult, I find it thrilling to look at a bird or a deer or a cow and realize that the same life force that runs through me, and through the rest of us, also runs through that animal. I can feel a powerful connectedness that lies at the heart of love and spirituality. Unfortunately, although animals can be receptive to our love, our society tends to treat them as commodities. In factory farms, for example, the cruelty inflicted upon the animals is almost indescribably severe. I don't tell people that they should be vegetarians or where they should draw their lines. I do, however, want them to know about this suffering so that they can make their own choices. It's helpful to ask, "What does my life stand for?" so we do not find ourselves supporting something that violates our essential values.

Sadly, many of us are estranged from ourselves, from one another, and from nature. Half of all marriages end in divorce, families are scattered across the country, children grow up shuttling back and forth between parents and stepsiblings. During times like these, we can benefit from remembering that the key to love is to love what is available, rather than to reserve all our love for one person, idea, or thing. Instead of waiting for perfection or for the ideal, and instead of closing our hearts to those with whom we disagree, we can love everyone we come into contact with. We can even act loving toward people we do not know and have never met.

There are several toll bridges in the Bay Area, where I live. Not too long ago, some people began paying the tolls of the cars immediately behind them as "random act of kindness." The drivers of these "cars behind" were undoubtedly surprised and delighted to be told that "your toll has been paid by the car ahead of you." This is an example of a spontaneous gift, one given without expectations of or demands for anything in return. I did this for a while, then had an unusual insight. Why not perform a random act of kindness for someone I could see and briefly meet? Such people were right in front of me breathing auto exhaust all day long while collecting tolls from countless cars. So I began giving "tips" to the toll takers. I'd say, "Keep the change," smiling as I drove off. These moments of personal contact were even more valuable to me than the more impersonal act of paying the toll for the car behind me.

There is a little of Donald Trump and a little of Mother Teresa in each of us. Part of us wants to acquire and rule, while another part of us yearns to be of service to others, to love, care for, nurture, and protect. A great way to do so, while simultaneously feeling an integral part of the world, is simply to love others: your friends, your neighbors, your relatives, and even your "opponents." Give away your love, freely and without expectation. Give it away, and soon your life will be filled with love, and you will have set others on the path of love and peace.

Breathing In Love

by *Jean Shinoda Bolen, M.D.*

"I think people don't place a high enough value on how much they are nurtured by doing whatever it is that totally absorbs them. Whenever people are totally caught up in what they are doing — their passion — a timeless quality exists in which they are expressing the real essence of their authentic self. And this genuine essence, this authentic self, thereby helps their inner love grow."

L OVE IS AN ENERGY that surrounds us, an energy to which we give particular form through an open heart. It logically follows that the more we open our heart, the more our lives are filled with love; the more love we give away, the more we become filled with it.

On a physiological level, our bodies function best if we breathe deeply and fill our lungs with oxygen. However, unlike the body, where the breathing mechanism normally happens whether we want it to or not, we must consciously fill our heart and our lives with love in order to live lives rich in love and its blessings. We need to take love in and send it back out again. The more we engage in this cycle, the healthier we become and the more our lives are filled with love. Just as the physical heart fills and empties almost one hundred times a minute, the "invisible heart" needs to do the same thing. It needs to keep moving— love in, love out, giving, receiving. Unlike the physical heart, which operates instinctively, the soul heart takes in and gives out as a choice. We must choose to fill our heart with love from the people in our lives and from the love that exists in nature and the universe. To breathe in love, to receive it, we need to see the beauty and open our heart to it. We need to meditate on what is peaceful. Once we are "filled up" in this way, we once again have an abundance of love to send out into the world.

We give our love to the world from that place of soul where we share the inner side of ourselves with others. We have a choice about how we show our soul place. If a soul is filled with love, a soul place is very different from one that is filled with obsession, anger, or resentment. If the psyche is filled with these negative feelings, there is no room for love to move through us. It is the equivalent of a lung that has emphysema or a physical body that is disabled and hasn't learned to function optimally.

We come into the world ready to receive and learn about love, and to give it back. A baby is born into the world as a lovable, vulnerable bundle, capable of evoking love and actually needing it to physically grow. Babies who aren't loved die, even if all their physical needs are taken care of. Without touch, smiles, and comforting affection, they fail to thrive, they stop growing, and they eventually die of depression. It's as if our very matter, our cells, require a certain amount of love even to grow on a physical level. As adults, we no longer need love to grow physically; nevertheless, it remains an essential nutrient for the soul.

We are born into this world wanting most of all to be loved. Babies who come into a healthy environment bring joy just by being born. When we are babies, the world smiles at us and we smile back. We have the sense of being in a friendly universe that loves us. That feeling is what we all hope for, but it doesn't always happen. Sometimes we are either denied love or loved so conditionally that we have to suppress entire parts of ourselves to be acceptable. Then the natural order, the way things are supposed to be, is upset. A common response to feeling unloved is to begin using defensive maneuvers. People who feel unloved feel they must accumulate and use power to protect themselves. This obsessive interest in power limits faith and eventually limits accomplishments. When you are bound up by feeling conditionally accepted or trapped in co-dependent types of behavior so that others value you, your interactions with the world no longer have to do with love but are motivated by the intense desire to feel accepted.

So much of what brings people into consultation offices, both psychological as well as medical, has to do with their unhappiness: feeling as if they, as individuals, don't matter. A self-negating internalized critic, a harsh judge, has taken over. This critic assumes that the person will be what someone else expects, rather than being his or her own true self. There is a discrepancy between the self the person really is—spontaneous, instinctive, and natural—and who he or she presents to the world. This dichotomy creates an enormous amount of unhappiness that eventually manifests itself in physical and psychological symptoms. I believe that at the root of this problem is a lack of that essential nutrient, love.

I think there is some kind of perception, deep within us, that knows whether there is love in the environment or not. I don't think we are consciously aware of it, any more than we are consciously aware of the percentage of oxygen in a polluted environment. But at some instinctive level, just as we know whether we are breathing in good air or not, we know whether there is love around us. This awareness is important, because when the love gauge reads "low," we can consciously choose to bring love back into our environment through our conscious choices.

Many years ago I made a kind of rule for myself that I wouldn't agree to do anything unless it was fun and meaningful. Fun for me has to do with the quality of the people involved, their openheartedness. If they are fun to be with, then I can be myself and laugh and, if necessary, cry. I can be honest, and there is no need to put on a false face. I love Anne Morrow Lindbergh's words that being insincere is the hardest work there is. So whenever I have the choice, I ask myself, "Is it fun? Is it meaningful?" If the love energy will flow naturally and fully, then I can go ahead. In the same way that we can choose to bring in love, we also have to know when to move away from those situations that take love out of our lives. If you sense that someone is doing something out of unlovingness, and you know you'll be affected by it, there is a real need to say no. In order to fill our lives with love, we must learn to think and act selectively.

I think people don't place a high enough value on how much they are nurtured by doing whatever it is that totally absorbs them. Whenever people are totally caught up in what they are doing—their passion—a timeless quality exists in which they are expressing the real essence of their authentic self. And this genuine essence, this authentic self, thereby helps their inner love grow. The activity could be anything: doing brain surgery, straightening up a room, or painting a picture. Whatever it is, if it makes their heart happy, they are extending who they truly are, not only into what they are doing but into the love that flows through the universe. What love could be greater than giving our world the gift of our authentic selves?

BEING LOVE

BY *Ram Dass*

"Remember, we are all affecting the world every moment, whether we mean to or not. Our actions and states of mind matter, because we're so deeply interconnected with one another. Working on our own consciousness is the most important thing that we are doing at any moment, and being love is the supreme creative act."

THE MOST IMPORTANT aspect of love is not in the giving or the receiving: it's in the being. When I need love from others, or need to give love to others, I'm caught in an unstable situation. *Being* in love, rather than giving or taking love, is the only thing that provides stability. Being in love means seeing the Beloved all around me.

I'm not interested in becoming a "lover." I'm interested only in being love. In our culture we think of love as a relational thing: "I love you" and "you are my lover." But while the ego is built around relationship, the soul is not. It wants only to *be* love. It's a true joy, for example, to turn someone whom you don't initially like into the Beloved. One way I practice doing so is by placing a photograph of a politician with whom I intensely disagree on my *puja* table — my altar. Each morning when I wake up, I say good morning to the Buddha, to my guru, and to the other holy beings there. But I find it's with a different spirit that I say, "Hello, Mr. Politician." I know it sounds like a funny thing to do, but it reminds me of how far I have to go to see the Beloved in everybody. Mother Teresa has described this as "seeing Christ in all his distressing disguises." When I realized that Mother Teresa was actually involved in an intimate love affair with each and every one of the poor and the lepers she was picking up from the gutters in India, I thought to myself, "That's the way to play the game of love." And that's what I've been training myself to do for the past quarter century: to see and be with the Beloved everywhere.

One of the interesting aspects of seeing the Beloved in this way is that it doesn't require the other person to see him- or herself as the Beloved. All that's necessary is that I focus my own consciousness properly. It's interesting to notice, though, how warmly people respond to being seen as the Beloved, even if they don't know what's happening. (Of course, all this assumes that your feelings are genuine and that you aren't compelled to act on them or to lay any sort of trip on the other person. The idea is simply to live and breathe among the Beloved.)

The way I work at seeing others (like the politician) as the Beloved is to remind myself, "This is another soul, just like me, who has taken a complicated incarnation, just as I have. I don't want to be in his incarnation any more than he wants to be in mine. But since I want to rest in my soul and not in my ego, I would like to give everybody else the opportunity to do the same."

If I can see the soul that happens to have incarnated into a person that I don't care for, then my consciousness becomes an environment in which he or she is free to come up for air if he or she wants to. That person can do so because I'm not trying to keep him or her locked into being the person he or she has become. It's liberating to resist another person politically, yet still see him or her as another soul. That's what Krishna meant when he said, "I'm not going to fight, because they are all my cousins on the other side." We may disagree with one another in our current incarnation, but we are all souls.

A story I have told many times reinforces this point. Some years ago I put out a set of records called *Love, Serve, Remember.* The records — which had music, readings from the Gospel of John, and all kinds of neat things — came in an album with a beautiful booklet with text and pictures. It was a wonderful package, and we sold it by mail order for about $4.50.

I showed the album to my father. Dad was a wealthy Boston lawyer — a conservative Republican, a capitalist, and, at the time, the president of a railroad. He looked over the album and said, "Great job here! But, gee, you know — four and a half dollars? You could probably sell this for ten dollars — fifteen dollars, even!"

I said, "Yeah, I know."

"Would fewer people buy it if it were more expensive?" he asked.

"No," I replied. "Probably the same number would buy it."

"Well, I don't understand you," he pressed on. "You could sell it for ten, and you're selling it for four-fifty? What's wrong, are you against capitalism or something?"

I tried to figure out how to explain to him how our approaches differed. I said, "Dad, didn't you just try a law case for Uncle Henry?"

"Yeah," he replied, "and it was a damned tough case. I spent a lot of time in the law library."

I asked, "Did you win the case?" And he answered, "Yeah, I won it."

Now, my father was a very successful attorney, and he charged fees that were commensurate with his reputation. So I continued. "Well, I'll bet you charged him an arm and a leg for that one!"

Dad was indignant at the suggestion. "What, are you out of your mind? That's Uncle Henry—I couldn't charge him!"

"Well, that's my problem," I said. "If you find anyone who isn't Uncle Henry, I'll rip them off."

The point I was trying to make is that when you see the Beloved all around you, everyone is family and everywhere is love. When I allow myself to really see the beauty of another being, to see the inherent beauty of a soul manifesting itself, I feel a quality of love in that being's presence. It doesn't matter what we're doing. We could be talking about our cats because we happen to be picking out cat food in the supermarket, or we could simply be passing each other on the sidewalk. When we are being love, we extend outward an environment that allows others to act in different, more loving and peaceful ways than they are used to behaving. Not only does it allow them to be more loving, it encourages them to be so.

In 1969 I was giving a series of lectures in New York

City. Every night, taking the bus up Third Avenue, I got the same extraordinary bus driver. Every night it was rush hour in one of the busiest cities in the world, but he had a warm word and a caring presence for each person who got on the bus. He drove as if he were sculling a boat down a river, flowing through the traffic rather than resisting it. Everyone who got on that bus was less likely to kick the dog that evening or to be otherwise hostile and unloving, because of the loving space that driver had created. Yet all he was doing was driving his bus. He wasn't a therapist or a great spiritual teacher. He was simply being love.

Remember, we are all affecting the world every moment, whether we mean to or not. Our actions and states of mind matter, because we're so deeply interconnected with one another. Working on our own consciousness is the most important thing that we are doing at any moment, and being love is the supreme creative act.

6.

Remembering to Love

"There is always something left to love. And if you ain't learned that, you ain't learned nothing."

— LORRAINE HANSBERRY

A Raisin in the Sun (1959)

Heart Lessons

BY *Bernie Siegel, M.D.*

"So I began to stop and think when somebody entered the room: If I love this person, how would I behave toward him or her? And, of course, what I found was that the more I acted this way, the more loving and sensitive I became. And the other people are changed by simply being loved; it really becomes easier to love them. With this basic approach, over time I changed myself, my body, my state of health, my relationships, and many other aspects of my life."

THIS IS THE ESSENCE of how I help myself remain aware of my feelings: I write a poem whenever something moves me. This one came after watching a story on television about Lassie.

> I love Lassie, Lassie loves me.
> Lassie is love.
> A dog, a dog, a dog teaches love.
> I'm going to set my sights on becoming a dog.
> I have a role model now.

So that's how I manage. Whenever I wonder how to be more loving, I behave as if I were Lassie.

Love is so important. When we're in pain, if someone is there for us, loving us, we receive the greatest gift in the world and we ultimately hurt a lot less. I hope that someday we shall reach a point where it is normal for people to love well and fully. It's certainly not that we don't have enough information about how to love, but many of us don't have the ability, because we weren't loved ourselves. The best way around this problem is to practice and rehearse loving behavior daily.

Years ago I asked the anthropologist Ashley Montagu how I could be a more loving human being. I said, "For example, if my mother-in-law moves into my house and I want to have a better relationship with her, be more loving with her, what can I do?" And he said, "When your mother-in-law comes in the room, behave as if you love her." I thought this advice sounded superficial, but then I realized that I really wanted to achieve this mindset. I wasn't trying to fool my mother-in-law or my wife or my children or anyone else. I only want to love them more. So I began to stop and think when somebody entered the room: If I love this person, how would I behave toward him or her? And, of course, what I found was that the more I acted this way, the more loving and sensitive I became. And the other people are changed by simply being loved; it really becomes easier to love them. With this basic approach, over time I changed myself, my body, my state of health, my relationships, and many other aspects of my life.

Learning to love more effectively merely involves performing and practicing like a movie star or an athlete. When someone says to actors or athletes, "Oh, you're such a lucky person to be born with this skill," they look at the person as if to say, "Wait a minute, I am a wonderful performer or athlete, not because I was born with this skill, but because I spent a lot of time practicing and rehearsing and working my way up." So becoming a lover works exactly the same way—rehearsing and practicing. Find role models. A person could say, "What would the Buddha or Jesus do in this situation? Or Moses, Confucius, Gandhi, the Dalai Lama, Mother Teresa, Martin Luther King, Jr.?" Or just imagine how a loving mother would act. And if that's too hard, then you can always go back to "What would Lassie do?" A dog will lick your face, even if you ignore it. Unless repeatedly abused, a dog will lick your face, even when a vet has amputated a limb or is about to put it to death. It simply doesn't hold on to hostility. It is here to love, be loved, and along the way teach us a few things.

All the world's a theater, and we can choose how to act. We're given a lifetime to practice and can become as good as we want to be. But we must remember that we cannot perform well all the time. Therefore, we need to be forgiving of ourselves and others, recognizing that we're doing the best we can at any moment.

As a physician, I have found that being good at loving has nothing to do with physical health. There are plenty of wonderful lovers out there who are missing parts of their bodies or the ability to move. I call these "the healthy people," but it has nothing to do with the state of their bodies or their physical health. Sometimes, in fact, it takes the threat of death for people to pay attention to love and to make it a priority. Our mortality can be a great teacher.

It's hard for people who don't know how to play, who've lost that childlike quality, to be lovers because they are more likely to be hostile. Love and play go together. People who have studied pathological killers say that many of them just don't know how to play. They can't kid around. Everything is serious.

Laughter brings out the child in everybody. It diffuses much of the fear and resentment people have of one another, making it easier to be loving. Just look at your baby picture and you'll know how easy it is to love that child. Now look in the mirror. Do you have the same feelings? Why not?

To encourage love at the hospital (this can also be done in any office), I give out rainbow pins with people's names that say, "You make a difference." If I saw people acting in a loving way, I would get their names and give them pins and thank them. Just think, if everybody who was dedicated to love wore a symbol, you would behave differently toward them when you saw them.

I was lucky to be brought up loved. Not that everything I did was liked, but I knew that I was loved — and knowing this gave me the ability and freedom to be who I wanted to be. Because I had my parents' support, I didn't need everybody else's approval and I could be loving and free. The benefit of this kind of support is that when you want to be different, you can, because you know you will always be accepted. When I married, I always knew that I could come home to a loving person who accepted me. So, if I were a little bizarre, crazy, or whatever, I had a place to go. Even when disturbing things happened to me, I knew I could go home, where I was still number one.

Sadly, others are not so fortunate. People who have not been loved as children are often in a great deal of pain, even if they do not show it outwardly. We need to communicate about the pain we suffer and listen to one another in order to heal. We can't assume that everyone thinks or feels like we do.

I suggest that we have an American Society for the Prevention of Cruelty to Humans, like the ASPCA. Basically, I want people to love themselves and others as they would a pet. Some people feed themselves things they would never feed their pets. They'll take drugs they wouldn't give their pets. People exercise their pets, while they themselves just sit around. They hug their pets but not their own families. People need to be as kind to themselves as they are to their pets. We have the information but not the inspiration.

In my practice, I've often seen that people wouldn't take the necessary steps to stay healthy. I learned that for most people wellness becomes a spiritual journey. So in trying to inspire people, I ask them, "Why are you here? Why were you born? Why is the world the way it is? What is all this about?" And my answer is that we're here to learn to love more fully, to be God or angels in disguise for one another, to show our love, to show our compassion, to be active in creation. That is the reason and the meaning behind our lives. Each of us has a choice about how to love the world in our unique way.

Wherever I lecture, I hear people complaining about how other people act at work or at home. They often let their irritations ruin their lives. To have a happy life, we have to practice loving people, including their imperfections, which means learning and practicing tolerance and compassion. If you are here for a limited time, would you rather spend it being irritated or being loving?

Here's a story about how I once handled a disagreement with my wife, Bobbie. The handles broke off some cups because of the way I put them in the dishwasher. My wife wanted to throw them out. I didn't. I thought they were still useful. So I just put the cups in a bag to hide them and prevent divorce proceedings. I took them to our vacation house where my wife wouldn't see them as often. One morning while we were on Cape Cod, I went out jogging as usual with a plastic bag to pick up either things that God leaves me along the way or recyclables. I was running along and saw a cup with a broken handle lying in the road. I knew it was a message from God. So I ran over, picked it up, turned it over, and saw a drawing of two fat elephants hugging under mistletoe. Inscribed on the cup was "I love you just the way you are." I brought the cup home and showed it to Bobbie. Now the cup sits on a shelf in our house, reminding us every day of the real message of life. (The other cups are now accepted and used by my wife.)

When you're a lover, you don't destroy — whether it's nature, society, or an individual. Children who have plants and animals learn to care and nurture a reverence for life.

At any given time, our five children used to have up to a hundred creatures in our home, including three dozen turtles in kiddy pools, lizards, dogs, skunks, and crickets. I tried to teach my kids that if they had a life in their hands, they cared for it and eventually became an expert in its care. I think a child brought up this way is going to be a lot different as an adult from one who learns that suffering is meaningless and it's okay to kill a neighbor or torture animals or that a neighbor isn't the right color, shape, or whatever. As our son Jeff said, "The animals get along because they're all the same color inside." So are we.

I suggest that people keep a journal or write a poem every day, like the one I wrote about Lassie. It helps them get in touch with all aspects of life, including the painful ones. It's important to write not only about the tough stuff, which we tend to remember, but also about the good and funny events. If people can see the humor in a tense situation, then they can laugh and diffuse the anger.

It's great when parents can act childlike, because their kids notice and then feel free to behave that way. Making others laugh is such a loving act, because if love didn't exist between people, they wouldn't be interested in laughing or in making another person laugh. Perhaps if we can all become a little less serious, laugh more often, and act more loving toward ourselves and others, we can live in a more loving world and, as this book suggests, we can all fill our lives with love.

THE ATMOSPHERE OF LOVE

BY *Daphne Rose Kingma*

"We need to change our vision of love to realize that we live in a universe created and sustained by love and that we're able to experience this love in every venue in our lives — in our language, in our sexuality, in our friendships, in our work, in our service, in our suffering, in our transformation, in our living, and in our dying."

I REMEMBER A CERTAIN period in my life when, to my great joy and amazement, I discovered that my life was filled with love. As a child I had observed people in the small scenes of their relationships — at church, at the park, waiting for the trolley — and I remember thinking, "Oh, isn't that beautiful, isn't that wonderful, look at how they're talking with one another, look how they're holding hands, how they're comforting one another." This was very moving to me. And then at some point in my life I suddenly realized that I too was living that experience.

We tend to think that love is going to be the exception in our lives, that if we're really, really lucky we're going to have an experience of love, we're going to fall in love, or we're going to have a lover or a great friend. But the truth is that love is really the ground of our being. It's the atmosphere in which we experience everything we undertake: it's everything we are, it's every person we encounter. We need to change our vision of love to realize that we live in a universe created and sustained by love and that we're able to experience this love in every venue in our lives—in our language, in our sexuality, in our friendships, in our work, in our service, in our suffering, in our transformation, in our living, and in our dying.

Unhappily, it's part of the human mental structure to create an idea—literally an idea—that love is a thing apart from us, a thing we can isolate as a particular experience. We need to change this view, move it from the foreground to the background. We need to take love from the particular to the universal. This, above all, is what can bring more love into our lives.

There are many ways to acknowledge that love is not a thing apart, that it is, in fact, a part of everything we do, think, and feel. Some people say affirmations; some put their energies into looking for someone with whom to share their lives. But no matter how we go about coming into the love that is always there for us, we all need to proceed with two attitudes: intention and surrender. We all have masculine and feminine energies: intention is the masculine; surrender, the feminine. And it's a paradoxical combination of those energies that brings love into our lives. This means that love is both something we have to consciously pursue (proceeding with intent) and something that we must simply let happen (or surrender to). So, for example, we may take action by saying, "I'm now looking for a partner to love" or "I'm going to make a list of every beautiful thing that happens to me so that I'm aware that every day I'm being loved in some form or another." Or we may surrender, saying, "I'm going to be available to the unexpected love that is being offered to me moment by moment," whether it comes from the stranger who pays you a compliment or from the workmen who are improving your house, or whether it's a breathtaking experience with your beloved in a moment of exquisite intimacy in a sexual encounter, in a moment of shared grief, in a moment of expressed vulnerability. We need to be both open to receive and also actively and consciously seeking to receive. If you approach life this way, then love becomes not an exception in your life, but the very context in which you experience life.

There are many ways we take love for granted, things that happen every day and are so much a part of our lives that instead of seeing them as love, we treat them as invisible. To see them and receive them all as gifts of love, we need to move beyond the very particular, finite, romantic view of love and into the infinite frame. Now, of course, romantic love is absolutely delicious, embracing as it does the "falling in love" part where there is sexual attraction and a dream of the future. But if we're stuck thinking that's the only form that love can take, without it we'll feel we're not experiencing love at all.

I believe that we have an opportunity, in this final decade of the century, to expand and blossom our love consciousness, to change our definition of love, and to realize that love is available to us in every moment in the most surprising forms. I'll give you an example: I was in Hawaii a few weeks ago. I was very weary, from a vast fire that happened to my house. I was lying on the beach, incredibly exhausted. I didn't want to talk to a living soul.

And a little girl came up to me with a pinwheel and said, "Can I sing you a song?" She sang a beautiful little song about friendship. The last line was "So I'm singing you this song and I want to be your friend, will you be my friend, too?" It was an absolutely exquisite gift. I will never see her again, I don't know her name, but we had an experience of deep connectedness and true love in that moment on the beach. There are hundreds of these moments in life that are so tiny that they don't register on this chart that we've all built about what love is. We think love has to look a certain way, have a certain outcome. But we're constantly gifted with such moments, experiences that are just breathtaking in their purity and their absolutely consecrated perfection.

When we zero in on a narrow definition of love, we lose sight of all the love we are actually receiving and our lives lack a sense of richness, even though we are constantly being blessed with the riches of love. Instead of feeling immersed in love, we're always one step removed from it, sort of waiting for it to happen to us. Yet love is really the atmosphere; it's all around us. Recently I had a lot of workmen here, repairing the damage from the fire. And I felt that they were blessing me, loving me through their craftsmanship and their kindness and their willingness to be a part of this restoration and renewal of my life. They were in good spirits and they all did their work so beautifully; this was an experience of love. They were giving their gift, and I was able to love them by receiving it and by participating in their lives and their livelihood by paying them.

These are all transactions of love, although we don't tend to think of them this way. But this is how love is the very atmosphere that we live in. It's like the air. If we didn't have air, we would not be able to sustain our lives.

And love, like the air, is a continuous, constant, life-giving presence that sustains us all, literally, in ways that we don't even know and can't comprehend.

There is an incredibly beautiful elegance in all of our interactions with people and nature. In my own life, recently I have been asking for many transformations because an era of my life is ending. I intuitively sensed that I was ready to take on another chapter of my life. And this new beginning was given to me in the form of a wandering troubled person who set my house on fire. In a sense, this person, whom I didn't even know, gave me the gift of liberation and transformation. I won't ever see him or know him, like the little girl at the beach, but on a soul level, I want to say thank you. Thank you for being the suffering person whose action set me free.

I think that we're all being asked, in a very profound way at this time in history, to reconnect with the truth that love is the very atmosphere in which we live. We are being invited to overcome the mechanistic relationship to love that has created the tremendous catastrophe that we're perpetrating on the planet. As the world was conceived, there was an interrelationship between human creatures and animals and plants and trees that was perfectly balanced. This was a relationship of love.

Then we got the idea that we needed to make a distinction between "mine" and "yours," "ours" and "theirs"; we entered into that atmosphere of love in a very controlling and divisive way, which robbed us of our understanding of the world, that it is part of an infinite universe we can't even begin to comprehend, a universe that is the embodiment and the enactment of infinite love. We're living out our little part of it, and we're trying to decide what it means. But we have a very limited perspective, so we say,

"Well, this can't be love because it doesn't feel like my idea of love." But the truth is, if we changed our idea of love, we would suddenly comprehend it. We've asked love to fit our definitions instead of being open for love to teach us what it is.

I believe there are two things that all of us can do on a very simple level to have a greater experience of love: express love and receive it. We have thousands of opportunities every day to express love — with our bodies; with our language; with our choices; with our relationships to our possessions, to our children, to the other people we love, and to strangers on the street. If we start expressing the truth of our connection to other people, we will begin to feel more love, to feel that the world is a more harmonious place, that we belong in it and that it is a gracious, genteel, compassionate environment. We can say to the stranger or the friend, "You are beautiful" or "I see that you are suffering and I reach out my hand to you" or "You're blessing me with your wisdom" or "You're kind" or "Your words are touching." Conversely, when they are offered to us we can receive all these minute, beautiful gifts, taking them into the infinite brilliance of our hearts and minds and be transformed by them. For there *are* incredible gifts, every day. Just being alive is a gift. Just waking up is a gift. You may be doing some awful chores on this particular day, but it's a beautiful day: you're alive, you're here.

It's so easy to let all these gifts go unnoticed and unmentioned. We need to acknowledge them openly — for the world and for ourselves, because when we don't openly express ourselves about them, it's not just that the other person doesn't get the compliment, it's that we ourselves are not reminded that life is generous and good and that we are constantly in the presence of love. Conversely, every time we do speak up about them, love becomes part of our body of memory. I use the expression *body of memory* because it is in our bodies that we carry these memories of an infinity of love experiences that I believe reach back even beyond this lifetime. Every time we do acknowledge these love moments, on a molecular, cellular level, our bodies are being reminded that life is graceful and gracious. And that becomes our world. We allow the flow of love to come in; we know we're in a sea of love, a bath of love, an atmosphere of love that's constantly accessible if only we are willing to receive it. And when we receive it, we can say to ourselves, "Thank you, I've been touched, honored, recognized" — and the true miracle of our being here in life has been momentarily celebrated and acknowledged.

Sharing love takes many forms: words and gestures and passion and things we create such as art and music and literature, film, and theater. In the world of love there is a constant dialogue and choreography of expression and reception. There is also the internal personal stance that says, "I'm going to be very still and know that everything is working beautifully; my life is, at every second, meaningful and rich beyond bounds." To come to this place, all we really have to do is understand that love is the atmosphere, the very air we breathe. Then we can give love and receive it — breathe out, breathe in — and love will always fill our lives.

LOVE AND LETTING BE

BY *John Welwood, Ph.D.*

"To love a person for who he or she is — apart from our desires and projections — calls on us to wake up from our dreams and fantasies. It brings us up against the obstacles to love — all the places where we are tight or closed down inside. If you are willing to work with these obstacles, you start to open up in new ways and become more fully engaged."

TO TRULY LOVE people, we must first be able to let them be — let them be who they are, not who we would like them to be. True love involves loving people's *being*, not just their personality, their looks, or what they do for you. To do so requires a certain kind of discernment, or awareness, of who a person really is. True love never tries to tell someone who or what he or she should be. The same is true for loving yourself. You have to learn to see who you really are, behind all your thoughts and images about who you are.

Though love is often shrouded in projection and imagination, it is really about truth. Truly loving calls on us to wake up and see things as they actually are, see the truth about ourselves and about the ones we love.

Love is much more than showering someone with positive feelings. Many parents "drown" a child in "love," without seeing who the child really is. They see their *version* of the child, and love that image. This happens between lovers as well: we may love our image of the other, or our image of ourselves when we are with that person.

How to see the truth? It helps to take some time out of our busy lives every day to tune in, through meditation or just sitting quietly, to connect with who we really are, underneath our personality, underneath our mind, underneath our thoughts, emotions, and plans — everything we know or think about ourselves. Simply being present, being ourselves, feeling and contacting who we are, in a quiet, nameless way. It's also good to do this with others, to practice opening ourselves to them just as they are, without trying to make them fit into some agenda we might have.

Tuning in to who another person really is — as opposed to who you would *like* him or her to be — is very challenging. It brings us up against obstacles: our hopes, fears, and needs, or our desire to control ourselves and everything in our surroundings. Love without awareness easily becomes distorted. It can become a tool for controlling others and can be given as a reward or withheld as a punishment for behavior that's deemed either "good" or "bad."

But true love is never an instrument of control. It involves letting someone be. This freedom is not something passive. Instead, it involves active support and encouragement. You want someone you love to flourish in his or her own particular way, so you give this person the space to do just that. This is true nourishment. It's the opposite of "smothering with love." Those who smother with love are not giving the loved one space to be who he or she is — they're trying to make the person an extension of themselves.

To love a person for who he or she is — apart from our desires and projections — calls on us to wake up from our dreams and fantasies. It brings us up against the obstacles to love — all the places where we are tight or closed down inside. If you are willing to work with these obstacles, you start to open up in new ways and become more fully engaged. Your love is put to the test. You go through a baptism of fire and may even wonder, "Do I really have what it takes to love someone, or even love myself?" But when love is aligned with the truth, existing in the service of the truth, then it eventually conquers all — all the obstacles to being who we really are. We come out of that fire more real, more open, and truly loving.

My work as a psychotherapist is not about "helping" my clients or "fixing" them, or giving them answers or advice. It's mostly about providing a space in which they can let go of the chains that keep them from being who they are. I try to provide an open space of truth and inquiry that's full of encouragement for them to be themselves. I don't have any particular agenda and don't suggest that my clients have an agenda for themselves. I just give them the opportunity to look at what's going on, feel what they feel, open themselves to their experiences, and develop some insight into their situations. Once they can respond to this invitation, the rest of the process almost happens on its own.

This kind of being-with does not require a "gushy" kind of love, but something more like compassion. It's warm, it's inviting, and it allows a person to unfold, like a flower. In more than twenty years as a therapist, I've found that this is the most powerful thing in terms of helping someone. This compassion doesn't involve a lot of instruction. It just provides a space, a permission, an encouragement, a support, and a presence. In that kind of space, people can begin to find their own way and blossom.

This is what we all really want, what our heart wants, what our soul wants — this space to just be. This is also what we wanted from our parents. We wanted them to be *present* with us. We wanted them to see who we really were. That kind of presence and support is the most valuable thing you can give a child. But instead, what many parents give their children is the message "We love you when you're like this, and we're critical of you when you're like that." That kind of conditional love is a form of control, because it is used as a reward or punishment. So we grew up learning to do the things we were rewarded for. And that became a prison.

You can continue to live in the prison that you and your parents constructed together, doing things so that you'll get the rewards of "love." But this is like being a rat in a cage, pressing the bar to get food. You keep pressing that bar, trying to get the same empty kind of rewards and reinforcement from other people that you got from your parents, because you didn't get the real thing — genuine recognition and acceptance.

But the truth is that you are valuable and beautiful just as you are. Your very nature *is* beauty; *is* value; *is* love; *is* presence, openness, and clarity; *is* richness, power, and generosity. These qualities are already who you are. Once you recognize this about yourself and about others, you are able to give and receive love freely.

When the obstacles to love arise, and inevitably they will, it's important to open yourself to seeing and feeling what is coming up, to develop a willingness to inquire into what is happening, and to enlarge a capacity to let yourself have your feelings, whatever they may be. Every time you try to block or suppress some feeling or perception, you actually disconnect from yourself. And if you are not connected with yourself, it's impossible to truly connect with others.

I try to meditate every day. I find that it helps me sharpen my awareness and perception. This is very important. It is also helpful to set aside time to pay attention to my feelings, to inquire into them, and to let myself hear what they are trying to tell me. My wife, Jennifer, and I also set aside special time for what we call "truth telling." We each try to say what we're going through and then really try to hear what the other has to say. Often it's difficult to hear the other person's truth, but we try to give each other this kind of space and presence, which has been very helpful to us. What is most simple (and difficult) is just to reveal your experience to someone and to hear and understand what it's like for the other person as well. When my wife and I reach the point where we can simply hear and understand how the other feels, we feel loving again, even when struggling with a very difficult issue. Then, even if we still have not reached agreement about what we are discussing, we can usually find a way to work it out.

Love and awareness *are* our essential nature. They are always already present, so it's a question of being able to tune into that and clear away the obstacles, which are mostly mental. Our habitual thought forms are like clouds in the sky. The vast sky of love and awareness is always open and always calling to us, even though the clouds may sometimes block it. The key is to tune in to this vast sky behind the clouds and to know that it's our true nature. The clouds evaporate when we bring the warmth of our hearts to bear on them. Awareness and compassion for ourselves and others chases away those clouds and eventually allows us to reconnect with our true nature — which is love, caring, openness, and warmth.

LIVING FROM THE HEART

BY *Helen Hunt, M.A.*

"Empathy cannot happen from the mind. It is a pure heart function. Often it is the proverbial breaking of the heart that ushers in the powerful onset of empathy. Though pain may crack the heart open — leaving us raw — rather than taking something away from us, it offers us a chance to be present to our own life process, to feel the heart stirrings — even though there is pain."

T HE CAPACITY TO LOVE, to develop in heart and empathy, is fundamental to our worldwide survival. We are inherently connected with all other beings on this planet. Within nature, we are all interrelated, inexplicably linked together to form the miraculous whole called earth. This awareness enables us to fulfill our destinies within the human collective — while contributing our uniqueness to the healing of the world.

One of the most common dis-eases in our society is the feeling of isolation. People go into therapy feeling alone.

They not only feel isolated but feel alone in this feeling of isolation. This isolation manifests itself in so many ways, from the inability to form or stay in a relationship, to the experience of "being outside looking in," "cut off," "left out" wherever we go. The sense of isolation is paralyzing to the spirit. If people are convinced that they are alone and unapproachable, their heart is cut off from others. They cannot engage with others or with life, for they have ceased to engage with their own heart-self. The joy and fulfillment of sharing love seems forever unattainable.

Love is the experience of a constant opening to self and others — the willingness to receive and send the joy of a shared life, a shared moment. It is deeply gratifying on a personal level to feel cherished and to be able to cherish someone. On a more abstract level, this shared love is the way to feel a part of the human family.

Loving is very important to me on a personal level. But I am also aware that there is an effort going on in society to understand what love is and what heart is — what it would mean for the world if we all engage in relationships from the heart. While I don't have all the answers, I would offer that heart wisdom is different from head knowledge. As we learn the lessons that only the heart can teach, our perspective shifts to encompass a greater reality, bringing grace into our lives.

I have a colleague who identifies her goal in life as being a "heartist." A worthy goal for any of us today! Western society is consumed with problem solving, long-term planning, and heightened time efficiency. We prioritize the cognitive process to analyze ourselves and others. While there is nothing wrong with this — cognition has certainly served us well in many ways — the heart has information for us as well. Our head allows us to access information rationally. Through our heart, we access trans-rationally. The capacity to be open to and engage in the trans-rational is essential to living a full life. The two — head and heart — must function in balanced harmony.

To understand this idea we have to put our head knowledge into context. We are part of the Cartesian age of industrialization and mathematical excellence. We've been part of a philosophical evolution that has appreciated the mechanical, the logical. In addition, our modern era has brought a focus on individuality and a strong need to honor the individual. A person working from the head, this philosophy maintains, thinks of his or her own self-interest, how to self-protect, how to become the best individual possible. I think our use of logical instincts and societal training to protect our sense of self, our personhood, is ingrained in many of us. While this process of individuating has been one of the most exciting developments in the last two centuries, if we are exclusively cognitive, then the feelings — the heart — shut down. We run into the danger of shrinking down toward a one-dimensional way of life — instead of honoring our multi-dimensional reality.

"I know the words but I don't yet know the tune" is the plight bemoaned by some of my friends who have achieved their educational goals, amassed plenty of material goods, and have challenging careers, yet still feel empty in life. This saying sums up the difference between living a life in which the heart is involved and one in which the heart is closed. You can't "know the tune" if you aren't engaged in the full rhythm of life. For the tune of life is embedded in the heart. It is the heart that stirs our melody of joy.

And it is Delores Williams, a feminist theologian who

represents a womanist perspective, who clarifies that in the black church, it is not the sermon but the singing that moves the spirit from person to person, galvanizing the congregation. She and other feminist theologians recognize the need to move away from the intellect, so as to develop a greater openness to that part of us that is translogical. It is from this place that the heart truly speaks to us.

We are all a part of this large, worldwide human family here on earth. As with ripples in a pond, all we do affects not only those immediately in our lives, but all other life on earth. This may be why another feminist theologian, Carter Heyward, speaks of her understanding of upholders of the Judeo-Christian heritage being challenged to band together as "justice-seeking friends" searching for a "right relationship" with others in the world. Martin Buber spoke of the sacred being manifest when a relationship shifted from an "I / it" to an "I / thou," in which the other was held in esteem equal to the concern about oneself. Those who live from the heart do so contextually, focusing not only on the individual but on the collective as well. Living from the heart offers the ability to look into another's eyes, see into his or her life, so as to cultivate an understanding of what it's like to walk in his or her shoes.

"Heartists" are also aware of the ripple effect of present behaviors on the future. Within certain Native American traditions, the seventh generation policy is used in all decision making. Instead of thinking only for today, they base decisions on the impact those decisions will have on the next seven generations. Sensing the future in this way requires awareness of our interconnectivity and the capacity for empathy. A person who is functioning from the heart assesses problems with an eye focused not only on the individual but also on what is best for the collective.

Empathy cannot happen from the mind. It is a pure heart function. Often it is the proverbial breaking of the heart that ushers in the powerful onset of empathy. Though pain may crack the heart open — leaving us raw — rather than taking something away from us, it offers us a chance to be present to our own life process, to feel the heart stirrings — even though there is pain. As my friend Sara says, "The only thing wrong with pain is when we run from it."

A commitment of love that invited me into my heart was a story told to me by a Santa Fe artist, Dominique Muzart. She and a group of friends were concerned about pollution of the Rio Grande. So they created — from their heart and their faith — a ritual. Every morning they went down to the Rio Grande and took bits of trash out of the river, saying a Hail Mary as they lifted out each empty beer can or paper cup. They would meditate on the slow current in the river and say a prayer, visualizing the river as a large rosary. Each piece of trash, a bead.

I was moved when I heard that story. I was living in New York at the time, and had a fifteen-block walk from my apartment to my office. Usually, during that walk, I would be preparing to inundate my assistant, Elizabeth, with all the challenges we would be confronting that day. But after I heard this story, I began to shift my focus during my walk to work. I, too, would pick up pieces of trash, quietly offering a Hail Mary as I placed each piece in a city receptacle. By the time I'd arrived in my office twenty minutes later, I'd had all sorts of encounters with squirrels and dandelions (one of the few tenacious plants that struggle through the concrete cracks) as well as the occasional trash collector who offered a broad smile when he realized I was helping keep the city clean. Walking into my office, I felt grateful for the chance to live the hours in the day ahead. I felt connected to myself; and it was a process that transported me out of my head — that mighty list-making machine — and into a place that is difficult to articulate but offers such sustenance and nurturance for me. Such a simple ritual completely shifted my perspective for the rest of the day.

We all know exercise is good for us, but how easy is it to maintain a regimen? Similarly, though living from the heart offers rich rewards, this state is difficult to achieve and maintain. Looking at "family as a spiritual practice," we can reinterpret the dissension that inevitably erupts as an invitation to heart exercise. My husband, Harville, and I have a blended family, with kids ranging from age twenty-six to ten. We are blessed / cursed with the challenge of surviving all the developmental crises going on simultaneously! In a wild and woolly household, things can get quite chaotic. When frustrated with each other, Harville and I occasionally say, "Talk to me like I'm someone you love." This is a reminder that it is not just the content that gets conveyed but also the delivery. Can we talk in a way that invites the listening?

Genuine loving — a love that does not strive to change or to control — means actually caring for someone else's welfare as much as you care for your own. Genuine loving has the potential to be the woof and warp — the foundation — of our every interaction.

Pain is often the impetus that motivates us as we strive to open fully to ourselves, to others, and to life. Our spiritual practice can put both the pain and the capacity to love into a framework. The faith and the belief in rebirth and resurrection that is a part of my spiritual practice is my bedrock as I maneuver the currents of life — reminding me that there are continuous cycles. The concept of life, death, and resurrection is alive everywhere, and perhaps most profoundly felt in nature. The seasons come and go — winter following spring following winter. If we look at pain as being the "winter" of our lives, then the sure knowledge that we will again experience our own "spring" can help offer a larger perspective and allow us to cultivate the compassion and patience to await our personal thaw.

The heart grows when it is in covenant with someone else. While there is intimacy, there must also be boundaries. Anger, for example, is one face of love. Anger, so often seen as negative within our society, can be a cleansing force. It is crucial for us to understand the role of anger in moving into the heart. And dealing with anger — our own and others' — means setting and accepting limits. These limits, though initially they may not seem to, help us as we move toward genuine love.

We have to work on learning to make one another safe so that we can evolve and heartwork can happen. A clear standard is set in I John 4:18: "There is no fear in love; but perfect love casteth out fear." So genuine love has a lot to do with safety. Without clear boundaries, which act as a protection of the self, we do not feel comfortable opening up to intimacy. And it is empathy for one another's point of view that also aids us in feeling safe. As we work on our boundaries and empathy, we open to intimacy and experience genuine love.

That is where a spiritual practice comes in. Beyond the fractured nature of much of our lives and relationships, there is a unifying whole. Most scientists recognize that there is a higher intelligence in operation. Just developing a sense of that higher sphere can, I feel, help us minimize the fear we have of one another, the fear of making mistakes, the fear of our anger. Just as pain and anger help us in our growth, so too do mistakes. To assume that we can be perfect, or to attempt to strive toward perfection, is instantly demoralizing. Perfection is a goal that lies forever outside our grasp. Rather, we need to embrace our mistakes and learn from them. Each mistake can bring us closer to genuine love. And as the love grows, our lives grow — and we can live a life full and complete, thinking with our heads but living from our hearts.

A MIXTURE OF LOVE

BY *Shakti Gawain*

"I believe that, as eternal spiritual beings, we have taken physical form in order to experience a unique, amazing, and fantastic (although often difficult) journey as human beings. We are here to learn about both kinds of love: human love, with its needs and desires and inconsistencies, and spiritual love, with its all-encompassing benevolence."

I BELIEVE THAT there are two basic kinds of love: spiritual love and what I call "human love." Spiritual love manifests itself when we are deeply connected to our own essence (our spirit), to the life force and the oneness. It's a kind of open, expansive feeling of affiliation with all of life. It is unconditional love. Human love, on the other hand, involves our personal needs on physical, emotional, and mental levels. It's not unconditional love.

What we commonly refer to as "love" is usually a mixture of these two and appears in many different forms—

as the love between a parent and child, the love between friends, or the love between romantic partners. A lot of people (especially those who are spiritually inclined) focus on giving and receiving unconditional love, as if this is the purest and best form of love and as if human love were somehow inferior. But the truth of the matter is that we can only feel unconditional love when our physical, emotional, and mental needs have been met. Unconditional spiritual love is blocked when we are emotionally wounded, when we don't know how to take care of ourselves, or when we don't live by our own sense of truth. Only as we heal our emotional wounds and care for ourselves on all levels can we begin to experience truly unconditional love.

I believe that, as eternal spiritual beings, we have taken physical form in order to experience a unique, amazing, and fantastic (although often difficult) journey as human beings. We are here to learn about both kinds of love: human love, with its needs and desires and inconsistencies, and spiritual love, with its all-encompassing benevolence. Some people try to bypass the human experience. Thinking that human love is somehow less important or on a lower level, they attempt to directly access the "higher plane" of spiritual love. But we can't recognize and satisfy the needs of others until we learn how to recognize and satisfy our own human needs. We must learn to love ourselves, including the parts that we believe are bad. Too many people try to love without allowing themselves to experience "bad" feelings, such as anger, sadness, or selfishness. These people try to be continually happy, loving, and giving—denying that they have any negative feelings. But this approach never works, for whatever we reject about ourselves eventually comes back to claim us.

But if we can learn to accept — even love — our hatred, our dependency, our needs, and our fears as part of the human experience, we can extend this love and acceptance to another. This is true compassion. When this is achieved, we can more easily connect to the life force, to the universe, and to a truly spiritual kind of love. So, true spiritual love begins with learning to love and accept ourselves.

In order to truly love and care for ourselves, we must tune in to our own needs, feelings, and energies — we must "stay close to ourselves" as much as possible. The more we are able to do so, the more connected we feel to ourselves. This, in turn, makes it easier for us to connect to others and to receive their love. To contact our inner selves, we must have some time alone every day, quiet time when we can take a break from the world, to simply relax and let it all go. I try to meditate a little bit each morning, even if it's only for five or ten minutes, just to get myself centered. But what helps me the most is getting outside for a while. I'll take a short walk or just sit quietly under a shady tree. Experiencing nature plays a very important role in my feeling connected not only to myself but to a larger entity. It also helps me put myself and my problems into perspective. Just walking through a grove of trees or seeing the great blue expanse of the ocean or listening to the birds sing helps me to remember that my problems and my being are just tiny parts of a much greater scheme. That knowledge can be very calming and very nurturing.

Once we get in touch with ourselves, with our feelings, needs, and desires, it's important to find others with whom we can be completely honest. Love depends upon honesty and the feeling that it's okay (and desirable) to express fully what's going on inside. But, of course, the other side of the coin is that both parties need to be supportive listeners. All of us need to feel heard. That's why just listening in a nonjudgmental way may be one of the most loving acts any of us can perform. Listening to and sympathizing with the other person's experience, even if our own experience is different, is the cornerstone of a loving relationship. True intimacy is attained only when both people feel secure enough to open up and share the deepest parts of themselves — their hopes, dreams, fears, and hurts. But this security comes about only through acceptance — and acceptance of another comes about only through acceptance of oneself.

I believe an important part of our work as human beings is to find ways to reconnect with that fundamental love that is the life force. It's not so much that we need to "get" it. It's there and has always been there. But many of us have somehow become separated from this love and need to find a spiritual practice that can help us reconnect. Regaining this connection to spirituality is achieved in exactly the same way that we regain our connection to ourselves — through quiet time when we are alone, when we simply stop all the busyness and center ourselves. Spirituality is found within us, not without. It's really just our natural state. All we need to do is to find out what is blocking us from it, and then start the healing process. The first step involves contacting our deepest core, accepting it, and loving it. For some this contact is achieved through meditation. For others it may be going to church, spending time outside, listening to music, or painting a picture. It can be anything — whatever gives you that sense of profound connection with life. The next step is to take care of our own emotional needs, since the foundation of every kind of love is truly loving and caring for ourselves.

The more we take care of our human emotional needs, the more easily we are able to love others, and the more we become attuned to spiritual love.

If you are searching for ways to add more love to your life, begin with loving yourself. Love is not something that comes to you when you are trying to "make it happen." In fact, in many cases the more you try to love or be loved, the more elusive love becomes. Learn to accept and appreciate yourself, learn to love even your "unlovable" parts, and you will see that love just blossoms within you and around you.

Love Is a Choice

by *Richard Carlson, Ph.D.*

"In the end, I think my greatest concerns will be, How much love did I have in my life? How did I share my love? Who loved me? Whom did I treasure? Whose lives did I impact? Did my life make a difference to someone else? How did I serve the world? I'm certain that my only concerns will be about how I did or did not fill my life with love."

MY NINETY-TWO-YEAR-OLD grandmother taught me, in her way, that love is all that truly matters and is the only real measure of our success as human beings. Grandma grew up in very difficult times, the only girl in a family of six men. The family lived in the middle of nowhere, and Grandma worked hard from the time she was very young. She survived the devastating depression of the 1930s and the grief of losing her two-year-old baby sister. Her experiences taught her to be tough and strong; her motto was "It's a good life if you don't weaken."

Although my sisters, cousins, and I all felt that Grandma loved us, I couldn't remember her ever directly telling us so. A few months before her death, though, that changed. She had lost almost all voluntary control of her body and could barely move, and she spent her days lying down with her eyes closed. I visited her, rubbing her back, sitting close to her. Grandma was so weak that she had to choose her words very carefully. And she used those precious words to tell me — not just once or twice, but frequently — how much she loved me. Her body was deteriorating, her possessions were of no further importance, her accomplishments seemed small, but she had one thing left that really mattered — love. In a life that was rapidly changing, love was the only constant force. Over and over she told me how much she loved us all, the whole family, naming us one by one. The love she shared was genuine and sweet; I'll never forget her words or the feeling behind them. On those last visits during her final days, I knew without doubt that her words of love meant more to me than anything else her life may have stood for.

What a gift she gave me! Sharing her loving last days taught me so much about life and love. I often think about how I will look back on my life, during my own last days. I know that I'll ask myself, "What was my life all about? What really mattered to me? What was I most proud of? How did I spend my time and energy? How will I be remembered?" I think of these questions now because, to borrow a phrase from Stephen Covey, I need to "begin with the end in mind." When I think this way, my goals — and my path to those goals — become so much clearer.

I doubt very much that when the time comes for me to die, I'll be saying to myself, "I wish I would have spent more time at the office" or "Darn it, I never did get my

bank balance as high as I wanted to" or "If only I had
taken one more stroke off my golf game or lost those five
pounds, my life would have been complete." In the end, I
think my greatest concerns will be, How much love did I
have in my life? How did I share my love? Who loved me?
Whom did I treasure? Whose lives did I impact? Did my
life make a difference to someone else? How did I serve
the world? I'm certain that my only concerns will be about
how I did or did not fill my life with love.

Many of us say, quite sincerely, that love is the most
important aspect of our lives. Even so, how often do we
focus instead on other things — winning arguments, getting what we want, wishing people were different, collecting achievements, consuming, seeking gratification, even
washing our cars? My best friend and coeditor of this
book, Benjamin Shield, taught me an important lesson:
"We vote with our actions." It's easy (and often tempting)
to pay lip service to love, but the truest measure of our
commitment to love lies in our actions. We may with good
intentions say one thing, but do something entirely different. We say, "My family is the most important part of my
life," yet we rarely find time to spend with them. Or we
might talk year after year about the virtues of putting others first, fully intending to help someone, yet never actually getting to it.

The questions you need to ask yourself are: "Is my
family really the most important part of my life?" "Do I
really want to spend time volunteering?" If we want our
love to flourish in our lives, we must make loving choices.
And we have to remember that love is not just a noun but a
verb as well. In reality, we do vote with our actions. True,
loving choices require true, loving actions.

Over the years I have seen that the people who do make

these real choices to fill their lives with love end up, virtually always, having the most satisfying and meaningful lives. When they not only say, "My family is important," but also make time for their loved ones, they receive a great deal of personal nourishment. Likewise, someone who actually makes the call and begins volunteering finds that there is tremendous satisfaction in working to help others. There are other, subtler ways we can make active choices as well. Someone who receives criticism and, instead of reacting and striking back, learns to take it in stride, realizing that the critic probably doesn't have enough love in his or her own life, is living out his or her loving choices. We have dozens of chances, every day, to make loving choices — choices that translate into warm feelings, gratitude, acceptance, positive relationships, and hope.

Having said that, I have to add that, of course, making loving choices is easier said than done. We are constantly confronted with obstacles that don't seem to warrant such a response. It's easy to think, "I'll be loving when . . ." and you fill in the blank — when my children start behaving, when my spouse acts differently, when my bills are paid, when my work is more fun, when I get through this stressful time, and so forth. What really nurtures a loving life, though, is our willingness to remain in a loving space and to respond with love during these more difficult moments. It's easy to be loving when everything is going smoothly and people are acting loving toward you. It's something else entirely to feel love for others (or for life itself) when you're in the midst of chaos or when other people aren't acting as you would like — when you're being criticized, when people are making demands on your time, when you do something nice that isn't appreciated.

One of my greatest challenges is the way I respond to

my children when their behavior is less than I expect. When I'm super-busy, trying to get everything done, and the two of them are firing requests and questions at me, in between having their own conflicts, I often react to the frenzied feeling in the room and demand that my children "act more loving!" But how silly that must sound to a four-year-old and a six-year-old! My intention is to teach them to respond to life with love, yet my actions — the tone of my voice, my frustrated demeanor, my demand-ing, judgmental words — are anything but loving. Here, as in so many other instances in my life, I'm hoping, even demanding, that others act loving, yet I'm unwilling to make loving choices myself.

I can always rationalize my own unloving reactions and behavior, of course. I can easily convince myself that it's appropriate to be angry in a certain situation. And that may even be true. So I give myself the benefit of the doubt. Yet shouldn't I extend that same courtesy to others when they act less than loving toward me? After all, from the perspective of my six-year-old, her behavior and reactions are as justifiable as my own. In fact, she has informed me in no uncertain terms, "Daddy, my life is way harder than yours!" And, you know, she may be right. She has a four-year-old sister following her around the house, whether she likes it or not. She's confronted daily with demands to learn to read and write and all the other difficult challenges of first grade. She has adults telling her what to do all day long. She needs permission to spend time with her best friends, even to go out of the front yard. And on it goes. The same is true for my four-year-old. From her perspective, her problems seem just as compelling — and they are!

How can I expect and demand that my children be

loving if I can't or won't do so myself? Doesn't the message my children receive from my example conflict with what I'm trying to teach them? Wouldn't they be getting the message to "act loving when everything is perfect, but at all other times go crazy"? And would the second part of the message be that "while you're going crazy, get frustrated that the people around you aren't able to act loving"?

I'm not suggesting that it's possible, or even appropriate, to act loving all the time or that you should act loving when you don't feel loving. What I am saying is that love begins in our own hearts. It is a choice. In a very real sense, to fill your life with love, you need to see love as its own reward. Giving and receiving must be seen as two sides of the same coin, different aspects of the same energy. Truly, it feels just as good to respond with love as it does to receive love. It's more important to be love that it is to get love.

When I do manage to keep my bearings with my children during those difficult moments — when I am love as opposed to demanding love — I notice how peaceful I feel and how quickly the immediate situation resolves itself. It's in these moments that I feel most proud of myself, contented and grateful for the gift of love. If I remain in a loving space, even in the midst of chaos, my family usually adjusts to my more peaceful state. The same is true for my wife. More often than not, she's the one (not I) who keeps her perspective while the rest of us act out. As she remains calm, the rest of us eventually come around. Responding with love is a powerful medicine.

When we do face the difficult times, we need to remember that circumstances don't make a person, they reveal him or her. If someone criticizes me and I fight back, all this says about me is that I'm a person who needs to fight. Yes, once in a while we do need to fight. But if I want my life to be filled with love, it has to start with me. After all, love comes from within each of us and is directed outward. Likewise, if I judge someone, my judgment doesn't really say anything about the person I'm judging. It merely describes me as someone who needs to judge.

If I want a life filled with love, I can't wait for the world and all the people in it to conform to my wishes. Actually it is the other way around. The love I want begins with me. As I make loving choices and fill my life with love, I start to notice that the people around me are also more loving. Then I receive the love I need. It's a circle of love that begins with me.

My wife and I have just started a ritual with our children that has helped fill all our lives with more love. We pretend that we have invisible antennae that are on the lookout for love. We sit, sometimes as a family and sometimes individually, and ask questions of one another, such as, "What went right today?" "What was the most loving act that you witnessed?" "What was the most loving thing you did for someone else today?" These questions help us think about the importance of love and remind us that there is good in the world — if we look for it. As we consciously consider the love in our lives, reflecting on love and loving choices, our lives can't help but be filled with love. Love becomes a habit. If our attention is on what's wrong, that's what we notice. If our attention is on what's precious, that too is what we see. It's not always easy, but it is pretty simple.

In our own little way, each of us affects the world with every choice we make. Either we are part of the problem or we are part of the solution. We either bring more love into the world or we get in the way. Each choice that we make along the way becomes an important step on the path of love. When being a source of love is our top priority, life becomes a magnificent, love-filled journey to be treasured.

Afterword

---

*"The best and most beautiful things in the world cannot
be seen, nor touched . . . but are felt in the heart."*
— HELEN KELLER (1880–1968)

WE HOPE THAT this book has, in some way,
inspired you to let more love into your life.
The movement of one grain of sand, some
believe, can affect the entire world. So too, the simple willingness to make love the foundation of our lives can begin
to bring more love into our heart and, subsequently, into
our world. A wonderful teacher affirmed that "the shortest
distance between two points is an intention." Often a simple
change of our intentions can create the beginning of a
whole new life.

We live in a culture that tells us love is "out there"
somewhere. If we earn the right income, drive the right
automobile, have the right hairstyle, and wear the clothing
that is in fashion, *then* we are worthy to find love or love
finds us. In contrast, the contributors to this collection
teach the simple, yet essential, understanding that love

truly does originate from within. In truth, our ability to give and receive love is directly proportional to our ability to love ourselves. We alone have the opportunity as well as the responsibility to create the love we desire in our lives.

It is comforting to be reminded that we already possess the most essential aspects of love in our heart. Accessing this love is most often a process of letting go of those obstacles that block love's expression. If we let go of those personal "speed bumps" along our journey, such as fear and low self-esteem, and truly let love in, moment by moment, we are well along our path to having the love we desire.

However, our intentions must be coupled with action. Japanese philosopher Takuan Soho once said, "One may explain water, but the mouth will not become wet." To make the words of the contributors to this collection truly our own, we must actively "push the envelope" of our ability to love. We wouldn't expect our bodies to get stronger and healthier without stretching and exercising. In the same way, by integrating intention with action, we must exercise our souls and minds and hearts to bring love into our lives.

Don't forget that loving is a process that must be attended to if it is to grow and thrive. It is our hope that, as you finish this book, it becomes not an ending but a fresh beginning. You will doubtless find, as have we, that just when you feel you have reached your goal, life offers your next lesson — yet another opportunity to live even more from your heart. Ram Dass said, "The ultimate test of even the most enlightened gurus is when they go home and spend a weekend with their parents!"

We feel honored to be a part of this project. We have worked with some of the most inspiring, loving people we have ever known. It has also been our honor to have *you* as our reader. It's our wish that this book affect your life in a positive light. It has ours.

With respect,

BENJAMIN SHIELD, PH.D.
2118 Wilshire Boulevard, Suite 741
Santa Monica, CA 90403

RICHARD CARLSON, PH.D.
P.O. Box 1196
Orinda, CA 94563

ABOUT THE
CONTRIBUTORS

JEAN SHINODA BOLEN, M.D.

Dr. Jean Shinoda Bolen is a psychiatrist, Jungian analyst in private practice, clinical professor of psychiatry at the University of California Medical Center in San Francisco, and internationally known lecturer. She is the author of *The Tao of Psychology, Goddesses in Everywoman, Gods in Everyman, Ring of Power,* and *Crossing to Avalon.* Dr. Bolen's latest book is *Close to the Bone: Life-threatening Illness and the Meaning of Life.*

She brings to all aspects of her work an emphasis on the quest for meaning and the need for a spiritual dimension in life, while also taking into account the powerful effects of archetypes within us and family and culture upon us. She appears in two widely acclaimed documentaries: *Goddess Remembered,* the first of the Canadian Film Board's trilogy on women's spirituality, and the Academy Award—winning anti-nuclear documentary *Women—For America, For the World.* Her words are published in many anthologies and recorded on many audiotapes. She lives in northern California, practices in San Francisco, and has a son and a daughter.

JOAN BORYSENKO, PH.D.

Joan Borysenko is a medical scientist, psychologist, and author whose vision is to reunite medicine, psychology, and spirituality in the service of personal and planetary healing. She is the author of the bestseller, *Minding the Body, Mending the Mind*, as well as *Guilt Is the Teacher, Love Is the Lesson; On Wings of Light; Meditations for Awakening the Source; Fire in the Soul: A New Psychology of Spiritual Optimism; Pocketful of Miracles*—a book of daily spiritual practice—and coauthor of *The Power of the Mind to Heal*.

Dr. Borysenko is cofounder and former director of the Mind/Body Clinic at New England Deaconess Hospital and was an instructor in medicine at the Harvard Medical School. She holds advanced degrees in cell biology and psychology.

NATHANIEL BRANDEN, PH.D.

The name Nathaniel Branden has become synonymous with the psychology of self-esteem, a field he pioneered over thirty years ago. He has done more, perhaps, than any other theorist to awaken America's consciousness to the importance of self-esteem to human well-being. He has been described as "the father of the self-esteem movement."

Dr. Branden is the author of fourteen books, with over 3 million copies in print. He lectures widely to professional and corporate groups. His books include *The Psychology of Self-Esteem, The Disowned Self, How to Raise Your Self-Esteem,* and *The Six Pillars of Self-Esteem.*

LEO BUSCAGLIA, PH.D.

Leo F. Buscaglia, Ph.D., has written thirteen books, most of which deal with the experience of love. At one time, five of his books appeared on the *New York Times* bestseller list concurrently. His first book, *LOVE,* has been a continual bestseller for twenty years. Over 18 million copies of his books are in circulation, and his work has been translated into seventeen languages.

Dr. Buscaglia continues to research, write, and lecture internationally. He is deeply involved in promoting the dynamics of giving and loving through his nonprofit Felice Foundation and his work with a myriad of philanthropic organizations.

Dr. Buscaglia lives and works in Nevada. He is professor-at-large at the University of Southern California, where he taught for nineteen years. It was here that his famous "love class" originated.

RICHARD CARLSON, PH.D.

Richard Carlson holds a Ph.D. in psychology and is a nationally known stress-management consultant and teacher in the field of personal development and happiness. For several years he wrote a newspaper column called "Prescriptions for Happiness," and he is the author of many popular books, including *Handbook for the Soul* (edited with Benjamin Shield), *You Can Feel Good Again*, *You Can Be Happy No Matter What*, and *Shortcut Through Therapy*, as well as his most recent book, *Don't Sweat the Small Stuff*.

Dr. Carlson is a frequent lecturer and a popular talk-show guest, having appeared on such shows as the *Oprah Winfrey Show* and *Sally Jessy Raphael*. He is married and the father of two children. He lives in Martinez, California.

DEEPAK CHOPRA, M.D.

Dr. Chopra is an international expert in mind/body medicine. He travels widely to give lectures and seminars and has appeared on major television and radio shows throughout the world.

He is the author of fourteen books, including the runaway *New York Times* bestsellers *The Seven Spiritual Laws of Success* and *Ageless Body, Timeless Mind*, as well as *Creating*

Health, Return of the Rishi, Quantum Healing, Perfect Health, Unconditional Life, Creating Affluence, Perfect Weight, Restful Sleep, and *The Return of Merlin.* His books have been translated into more than twenty-five languages, and he has produced more than thirty audiotape series.

Deepak Chopra is the focus of a critically acclaimed PBS special "Body, Mind, and Soul: The Mystery and the Magic," which began airing as a PBS fund-raiser in the spring of 1995. To date, this show has been one of the most successful PBS fund-raisers in history.

Dr. Chopra has been named as one of America's Top Five Speakers of 1995 by Toastmasters International.

STEPHEN R. COVEY, PH.D.

Dr. Stephen R. Covey is founder and chairman of Covey Leadership Center, a seven-hundred-member international firm. Its mission is to empower people and organizations to significantly increase their performance capability in order to achieve worthwhile purposes through understanding and living Principle-Centered Leadership. He is also founder of the Institute for Principle-Centered Family Living, a non-profit research and development group dedicated to transforming education and improving the quality of family and community life.

Dr. Covey has taught leadership principles and management skills for more than twenty-five years to leaders in business, government, and education. His consulting portfolio includes more than half the Fortune 500 companies, as well as thousands of midsized and smaller organizations.

Dr. Covey is the author of several books and numerous articles on leadership, personal and organizational effectiveness, and family and interpersonal relationships. His book *The Seven Habits of Highly Effective People* was a #1 *New*

York Times national bestseller, with more than 6 million copies sold. The book has been published in more than twenty-four languages. Other books include *Principle-Centered Leadership* and his latest bestselling book, *First Things First*. His leadership advisory magazine, *Executive Excellence*, is in its tenth year of publication.

BETTY EADIE

The daughter of a Sioux Native American mother, Betty Eadie is the seventh of ten children and was raised in rural Nebraska and on the Rosebud Indian Reservation in South Dakota. Ms. Eadie is the mother of eight children and the grandmother of eight.

At the age of thirty-one, Ms. Eadie was recovering in the hospital after surgery. She was expected to recover fully, but sudden complications arose and she died. Her near-death experience is considered one of the most amazing ever told. Ms. Eadie writes about her near-death experience in the book *Embraced by the Light*, which has sold over 4.5 million copies and was on the *New York Times* bestseller list for more than a year.

She has given hundreds of talks about her experiences and has made numerous television appearances in the United States and abroad. Ms. Eadie lives with her husband, Joe, in the Pacific Northwest.

SHAKTI GAWAIN

Shakti Gawain is a bestselling author and internationally renowned speaker/workshop leader in the world consciousness movement. *The Path of Transformation: How Healing Ourselves Can Change the World*, her newest book, is the latest in a distinguished publishing history in the human potential market, including *Creative Visualization* (more than

2 million copies in print), *Living in the Light* (more than 700,000 copies in print), *Return to the Garden,* and *Awakening.* She has helped thousands of people learn to develop and act on their own intuition and creativity.

She has appeared on such nationally syndicated shows as the *Oprah Winfrey Show, Good Morning America, Sonya Live* on CNN, *Larry King Show, Jim Bohannon Show, Leeza Show, America's Talking,* and *New Dimensions Radio.*

Ms. Gawain cofounded Nataraj Publishing with her husband, Jim Burns, and was cofounder of New World Library publishing company. She and her husband make their home in Mill Valley, California, and on the island of Kauai, Hawaii.

JOHN GRAY, PH.D.

John Gray, Ph.D., is the author of *What Your Mother Couldn't Tell You and Your Father Didn't Know, Mars and Venus in the Bedroom,* as well as the phenomenal bestseller *Men Are from Mars, Women Are from Venus,* which has sold over 3 million copies in the United States and is available in twenty-six languages around the world.

An internationally recognized expert in the fields of communication, relationships, and personal growth, Dr. Gray uniquely focuses on assisting men and woman in understanding, respecting, and appreciating their differences. For over twenty years, he has conducted public and private seminars for over 100,000 participants. In his highly acclaimed books and in his popular weekend seminar, "Men, Women, and Relationships," he entertains and inspires his audiences with practical insights and easy-to-use techniques that can be applied immediately to enrich relationships.

John Gray is a popular speaker on the national lecture circuit and has often appeared on television and radio programs to discuss his work. He has been interviewed on the *Oprah*

Winfrey Show, Donahue, Good Morning America, Eye to Eye with Connie Chung, CNBC, and CNN, as well as countless local television and radio programs across the country.

LOUISE L. HAY

Louise L. Hay is known as one of the founders of the self-help movement. Her bestselling first book, *Heal Your Body,* discusses the connection between mind and body. Her lectures and workshops include her healing techniques and positive philosophy and teach people how to create more of what they want in their lives, including more wellness in their bodies, minds, and spirits.

Louise Hay was able to put her philosophies into practice when she was diagnosed with cancer. After considering the alternatives to surgery and drugs, she developed an intensive program of affirmation, visualization, nutritional cleansing, and psychotherapy. Within six months she was completely healed of cancer.

In her 1980 *New York Times* bestseller, *You Can Heal Your Life,* she explains how our beliefs and ideas about ourselves are often the cause of our emotional problems and physical maladies and how, by using certain tools, we can change our thinking and our lives for the better. Over 3 million copies have been sold throughout the world.

In 1985 Ms. Hay began her famous AIDS support group, The Hayride, which soon had grown to a weekly gathering of eight hundred people. It was during this time that she wrote *The AIDS Book: Creating a Positive Approach,* based on her experiences with this powerful group.

She now heads Hay House, which publishes some of the most notable self-help authors of our time, and has established the Hay Foundation and the Louise L. Hay Charitable Fund, nonprofit organizations that support many diverse organizations, including those dealing with AIDS, battered women, and other disadvantaged individuals in our society.

Louise's most recent book, *Life!*, was published in 1995. Her monthly column, "Dear Louise," appears in over thirty world publications. She lives in San Diego, California, with three dogs, two rabbits, and a cat.

HARVILLE HENDRIX, PH.D.

Harville Hendrix, Ph.D., the founder and president of the Institute for Imago Relationship Therapy, is the author of the popularly acclaimed books *Getting the Love You Want: A Guide for Couples* and *Keeping the Love You Find: A Guide for Singles*. In addition, Harville and his wife, Helen Hunt, M.A., who has been his support in developing Imago Relationship Therapy, coauthored *The Couples Companion: Meditations and Exercises for Getting the Love You Want*. They also collaborated on *Getting the Love You Want: The Home Video*, for which Dr. Hendrix and Ms. Hunt were executive editor and executive producer, respectively. This award-winning series was introduced and endorsed by Oprah Winfrey when it aired on public television. A former professor at Southern Methodist University, he holds an M.A. and a Ph.D. in psychology and religion from the School of Divinity at the University of Chicago and a master of divinity from Union Theological Seminary in New York. He is a diplomate in the American Association of Pastoral Counselors and a member of the American Group Psychotherapy Association and the International Transactional Analysis Association. Harville Hendrix and Helen Hunt have six children.

HELEN HUNT, M.A.

Helen Hunt has worked within the secular women's movement for the past fifteen years. President of the Sister Fund, a women's fund whose mission is to empower women and girls socially, economically, politically, and spiritually, she has been instrumental in founding other women's organizations in New York and Dallas. Most recently, she has deepened her focus to include a spiritual component and has been taking courses in feminist theology at Union Theological Seminary in New York City. She is currently working on a study that she feels may unearth ways to wed the spiritual and secular as women globally band together to work toward dignity, equality, and justice. It is feminist theology, she feels, that will help usher in a focus on collectivity and interconnectivity, energies that are much needed within our world today. She currently lives in New Mexico with her husband, Harville Hendrix, and two of their six children.

BARRY NEIL KAUFMAN

Author, lecturer, and teacher, Barry Neil Kaufman is the cofounder and codirector of the Option Institute, a learning center in Sheffield, Massachusetts, that offers programs for those seeking to be happier, more effective, and more successful. The Option Institute assists people challenged by adversity, including families with "special" children, to find hopeful and loving solutions to their difficulties.

His book *Happiness Is a Choice,* a national bestseller, includes heartwarming stories of his twenty years' experience working with those challenged by adversity. His ninth book, *Son-Rise: The Miracle Continues,* was released in 1995. He is currently working on two additional books to be published in 1996: *A Sacred Dying* and *Outsmarting Your Karma (And Other Pre-Ordained Conditions).* Mr. Kaufman is the father of six children.

SAMAHRIA LYTE KAUFMAN

Samahria Lyte Kaufman has spent the last twenty years dedicating herself to the limitless possibilities that exist for each of us. It began when she and her husband, author Barry Neil Kaufman, began treating their own son from what professionals labeled the "incurable" illness of autism. This journey became the subject of a book and then an NBC-TV special movie presentation, *Son-Rise,* winning the Christopher Award and Humanitas Prize. In 1994 the book was updated in the publication of *Son-Rise: The Miracle Continues* (which contains the original story as well as the stories of five other families who used this method to heal their seemingly "hopeless" children). She also coauthored the book and screenplay *A Sacred Dying,* applying her work to the subject of death and dying. In 1983 Ms. Kaufman and her husband founded the Option Institute.

DAPHNE ROSE KINGMA

Daphne Rose Kingma is a poet, psychotherapist, and teacher of relationships who has been in private practice in Beverly Hills and Santa Barbara, California, for more than twenty-five years.

She is the author of *Coming Apart: Why Relationships End and How to Live Through the Ending of Yours; True Love: How to Make Your Relationship Sweeter, Deeper and More Passionate; A Garland of Love: Meditations on the Meaning and Magic of Love; Weddings from the Heart: Ceremonies for an Unforgettable Wedding;* the groundbreaking book on male psychology for women, *The Men We Never Knew: How to Deepen Your Relationship with the Man You Love;* and, most recently, *Heart and Soul: Living the Joy, Truth and Beauty of Your Intimate Relationship.*

Her books have been translated into nine languages. She

has lectured widely and is a frequent guest on the *Oprah Winfrey, Sally Jessy Raphael,* and *Donahue* shows.

JACK KORNFIELD, PH.D.

Jack Kornfield was trained as a Buddhist monk in Thailand, Burma, and India and has taught meditation worldwide since 1974. He is one of the key teachers to introduce Theravada Buddhist practice to the West. For many years his work has been focused on integrating and bringing alive the great Eastern spiritual teachings in an accessible way for Western students and Western society. He also holds a Ph.D. in clinical psychology. He is a husband, father, psychotherapist, and founding teacher of the Insight Meditation Society and the Spirit Rock Center (P.O. Box 909; Woodacre, CA 94973). His books include *A Path with Heart, Seeking the Heart of Wisdom, A Still Forest Pool,* and *Stories of the Spirit, Stories of the Heart.*

RABBI HAROLD KUSHNER, PH.D.

Harold Kushner is rabbi laureate of Temple Israel, Natick, Massachusetts, after serving that congregation for twenty-four years. He is best known for *When Bad Things Happen to Good People,* an international bestseller first published in 1981. The book has been translated into twelve languages and was selected by members of the Book-of-the-Month Club as one of the ten most influential books of recent years. He has also written *When All You've Ever Wanted Isn't Enough,* which was awarded the Christopher medal for its contribution to the exaltation of the human spirit, *When Children Ask about God, Who Needs God?, How Good Do We Have to Be?,* and *To Life!*

Rabbi Kushner was born in Brooklyn, New York, and graduated from Columbia University. He was ordained by the Jewish Theological Seminary in 1960 and awarded a doctoral degree in Bible by the seminary in 1972. He has five honorary doctorates, has studied at the Hebrew University in Jerusalem and the Harvard Divinity School, and has taught at Clark University in Worcester, Massachusetts, and the rabbinical school of the Jewish Theological Seminary.

STEPHEN AND ONDREA LEVINE

Stephen Levine edited the *San Francisco Oracle* in the late 1960s. After intense practice of mindfulness meditation under the tutelage of an American Buddhist monk, he edited the *Mindfulness Series* for Unity Press. He has written several books, including *Grist for the Mill* (with Ram Dass), *Who Dies?*, *Meetings at the Edge*, and *Healing into Life and Death*.

Ondrea Levine, along with her husband, codirected the Hanuman Foundation Dying Project. For the past twenty years, the Levines have worked with the terminally ill and those in crisis. Together they share a soul in the deep, high mountain woods of northern New Mexico. They write and teach and heal in tandem exploration. Their newest book, *Embracing the Beloved: Relationship as a Path of Awakening*, offers details of much of their ongoing process.

PATRICIA LOVE, ED.D.

Patricia Love, Ed.D., is licensed as a professional counselor and marriage and family therapist. She is a clinical member and approved supervisor in the American Association for Marriage and Family Therapy and the past president of the International Association for Marriage and Family Counselors. She has two books, *What to Do When a Parent's Love Rules Your Life* and *Hot Monogamy*, which she coauthored with Jo Robinson. Dr. Love has published several professional articles, has been interviewed by numerous popular magazines, and appears regularly on national talk shows. She is a master trainer and faculty member of the Institute for Imago Relationship Therapy founded by Harville Hendrix. She spends most of her professional time writing, speaking, and training. She is known for her down-to-earth style laced with humor and practical information. She lives in Austin, Texas, amid friends, family, and the lively Tejano culture.

VICTORIA MORAN

Victoria Moran is the author of several books, including *Shelter for the Spirit, Compassion the Ultimate Ethic,* and *The Love-Powered Diet.* Her articles have appeared in such publications as *Ladies' Home Journal, Vegetarian Times, New Age,* and *Creation Spirituality.* She has traveled extensively in India and Tibet and lectures throughout the United States on compassionate living and practical spirituality. She lives in Kansas City, Missouri.

HUGH AND GAYLE PRATHER

Hugh Prather is best known for his books such as *Notes to Myself, Notes on How to Live in the World . . . and Still Be Happy,* and *I Touch the Earth, the Earth Touches Me,* as well as many others. He has been called "an American Kahlil Gibran" by the *New York Times* and "one of the compelling, insightful, inspirational, spiritual authors of our times" by *New Realities* magazine. He is a father, minister, teacher, and therapist.

Gayle Prather is cofounder of the Santa Fe Grief Support Group, which has been developed to assist parents who have had children die. She is also the mother of three boys and has been the coauthor (with her husband, Hugh) of several books, including *A Book for Couples, Notes to Each Other,* and

I'll Never Leave You. He has written that "Gayle is simply the kindest, most egoless, most intuitive entity on the planet." Together they conduct nationwide workshops for couples. The Prathers live in Arizona.

RAM DASS

Ram Dass was born in 1931 as Richard Alpert. He studied psychology, specializing in human motivation and personality development. Ram Dass received an M.A. from Wesleyan and a Ph.D. from Stanford University. He served on the psychology faculties at Stanford, the University of California, and Harvard University.

In 1974 Ram Dass created the Hanuman Foundation in order to promulgate spiritual awareness and well-being for people living in Western cultures. The foundation developed the Living–Dying Project, designed to provide conscious care and support for the terminally ill and dying. It also developed the Prison-Ashram Project, designed to help prison inmates grow spiritually during their incarceration. Both projects now successfully carry on their work as independent nonprofit organizations.

Ram Dass has authored a number of spiritual and self-help books, including the classic *Be Here Now; The Only Dance There Is; Grist for the Mill* (with Stephen Levine); *Journey of Awakening: A Meditator's Guidebook; Miracle of Love: Stories of Neem Karoli Baba; How Can I Help?* (with Paul Gorman); and *Compassion in Action* (with Mirabai Bush).

In 1978 Ram Dass cofounded the Seva Foundation—an international service organization working on public health and social justice issues in communities throughout the world. His lectures and workshops have been a primary fund-raising and public relations source for Seva's activities.

Ram Dass continues to lecture and teach throughout the world on such topics as utilizing service to others as a spiritual path, aging and its awakening potential, the relationship of business and social responsibility, personal relationships, spiritual awakening and its techniques, and social activism. When not traveling, Ram Dass lives in San Anselmo, California.

JAMES AND SALLE MERRILL REDFIELD

James Redfield has pursued an interest in human potential for the past twenty years. He has received a B.A. in sociology and an M.Ed. in counseling. Mr. Redfield has had a fifteen-year career as a therapist with emotionally disturbed adolescents. He currently writes and lectures about the spiritual dimensions of human consciousness.

His first novel, *The Celestine Prophecy,* is a gripping adventure story full of intrigue, suspense, and revelation. In this story lies a compelling vision of the new spiritual understanding that is emerging in personal and global awareness. Currently, the hardcover edition of *The Celestine Prophecy* has 1.2 million copies in print and has been on the *New York Times* bestseller list for more than one hundred weeks, having reached #1. He has also published *The Celestine Prophecy: An Experiential Guide,* a workbook companion to *The Celestine Prophecy.* His latest bestseller, *The Tenth Insight,* was published in 1995.

In 1989, after a series of life-changing events, Salle Merrill Redfield began to experience a high degree of stress and anxiety. Already familiar with the comforting effects of meditation, she joined a meditation group and was soon asked to become the group's leader. This experience served as preparation for the group meditations Ms. Redfield would eventually lead in conjunction with her husband when they traveled throughout the world speaking about *The Celestine Prophecy*. The success of these group sessions inspired Ms. Redfield to record her meditations for the bestselling AudioBook *The Celestine Meditations* and to write her new book, *The Joy of Meditating*.

Salle Merrill Redfield currently lives in Alabama and Florida with her husband and is a regular contributor to *The Celestine Journal* newsletter.

JOHN ROBBINS

John Robbins is the author of the Pulitzer Prize–nominated international bestseller *Diet for a New America: How Your Food Choices Affect Your Health, Happiness, and the Future of Life on Earth* and *May All Be Fed: Diet for a New World*. Many of the nation's leading authorities on alternatives in health and ecology consider him to be one of the world's leading experts on the dietary link with the environment and health. His life and work have been featured in an hour-long PBS special, *Diet For a New America*.

Mr. Robbins has been a featured and keynote speaker at major conferences sponsored by Physicians for Social Responsibility, Beyond War, Oxfam, the Sierra Club, the Humane Society of the United States, the United Nations Environmental Program, UNICEF, and many other organizations dedicated to the public interest. He is the recipient of the 1994 Rachel Carson Award. When he spoke at the United Nations, he received a standing ovation.

The only son of the founder of the Baskin-Robbins ice cream empire, John Robbins walked away from a life of immense wealth to pursue "the dream of a society at peace with its conscience because it respects and lives in harmony with all life forms." John is the founder of the nonprofit EarthSave foundation, an organization that provides education and leadership for transition to more healthful and environmentally sound food choices, nonpolluting energy supplies, and a wiser use of natural resources.

GABRIELLE ROTH

Gabrielle Roth is the author of *Maps to Ecstasy,* founder of The Moving Center, artistic director of her theater company, The Mirrors and a former member of the Actor's Studio (Playwright & Director's Unit). Her evocative music albums, including *Tongues, Luna, Trance, Waves, Ritual, Bones, Initiation,* and *Totem,* are at the cutting edge of trance/dance music, and her revolutionary video, *The Wave,* has catalyzed people all over the world. Devoted to exploring and communicating the language of primal movement, ecstatic experience, and the journey of the soul, she currently resides in Manhattan, where she teaches experimental theater and trains others to use her methods in artistic, educational, and healing contexts.

SHARON SALZBERG

Sharon Salzberg has been practicing and studying in a variety of Buddhist traditions since 1970. She has trained with teachers from many countries, including India, Burma, Nepal, Bhutan, and Tibet. Since 1974 Sharon has been leading retreats worldwide. She teaches both intensive awareness practice and the profound cultivation of kindness and compassion.

Sharon is a cofounder and guiding teacher of the Insight Meditation Society in Barre, Massachusetts, devoted to offering meditation training in silent retreats of various lengths. She is also a cofounder of the integration of the Buddhist teachings into the modern world. She is the author of *Lovingkindness: The Revolutionary Art of Happiness.* The book is a guide to the specific practices taught by the Buddha for the cultivation of concentration, fearlessness, happiness, and a loving heart.

BENJAMIN SHIELD, PH.D.

Dr. Benjamin Shield is a therapist, educator, and lecturer practicing in Santa Monica, California, and teaches throughout the United States and Europe. He holds degrees in biochemistry and biology from the University of California, with advanced studies at the Boston University School of Medicine. His doctoral degree is in the field of health sciences.

His work focuses on the integration of body, mind, and soul, while helping individuals to reduce levels of pain and to access exceptional levels of emotional and physical choices in their lives. He believes that healing and spirituality share common denominators and are accessible to each of us. Benjamin Shield has been a frequent guest on television and radio talk shows.

He has authored numerous articles on psychology, healing, and spirituality. His most recent bestselling book, *Handbook for the Soul,* has been translated into numerous languages. His other books and tapes (also in collaboration with Richard Carlson) include *Healers on Healing, For the Love of God,* and *Sixty Minutes to Great Relationships.* Most recently, he was a featured guest on the BBC/Canadian TV series *Medicine or Magic?* and a contributing author to the book *Alternative Medicine.*

BERNIE SIEGEL, M.D.

Dr. Bernie Siegel began talking about patient empowerment and the choice to live fully and die in peace more than fifteen years ago. As a physician who has cared for and counseled thousands with life-threatening illnesses, Dr. Siegel, who prefers to be called Bernie, embraces a philosophy of living—and dying—that stands at the forefront of medical ethics.

In 1978 Bernie started Exceptional Cancer Patients, a specific form of individual and group therapy utilizing patients' dreams, drawings, and images. ECaP is based on "carefrontation," a loving, safe, therapeutic confrontation that facilitates personal change and healing. This experience led to his desire to make everyone aware of his or her own healing potential.

Just like his two previous bestsellers, *Love, Medicine and Miracles* and *Peace, Love and Healing*, the third of Bernie's ever-popular inspirational books, *How to Live between Office Visits: A Guide to Life, Love and Health*, breaks new ground in the art of healing.

The Siegel family lives in the New Haven, Connecticut, area. Bernie and his wife, Bobbie Siegel, have coauthored many articles and five children. The family has innumerable interests and pets. Their home resembles a cross between a family art gallery, a zoo, a museum, and an automobile repair shop.

Andrew Weil, M.D.

Dr. Andrew Weil is the author of six books, including the *New York Times* bestseller *Spontaneous Healing*. He is a graduate of Harvard Medical School and has worked for the National Institute of Mental Health. For fifteen years he was a research associate in ethnopharmacology at the Harvard Botanical Museum as a fellow of the Institute of Current World Affairs. He traveled extensively throughout the world collecting information about the medicinal properties of plants, altered states of consciousness, and healing. He is currently associate director of the Division of Social Perspectives in Medicine and director of the program in integrative medicine at the University of Arizona in Tucson, where he practices natural and preventive medicine.

JOHN WELWOOD, PH.D.

Dr. John Welwood is a clinical psychologist and psychotherapist in private practice. His books include *Awakening the Heart: East / West Approaches to Psychotherapy and the Healing Relationship, Challenge of the Heart: Love, Sex, and Intimacy in Changing Times,* and *Journey of the Heart: The Path of Conscious Love.* His most recent book is titled *Love and Awakening: Discovering the Sacred Path of Intimate Relationship.*

Dr. Welwood, along with his wife, Jennifer, conduct Journey of the Heart seminars based on the principles and practices of his books for individuals and couples who are interested in conscious relationships. The Welwoods live and work in the San Francisco Bay Area.

MARIANNE WILLIAMSON

Marianne Williamson is an internationally acclaimed author and lecturer. All three of her books—*A Return to Love, A Woman's Worth,* and *Illuminata*—have been #1 *New York Times* bestsellers.

Ms. Williamson has been lecturing professionally on spirituality and metaphysics since 1983, both in the United States and abroad. She has done extensive charitable organizing throughout the country in service to people with life-challenging illnesses.